The Road to Katyn

To our son Alex, taken from us in his prime.

The Road to Katyn

A Soldier's Story

SALOMON W. SLOWES

Edited by
WŁADYSŁAW T. BARTOSZEWSKI

Translated by
Naftali Greenwood

Blackwell Publishers

in association with the Institute for
Polish-Jewish Studies, Oxford

First published 1992

Blackwell Publishers
108 Cowley Road
Oxford OX4 1JF
UK

D804
.S65
S5713
1992

Three Cambridge Center
Cambridge, Massachusetts 02142
USA

British Library Cataloguing in Publication Data

A CIP catalogue record for this book is available from the British
Library.

Library of Congress Cataloging in Publication Data

ISBN 0–631–179674

A CIP catalogue record for this book is available from the Library of
Congress.

Typeset in 11½ on 13½ pt Galliard
by Graphicraft Typesetters Ltd. Hong Kong
Printed and Bound in Great Britain by Hartnolls Limited, Bodmin, Cornwall

This book is printed on acid-free paper.

Contents

List of Plates

Between pages 126 and 127.

Foreword

The story of Katyn is a story of murder, deception, lies, dishonesty, collusion, and political expediency. Few emerge from it with credit. It is a story describing how the Soviet Union, in complicity with Nazi Germany, proceeded to kill thousands of Polish officers – prisoners of war protected by the Geneva Convention – in an effort to eliminate all the patriotic elements of the Polish intelligentsia, and how the Western Allies maintained their silence in the face of the crime for fear of offending the successive Soviet governments. It is a striking example of the worst side of *Realpolitik*, which foresakes the principle for a short-term political gain.

The roots of the events described by Salomon Slowes in his memoirs go back to the end of the First World War. Both Germany and Russia emerged from that conflict defeated. The newly emerged Communist Russia signed the humiliating treaty of Brest–Litovsk, in which she ceded control of Poland, Lithuania, Estonia, Livonia, and Courland to Germany, and recognized the Ukraine and Finland as independent states. Germany, in turn, was only able to rule over these territories for eight months, since in November 1918 she herself was forced to sign the armistice treaty forfeiting large parts of her territory and nullifying the Brest–Litovsk Treaty. Germany was also obliged to pay enormous sums in reparation, which ruined the economy of the new Weimar Republic.

The decisions of the Treaty of Versailles were considered by a large majority of Germans to be totally unjust and were strongly resented throughout the entire inter-war period. German resentment was directed particularly strongly at the newly re-emerged Polish Republic. Poland was indeed a clear beneficiary of the Paris Peace Conference of 1919. One of the 'fourteen points' of President Woodrow Wilson's proclamation of 8 January 1918 stated that Poland should again be established as an independent state with free and secure access to the sea. This postulate was realized despite fierce opposition coming from Germany, which was supported in its objection by Lloyd George.

The territorial conflict between Germany and Poland went back a long way. After the defeat of the Teutonic knights in the fifteenth century, Poland had maintained control over so-called Royal Prussia (later West Prussia) until the end of the eighteenth century. Following the partitions of 1772, 1793, and 1795, Poland lost large parts of her territory to Prussia, Austria, and especially to Russia. The re-emergence of Poland after 1918, which was only possible after the defeat of all three partitioning powers during the First World War, was treated as nothing short of a miracle. The Poles regarded all the territories gained from Germany as a return to the original status quo, especially since the area of the so-called Duchy of Posen was the cradle of the Polish state in the tenth century and the site of its first capital. The Germans regarded the territorial losses of Western Prussia, the Duchy of Posen, and parts of Silesia as totally unjustifiable and opposed them vigorously. The loss of Western Prussia in particular posed problems for the Weimar Republic because it divided the new state into two parts with East Prussia– always a German territory – being cut of from the rest of the country. Furthermore, the settlement meant that Poland ruled over approximately 800,000 Germans.

However, the Polish Republic gained most territory from the Soviet Union, although it never reached its pre-1772 Eastern border. From the sixteenth century the westward expansion of Muscovy took place at Poland's cost. By 1795 the expanding Russian Empire had swallowed up most of the Polish-Lithuanian Commonwealth and in the nineteenth century attempted to eradicate all signs of Polish statehood by renaming the heart of

occupied Poland 'Vistula-land' and suppressing Polish education and culture. The post-1918 Polish state was interested in
regaining as much of the territories of the old Commonwealth
as possible.

Soviet-Polish relations in the years immediately following the
October Revolution were extremely complex and reflected a
desire on the part of the Poles to keep their new-found independence and on the part of the Russians to keep as much
of the territory of the old Empire as possible. In this respect the
Bolsheviks differed very little from the White Russians. The
imperial policy of the Whites cost them the support of the
Poles, Ukrainians, and the nations of the Baltic Republics and
sealed the fate of the Civil War. The Polish government in
particular refused to fight on the side of General Denikin since
it considered the Bolsheviks to be less dangerous to the Polish
state in the short term. Despite his early rhetoric about the
right of self-determination of nations, Lenin – watching the
Communist revolutions springing up in Germany and Hungary –
attempted to spread the Communist gospel throughout Europe
and to recreate the Russian Empire ad the Soviet one.

In the autumn of 1919, the first skirmishes between the Red
Army and the Poles occurred. Early in 1920, Marshal Pilsudski,
head of the Polish Armed Forces, faced with Soviet preparations
for the attack, moved swiftly eastwards and occupied Kiev. The
Soviet General Tukhachevsky and the cavalry of Marshal
Budyonny pushed the Polish forces back to the Vistula where
on 15 August 1920 the so-called 'miracle of the Vistula' was
enacted and the Soviet forces were completely defeated in what
Lord d'Abernon called 'the eighteenth decisive battle of the
world'.[1] The Soviets conceded large areas to Poland and signed
a peace treaty in Riga in March 1922 that defined the Polish-
Russian border until 1939. Until the withdrawal from Afghanistan in 1989, the 1919–20 war with Poland was the only
one the Soviet Union ever lost. The Soviets have not reconciled
themselves to these territorial losses.

Thus both Germany and the Soviet Union perceived themselves to be the victims of the Versailles Treaty and marginalized
by the new order (Germany because of the war, Russia as a

result of turning Communist). The secret collaboration to undermine this post-war order was considered by both sides to be of definite advantage. They had established diplomatic relations already in 1921 and followed a year later by signing the Treaty of Rapallo. The Weimar Republic skilfully evaded the restrictions imposed on it by the victorious allies by secretly building, testing, and developing new weapons in the Soviet Union. The cooperation between the Red Army and the Reichswehr continued unabated until Hitler's rise to power and enabled the Germans to build aircraft and tanks which were later to be used in the Second World War. The Soviet Union also provided a convenient training ground for the German Army.

Hitler himself was strongly anti-Communist, he regarded the Soviet Union with distrust and spoke openly about the crusade against Bolshevism. In 1936 during the Spanish Civil War, Hitler and Stalin supported opposite sides. However, both regimes were united in their contempt towards democratic countries and both rejected the territorial settlements stemming from the Versailles Treaty. By 1939, after the Anschluss and the invasion of Czechoslovakia, it became clear that further German expansion had to take place in Poland and that German–Soviet interests coincided once more. The subjugation of Poland was clearly an interest shared by both.

A large proportion of Germans supported Hitler's assault on the Versailles Treaty and the creation of the *Grossdeutschland*, which included Austria and the Sudetenland. Few however relished the prospect of a war, especially since it would have been a war on two fronts. This was also the generals' nightmare and the cause – as they saw it – of the defeat in 1918. In order to carry his General Staff with him, Hitler needed to reassure them on that score. After various overtures that stipulated that Poland should join the Anti-Comintern Pact and participate in the invasion of Russia in exchange for various territorial benefits proved unsuccesful, Hitler began to contemplate an agreement with Stalin. With the threat of a war increasing, Britain and France signed a mutual assistance pact with Poland, which guaranteed assistance to that country in the event of German aggression. It is now known, however, that this was meant purely as a deterrent to Hitler and that neither country had the intention of assisting Poland militarily in the event of war. At the same time, British and French governments negotiated with the Soviet Union about the possibility of extending Soviet help to Poland in the event of war. The Russians were ready to agree provided that Poland allow them to move in the Red Army. The Polish government rejected this, fearing (with justification given what happened in the Baltic states in 1939–40) that, once there, the Soviet troops would never leave the country.

Thus the Soviet Union found itself in a position to be wooed by two opposing camps. Stalin knew that Hitler could not start a war with Poland, and by definition with Britain and France also, without securing his eastern flank. He could assume that the war between Germany, Britain, and France would be long, bloody, and exhausting and that it was bound to weaken at least one participant in it, thus improving the Soviet position *vis-à-vis* the rest of Europe. He was ready to talk to both sides in order to secure the best possible deal for his country. It very soon became apparent that the Western democracies could not offer him very much. What he could achieve by cooperating with Britain in France was peace, but this was not necessarily to his advantage. Since Poland steadfastly refused him the right to station the Red Army there, there was no question of any territorial gain at her expense by agreeing to the Western propositions. The democracies were simply unable to trade the territory of an ally for peace. Hitler, on the other hand, did not have such constraints and was able to offer Stalin much more. Thus the German-Soviet talks ended in success when, on 23 August 1939, both countries signed the non-aggression treaty popularly known as the Ribbentrop–Molotov Pact. The anodyne official document was accompanied by a secret additional protocol concerning the delimitation of German and Soviet spheres of interest in Eastern Europe. This protocol clearly indicated that the name of the pact was a misnomer, since it openly referred to partitioning the territories of the Baltic States, Finland, Poland, and Bessarabia between Germany and the Soviet Union.

Until 1989, the Soviets denied the existence of this secret protocol, despite the fact that a copy of it was found in Germany after the war, partly because they did not like to admit that they had acted in collusion with Hitler and practically enabled him to start the Second World War, and partly because after 1945 they retained all the territorial gains granted them by the Ribbentrop–Molotov pact and its subsequent revisions.

With the Soviet guarantee of support, Hitler felt able to attack Poland on 1 September 1939. Stalin joined him on 17 September, occupying Eastern Polish territories allocated to him by the secret protocol. The official explanation for this 'stab in the back' was that the Polish state showed 'internal insolvency and obvious impotence' and ceased to exist and that nobody knew the whereabouts of the Polish government. Therefore, the Soviet Foreign Minister, Molotov, concluded, the treaty of non-aggression between the Soviet Union and Poland ceased to operate and the Soviet Union had to act to protect 'its blood brothers, the Ukrainians and Byelorussians inhabiting Poland, who even formerly were nations without rights and who now have been utterly abandoned to their fate. The Soviet Government deems it its sacred duty to extend the hand of assistance to its brother Ukrainians and Byelorussians inhabiting Poland.'[2]

In reality, the Polish Army continued to fight the Germans for another three weeks and the Polish Government evacuated to Romania only after the Soviet attack took place. What followed was in practice the fourth partition of Poland. Stalin was very clear on the need to destroy the state when he conveyed to the German ambassador Schulenburg his view that 'in the final settlement of the Polish question anything that in the future might create friction between Germany and the Soviet Union must be avoided. From this point of view, [Stalin] considered it wrong to leave an independent residual Poland.'[3]

The Soviet Foreign Minister, Vyacheslav Molotov, openly referred to Poland as the bastard of the Versailles Treaty. In a speech of 31 October 1939 to the Supreme Council of the USSR he condemned Britain and France for trying to fight Nazi Germany in a war against ideology: 'It is therefore not only senseless but criminal to wage such a war as a war for the "destruction of Hitlerism" camouflaged as a fight for "democracy".' He then stated that after the invasion of Poland 'subsequent events fully confirmed that the new Soviet German relations were based on a firm foundation of mutual interests.'[4]

Molotov's speech had only publicly confirmed the agreements signed by the Soviets and the Nazis shortly before. On the 28 September 1939, the Third Reich and the Soviet Union signed a treaty which was to seal the fate of Salomon Slowes and his colleagues. The little-known Boundary and Friendship Treaty which specified the precise division of the territory, included confidential and secret additional protocols, one of which was devoted to the 'solidarity of both parties in the suppression of Polish agitation of their territories'. The protocol stated that 'both parties will tolerate in their territories no Polish agitation which affects the territories of the other party. They will suppress in their territories all beginnings of such agitation and inform each other concerning suitable measures for this purpose.'[5] These two phrases were in effect a death warrant for hundreds of thousands of Polish citizens.

Between January and March 1940, meetings between Nazi and Soviet officials which took place in Krakow decided the practical measures to be taken against this 'Polish agitation'. No documents from these discussions appear to have survived, but the circumstancial evidence linked to the NKVD–Gestapo conference in Krakow in March 1940 suggests that it was then the idea to establish a concentration camp for the Polish élite in Auschwitz was born and a solution was found to deal with the Polish élite on the territory occupied by the Soviet Union. Despite vigorous Soviet denials, it appears that the murders of Oswiecim and Katyn were conceived at the same time and in collusion. The Nazi and Soviet goals were the same – to eliminate the stratum of Polish society that was able to lead the resistance against their rule. Oswiecim was built originally as a concentration camp for the Polish élite which, for the first twenty-one months of the camp's existence, was its main victim. Katyn and other still unknown places were the Soviet solution to this problem.

The degree of collusion between the two regimes in this

sphere is quite well documented. There are a number of testimonies coming not only from the Poles but also from German
Communists who were exchanged by the Soviets for Polish
troops of Ukrainian and Byelorussian nationality, for instance,
and who ended up in respective concentration camps.[6]

The Soviet Union occupied 51.6 per cent of pre-war Polish
territory with 37.1 per cent of her population. The Soviet secret
police, the NKVD, had immediately begun to resettle Polish
citizens considered to be undesirable. Over 1.6 million Poles
were sent to the Soviet Union in a series of deportations of
which almost half a million ended up in labour camps – including
a quarter of a million children – and around 200,000 as prisoners
of war. Among them were around 15,000 officers – professionals, cadets, and reserve officers. The reservists represented the
best elements of Polish society: lawyers, doctors, university
lecturers, clergy of all denominations, and artists and came largely
from the middle class and nobility. Among them were about
1,000 Jewish officers including Major Baruch Steinberg – the
Chief Rabbi of the Polish Army, and Salomon Slowes.

The officers were separated from the ranks and kept in three
special camps at Kozielsk (approximately 4,500), Starobielsk
(3,920), and Ostaszkow (6,500), located deep within Soviet
Russia and the Ukraine. In the Ostaszkow camp there were also
some soldiers of the Border Guards, intelligence and police
officers, and military policemen. The camps were guarded not
by the Red Army but by special units of the NKVD. The
prisoners were treated correctly, although they were frequently
interrogated and various attempts were made 're-educate' them
and to persuade them to cooperate with the Soviet authorities.
Despite this, the prisoners were on the whole optimistic since
they expected the Anglo-French forces to destroy Nazi Germany and to humiliate the Soviet Union. Slowes, and others,
describe life in these camps in great detail.

In April 1940 the Germans began to construct Auschwitz
and the NKVD started to wind up the three POW camps. The
prisoners of Kozielsk, Ostaszkow, and Starobielsk disappeared
and only 448 of them were seen alive again. The testimonies of
those who survived, the discoveries made by the German Army

in 1943, and the admissions made by the Soviet Government in 1990 leave no doubt as to what happened to the Polish officers who were Soviet prisoners of war. The memoirs of Salomon Slowes are a rare testimony and the only ones written by a Jewish officer.

In April and May 1940, 124 prisoners of Ostaszkow and 79 of Starobielsk were despatched to another camp in Pavlishchev-Bor which also took 245 inmates of Kozielsk. The exact fate of the other inmates of Ostaszkow and Starobielsk remained unknown until 1991. The Soviet authorities have now admitted that the prisoners of Starobielsk were executed by the Kharkov NKVD, and those of Ostaszkow were murdered in the village of Mednoye near Tver. In August 1991 the joint Polish-Soviet team supervised the exhumation of graves in these locations, which conclusively proved the fate of the other officers.

The prisoners of Kozielsk were dispatched at the beginning of April 1940 to Gniezdovo Station by train and from there driven in lorries to a forest in Katyn near Smolensk. There, their hands were bound behind their backs. Some were gagged with sawdust. All were killed by pistol shots in the back of the head and those who apparently resisted were also bayoneted. They were laid down one on top of the other in ditches.

The remaining 448 people in Pavlishchev-Bor were intensively interrogated by the NKVD and were under severe pressure to break solidarity with other inmates and to cooperate with the Soviets. Slowes confirms that out of desperation a number of officers (around thirty) began to claim German origin, hoping that since Hitler was Stalin's ally they would be able to regain freedom. Indeed twelve of them were later released on the intervention of the German ambassador. The remaining eighteen did not pass the test of 'Germanness'. Some prisoners of Pavlishchev-Bor were removed from the camp and sent to various prisons.

On 13 June 1940 the remaining prisoners were moved to a camp in Griazowietz where conditions improved and where they were able to receive letters. By August 1940 the NKVD began to spread rumours of a possible formation of a Polish Army in the Soviet Union since the 'non-existent' Poland supposedly had common interests with that country. About 50 officers decided to accept an offer of cooperation with their captors and created a kind of discussion group which studied Communist history and politics. As Slowes mentions, the group was ostracized by the majority of inmates and even attacked. Some of those who collaborated were Jewish, which enabled the NKVD to arrest those who fought them on the pretext of anti-semitism. There is no doubt that some of the officers were indeed anti-semitic, but their anger was primarily directed against any of their colleagues who collaborated with the enemy. The prisoners remained in Griazowietz until the summer of 1941. The only exceptions were thirteen pro-Communist officers taken to Moscow in September/October 1940.

The reasons for the execution of 14,500 officers and cadets and for keeping a few hundred others alive although speculative are fairly clear. Stalin, like Hitler, was removing the leadership of the Polish nation in preparation for a permanent takeover of the country. The remaining officers were to be converted to Communism and used as puppets in pro-Soviet regime. The Soviet indoctrination was not very successful. Nevertheless, it enabled Stalin to find a small number of individuals who were later used as the core of the Polish Communist army and government. As Heller and Nekrich concluded, 'the Katyn massacre was entirely in keeping with Stalin's political aims.'[7]

Salomon Slowes and other remaining non-Communist officers were saved by the German attack on the Soviet Union in June 1941. In July 1941, the Polish-Government-in-Exile signed a treaty with the Soviet Union which re-established diplomatic links between the two countries and stipulated the release of all Polish prisoners from the camps and prisons. This was followed two weeks later by a military agreement that provided for the establishment of a Polish Army made up of Polish citizens who had been deported to the Soviet Union. General Władysław Anders was nominated as the commander of the army. One of the problems he encountered in forming the Polish Armed Forces was the severe shortage of officers. The Soviet Union had taken prisoner 45 per cent of the Polish officer corps but only a few hundred of those were located. Some of them survived in POW camps posing as ordinary soldiers, others in Griazowietz, but there was no sign of the rest. General Anders established a commission headed by Jozef Czapski, described by Slowes, whose role was to investigate and find the missing officers. Despite the vigorous search, he drew a blank.[8]

The Soviets gave various and conflicting explanations for the absence of these prisoners. They were supposedly released by their captors, overrun by the invading German army, or they escaped to Manchuria. During some private conversations the head of the NKVD, Beria, and his deputy Merkulov, mentioned that 'a mistake had been made' without elaborating on the meaning of this statement.[9] The Poles suspected that the missing officers could have been sent to hard labour camps in the far north of the country, but they were never able to confirm their suspicions. By August 1942 the entire Polish army in the Soviet Union was evacuated to Persia without the missing soldiers and without gaining any clear information about their fate.

The mystery was resolved in April 1943 when the German army discovered the graves of 4,443 Polish prisoners of war buried in the Katyn forest on NKVD property. The discovery was a godsend for the Nazis who immediately decided to use it for propaganda reasons in order to break the Anglo-American-Soviet coalition. They sent an international commission made up of specialists in pathological medicine coming from the countries overrun by Germany and allowed a Red Cross team from occupied Poland to conduct their own investigations. Both came to the conclusion that the crime must have been committed in 1940 and not in 1941 as the Soviet Union had begun to chain immediately after the discovery of the bodies. There were numerous proofs of that, including the lack of any objects dating from after April 1940, the decomposition of the bodies, and the fact that the pine trees growing on the graves were three years old.

The Soviet denials were greeted with some incredulity by the Polish Government-in-Exile which asked the International Red Cross to conduct an enquiry. The Nazis, trying to build capital out of the discovery, approached the Red Cross at the same time, which gave Stalin an excuse to attack the Poles. In a telegram to Churchill, he wrote that: 'the fact that the anti-Soviet campaign has been started simultaneously in the German and Polish press and follows identical lines is indubitable evidence of contact and collusion between Hitler – the Allies' enemy – and the Sikorski Government in this hostile campaign.'[10] The Soviet press published articles entitled 'Polish Collaborators of Hitler' and strongly attacked the government of General Sikorski. Stalin therefore used this opportunity as a convenient pretext to break diplomatic relations with the London Poles despite the mediating efforts of the British Government. The British found themselves in a very difficult position since they desperately needed Soviet help in the war against Hitler. Already in October 1939 when the Hitler–Stalin collaboration was flourishing, Churchill was drawing distinctions between the German and the Soviet attitude, and in the House of Commons Lloyd George – who was consistently anti-Polish – announced that there were many reasons 'for treating even the partition of Poland, in so far as the Russian part is concerned, in a totally different spirit from that part which appertains to Herr Hitler and the German government.'[11] By 1943, British public opinion and, to some extent, the Government was, in P. M. H. Bell's words, at 'the height of Russomania' with Stalin being more popular than Roosevelt among the general public.[12] Thus when the Katyn murders were revealed Churchill faced the dilemma of how to handle the affair. Mr (later Sir) Owen O'Malley, an Irish Protestant and British Ambassador to the Polish Government in London, prepared a long memorandum for Antony Eden on the issue of Katyn. In it, he stated that in view of the available evidence it was highly unlikely that the massacre was perpetrated by the Germans. While noting the political problems involved in blaming the Soviet Union for the crime and accepting the necessity of maintaining the alliance intact, he suggested that the British government's thinking about Stalin should be reconsidered:

Here at any rate we can make a compensatory contribution – a reaffirmation of our allegiance to truth and justice and compassion. If we do this we shall at least by predisposing ourselves to the exercise of a right judgement on all those half political, half moral questions . . . which will confront us both elsewhere and more particularly in respect to Polish-Russian relations as the war pursues its course and draws to its end; and so, if the facts about the Katyn massacre turn out to be as most of us incline to think, shall we vindicate the spirit of these brave unlucky men and justify the living to the dead.[13]

Senior members of the Foreign and Colonial Office agreed with the conclusion that the Soviet Union's guilt was a near certainty and were very distressed by the possible political consequences of the affair. Sir Frank Roberts commented on O'Malley's memorandum:

It is obviously a very awkward matter when we are fighting for a moral cause and when we intend to deal adequately with war criminals, that our Allies should be open to accusations of this kind . . . there is no point in our assisting German propaganda on these issues and there is no reason why we cannot maintain our own moral standards and values whilst at the same time endeavouring in every way possible to improve our relations with the Russians and incidentally perhaps to bring about an improvement in Soviet conduct.[14]

Consequently Roberts suggested the suppression of some parts of O'Malley's despatch which, according to him, were 'working up the maximum prejudice against the Soviet Union'. To their credit, (Lord) William Strang and (Sir) Orme Sargent rejected Roberts' suggestion and recommended that the document should be circulated to the War Cabinet in its entirety.[15] The dilemmas of the British Government were expressed succinctly in the remarks of Sir Alexander Cadogan:

The ominous thing about this incident is the ultimate political repercussion. How, if Russian guilt is established, can we expect Poles to live amicably side by side with Russians for generations to come? I fear there is no answer to that question.
And the other disturbing thought is that we may eventually,

by agreement and in collaboration with Russians, proceed to the trial and perhaps execution of Axis 'war criminals' while condoning this atrocity. I confess I shall find that extremely difficult to swallow.

However, quite clearly for the moment there is nothing to be done. As to what circulation we give to this explosive material, I find it difficult to make up my mind. Of course, it would be only honest to circulate it. But as we know (all admit) that the knowledge of this evidence cannot affect our course of action, or policy, is there any advantage in exposing more individuals than necessary to the spiritual conflict that a reading of this document excites?[16]

In the end, O'Malley's despatch was shown to very few. Churchill sent it to Roosevelt with a covering note which called it 'a grim, well-written story, but perhaps a little too well written. Nevertheless if you have time to read it, it would repay the trouble. I should like to have it back when you have finished with it as we are not circulating it officially in any way.'[17] The despatch became public knowledge only after being released in January 1972 under the thirty-year rule.

The immediate reaction of the Polish Government in 1943 had been strongly criticized by the British press for accusing the Soviet Ally of such an atrocity. The *Evening Standard* published a cartoon by David Low which encapsulated the public view on the matter. The picture showed a Polish officer supporting a wedge splitting a tree representing British-Russian-American unity while Joseph Goebbels was hitting the wedge with a hammer. The Pole was kneeling on a newspaper with the headline 'Polish Graves Frame-Up' and had the slogan 'Shortsighted Diplomacy' printed on his uniform. As Bell stated in his perceptive study of British public opinion, the British press had a 'concentrated attack of Realpolitik'. With the exception of Catholic and Scottish papers, the British press took a totally amoral stance with *The Times, New Statesman, Tribune,* and *News Chronicle* leading the attack on the Poles. The *New Statesman* went so far as to justify deportations and murder on the grounds that 'the Soviet Government, often with reason, would regard the landed aristocracy and the officer class of Poland in the light of Fascists and class enemies'. This Realpolitik of the British press went very far. E. H. Carr, a distinguished historian of the Soviet Union, later much criticized for his pro-Soviet stance by other historians, in his editorials for *The Times* consistently promoted the idea of establishing a Soviet sphere of influence in Eastern Europe as the only sensible outcome of the war and was therefore highly unsympathetic to the Poles.

Surprisingly, it was in the Foreign Office where moral doubts were discussed at length, although later suppressed on pragmatic grounds. There was also a clear minority of the population, especially among the older generation, Scots, and Northern Irish, which expressed sceptical and fearful attitudes towards Russia and expected a post-war conflict with her. With the possible exception of the working class, British public opinion had more doubts about Soviet behaviour than the press.[18]

It is difficult, however, to see what else the Polish government in London could have done. First, the government of General Sikorski was faced with severe criticism coming from the Polish Army in the Middle East which had just left the Soviet Union after years of detention in the camps and maltreatment by the Soviets of almost two million Polish citizens. All of them had bitter personal memories of the Soviets. The commander of the Polish Army in the Middle East, General Anders, was a political opponent of General Sikorski, the Prime Minister, whom he accused of being too accommodating to the Russians. There was the vexed territorial question of the Eastern Polish territories occupied by the Red Army in 1939, which Stalin wanted to incorporate into the Soviet Union after the war. Sikorski was under pressure from the British Government to accept the border changes. The Anders army consisted almost entirely of Poles from these territories who were adamantly opposed to giving them up to the aggressor who had started the war in the first place. There was a serious possibility of a mutiny if the Sikorski government totally ignored the discovery at Katyn, and of an open political challenge to the Polish Government. Secondly, as O'Malley noted in one of his despatches, some ministers in the Sikorski government had lost close members of their families in Kozielsk, Starobielsk, and Ostaszkow camps and therefore considered that a request to the Red Cross was the absolute minimum that they should do.

The discovery of the Katyn graves, although of great propaganda value to the Nazis, was also very convenient politically for the Soviet government. Ever since the victory in Stalingrad, Stalin and his generals knew that the final defeat of Germany was inevitable. His negotiating position had improved considerably and he could apply much more pressure on the Western allies. It is obvious that at least from that moment he was not going to accept any outcome of the war which would leave him with *less* territory than he was able to receive as a result of the 1939 pact with Hitler. From July 1941 onwards, his freedom of action was restricted, however, because he recognized the Polish Government-in-Exile in London which could never agree to cede voluntarily almost half of Poland's territory to an 'ally'. Stalin therefore needed a way to show that the Government was not the legitimate representative of the Polish nation in order not to be bound by their position during negotiations. The Polish response to the discovery of the Katyn murders provided him with a long-awaited opportunity. The Soviet Union announced that concern and doubts expressed by the Polish Government in London about the Katyn massacre and the fate of another ten thousand officers and NCOs who disappeared while in Soviet custody amounted to supporting Hitler and thus justified breaking off diplomatic relations.

Stalin acted cautiously at first because he was not sure what the British and American reaction would be. He was still totally dependent on the support of the Western Allies in terms of military equipment and no firm commitments had yet been made on the shape of East-Central Europe after the war. Nevertheless, he took some preparatory steps which accelerated after the British and American reaction to the break in diplomatic relations with Poland proved to be feeble. Emboldened by this, he began to create a Communist military and political Polish representative body in the Soviet Union. To this effect, as mentioned by Slowes, he kept some of the pro-Communist Polish officers alive – they were to become the core of the new

Polish infantry division. At the same time, he told those Polish Communists who had survived his pre-war purges and dissolution of the Polish Communist Party to form a Union of Polish Patriots (*ZPP*) to be run by the notorious Wanda Wasilewska.[19] In its weekly, eight days *before* the breaking off of relations with the London Poles, the Union published an article which openly stated that Poland should cede her eastern territories to the Soviet Union and possibly gain German lands in the West. Stalin's general aims had become apparent. Thanks to the excuse provided by Katyn, Stalin was able to create a totally unrepresentative body of people who were later to become the rulers of Poland.

During the Teheran Conference in November/December 1943, Roosevelt's lack of interest in Eastern Europe combined with his desire to secure Stalin's cooperation in organizing a post-war international order centred, as Roosevelt saw it, around the United Nations, resulted in his willingness to give away half of Poland and to have her subjugated by the Soviet Union (he also told Stalin that he was ready to accept the Soviet annexation of the Baltic states provided that this was done with *some* measure of approval by the local population). Roosevelt was happy to accept the shifting of Poland westwards provided this decision was not made public before the US general election in 1944 because it could be treated negatively by the population (in particular by six to seven million Americans of Polish extraction), which might lose him the vote. Stalin, being most accommodating, understood this little local difficulty.[20] Churchill, whose position was relatively weak and further diminished by Roosevelt's insistence on dealing independently with Stalin, thought pragmatically that it was not possible to stop the Soviets from taking over some of the eastern territory, although he was ready to fight for some parts of it (for instance Lvov). According to the minutes of the meeting between Churchill and Stalin, 'the Prime Minister demonstrated with the help of three matches his idea of Poland moving westwards, which pleased Marshall Stalin.'[21] Churchill was also not prepared to inform the Polish government about the proposed border changes. As his friend John Colville noted in his diary three months later:

The Polish question is coming to a head. Some people think that our attitude is a little reminiscent of Munich, but I am sure that the Poles' right course is to accept what they can get while still maintaining their right to fuller claims. O'Malley, our Ambassador, is evidently very much against selling out the Poles and points out that 'What is morally indefensible is always politically inept.'[22]

As Martin Gilbert concluded, 'Britain was prepared to urge the Poles to accept Stalin's concept of what the Polish-Soviet frontiers should be, but was not prepared to endorse a Soviet sponsored or Soviet controlled government in Poland.'[23] How this was to be achieved after the acceptance, in Teheran, of the principle of the Soviet sphere of influence in the area neither Churchill nor Gilbert clarified. The principles of the Atlantic Charter had been totally abandoned and Churchill's statements to the House of Commons that HM Government 'did not propose to recognize any territorial changes which take place during the war, unless they take place with the free consent and goodwill of the parties concerned' were forgotten.[24] Neither Roosevelt nor Churchill were ready to oppose Stalin decisively as had happened in the case of Finland which Stalin also wanted to subjugate. The compromise reached on Finland could possibly have been achieved if the Western allies had taken a much firmer line.

Western doubts were expressed only during the conference at Yalta which became a damage limitation exercise on their part since they tried to rescue what they could from Stalin's grasp. By February 1945, however, the military situation was totally different from that of November 1943. The Red Army had occupied almost all the territories which Stalin wanted to acquire in Eastern Europe and he was not going to accept any non-Communist governments there. As he said in his famous quote, 'Whoever occupies a territory imposes on it his social system, it cannot be otherwise.' Western military assistance had become irrelevant.

During the Nuremberg Trials the Soviets once again tried to blame the Nazis for the Katyn murder. It was the only crime to which the accused German officials steadfastly refused to admit and it soon became apparent that the Soviet testimonies were convoluted and inconsistent. The whole matter was dropped and the Allied judges ruled that since the crime was not committed by the Nazis, it should not be investigated any further. The Western Allies could not allow the Soviets to be explicitly indicted. When a counsel for the German General Staff and High Command asked at Nuremberg. 'Who is to made responsible for the Katyn case?', Lord Justice Lawrence replied, 'I do not propose to answer questions of that sort.'[25]

Between 1943 and 1951 the Department of State and the White House did their utmost to prevent the truth about Katyn reaching the general public. The Government suppressed a number of reports prepared by high-ranking American officers and diplomats in order to keep the Soviet guilt a secret. When one of the surviving officers described by Slowes, Jozef Czapski, was asked in 1950 to speak on the 'Voice of America', he was told not to include any mention of the massacre and forbidden to utter the name Katyn.[26] A number of Americans, however, felt deeply uneasy about this conspiracy of silence and thus in 1949 a private committee was established to investigate the Katyn crime, headed by a former US ambassador to Poland, Arthur Bliss Lane. It forced the Government to initiate an official investigation.

In 1951 the Katyn Select Committee of the US Congress unanimously found that the crime had 'beyond any reasonable doubt been committed by the Soviet NKVD' and added that, 'throughout our entire proceedings there has not been a scintilla of proof or even any remote circumstancial evidence presented that could indict any other nation in this international crime.' The Committee concluded that:

> the Soviets had plotted this criminal extermination of Poland's intellectual leadership as early as the fall of 1939 – shortly after Russia's treacherous invasion of the Polish nation's borders. There can be no doubt this massacre was a calculated plot to eliminate all Polish leaders who subsequently would have opposed the Soviet's plans for communizing Poland.[27]

These findings, supported by massive documentary evidence and testimonies, were accepted by most nations, with the obvious exception of the Communist states and, somewhat more surprisingly, the British Foreign and Commonwealth Office. For some obscure reason, successive Foreign Secretaries decided that it would be better not to accept the American findings. This was probably a result of an ill-conceived *Realpolitik* which stipulated that Britain should keep relations with the Soviet Union on an even keel. In 1953, the death of Stalin encouraged the British government in their belief that the situation in the Soviet Union would change substantially and therefore one should not antagonize the new Soviet Government by bringing up the Katyn story which even in 1944 Churchill thought to be 'of no practical importance'.[28] One suspects that once a decision to that effect was made, it was easier for the Foreign Office to evade the truth, which they did until the end. Forty-five years after Sir Owen O'Malley presented the FCO with convincing evidence of Soviet guilt, Lord Glenarthur, a Foreign Office minister, made the incredible statement in the House of Lords that there was no conclusive evidence that the Polish officers were murdered by the Soviet NKVD. Only after being challenged by the press did he admit that 'there was indeed substantial circumstantial evidence pointing to Soviet responsibility for the killings.'[29] Even after President Gorbachev had admitted Soviet responsibility, all the Foreign Office could come up with was 'we have long called for everyone to be open about this incident. We therefore now welcome the revelations from Moscow.'[30] This was the Foreign Office at its very worst.

The Poles were forced to accept the hated Communist government and the whole issue of Katyn was suppressed for almost 45 years. It was to become one of the key factors influencing Polish-Soviet relations. The huge majority of the Polish population had never accepted the Soviet explanations for the massacre which became a prime symbol of Soviet duplicity.

The Polish Communist line on Katyn from 1943 to 1989 has wavered between total suppression of any public mention of the name to sophisticated lies published by servile historians and journalists. After the US Congress Committee announced its findings, the Communist Government of Poland decided in 1952 to publish a book *Prawda o Katyniu* (The Truth About Katyn), 90 per cent of which was devoted to an attack on the United States and the rest repeated the official Soviet line about German guilt. For the rest of the period, all East European Communist parties maintained a wary silence, although numerous attempts were made to suppress any celebrations commemorating the victims outside purely Polish circles.

In 1976, the Soviet Government exerted considerable pressure on the British government to prevent Polish *émigrés* from unveiling a monument in London to the victims of Katyn with the simple inscription 'Katyn 1940'. The obvious point of contention was the date. The Soviets argued that it should either be 1941 or nothing. The *émigré* community was put under strong pressure from official British circles and was denied permission to erect the monument in the centre of London. It was eventually situated in a cemetery and the government of the time forbade its members and those of the armed forces to attend the ceremony to avoid offending the Soviets. A few honourable Britons refused to obey this unreasonable order.

Throughout the post-Stalinist period, there were consistent rumours in Poland that the Communist Government was just about to acknowledge Soviet involvement in the crime, but it was always decided that the issue was too sensitive and detrimental to Polish-Soviet relations to be safely breached. To many people in the West, this was difficult to understand. After all, the massacre took place many decades ago and could presumably be safely blamed on Stalin, together with many other atrocities. The fact that from the moral and legal point of view the Soviets had committed the hideous crime of murdering thousands of POWs was of little practical consequence. After Mikhail Gorbachev took power in the Soviet Union there was much speculation in the international press that he was on the verge of admitting Soviet guilt. This view did not take into consideration that the whole issue was of more than just historical importance. The key problem facing any Soviet leader was that of the legitimacy of the Polish government. The question of legitimacy went back to 1943 and the discovery of the mass graves at Katyn. The Soviet Government of the time shifted its recognition to a puppet Polish Communist organization precisely on the grounds that the legitimate London-based Government-in-Exile was hinting at Soviet involvement in the crime. The basis of legitimacy of the Polish Communist Government was that they supposedly represented the Polish people who in a sense withdrew their recognition from the London Government after their 'pro-Nazi stance'. The second part of this argument was that the Red Army liberated Poland from the Nazis and their reactionary supporters (who included anybody approving of the London Government). If one accepted that the Katyn murders were perpetrated by the Soviets, and that subsequently this action was supported by the Polish Communists, the whole post-war political edifice would be built on very shaky foundations.

Some circumstantial evidence to support this view can be derived from the behaviour of Mikhail Gorbachev on his visit to Poland in July 1988. At the time, many in the West anticipated that in order to improve Soviet-Polish relations he was going to admit to the Katyn massacre. Although in his address to the Polish parliament he denounced Stalin's deportations of hundreds of thousands of Poles to the Soviet Union there was no mention of the fate of the Polish officers. He finally admitted Soviet guilt only in September 1989. Between July 1988 and September 1989 a dramatic change occurred in Polish politics which made denials redundant. There was no longer any need to support legitimacy of the Polish Communist Government since after the June 1989 elections it was swept out of power.

In the meantime a joint Polish-Soviet historical commission had been established to investigate the matter. In April 1988 the obedient Polish Party historians issued a statement saying that the Soviet communiqué of 1944 about the Katyn murders was not 'credible', however they avoided the use of available evidence which would have decisively proven Soviet responsibility for the crime. Due to the political developments, the commission itself soon became irrelevant.

In August 1989 Tadeusz Mazowiecki, a journalist and Solidarity leader became the first non-Communist Prime Minister in Eastern Europe since 1948. The truth about the Katyn murders could for the first time be openly told in Poland. In October of that year the Polish Attorney General sent an official representation to his Soviet equivalent demanding the punishment of those Soviet citizens who were guilty of the murders. According to him the killing of Polish POWs had to be classified as genocide and as such does not fall under the statute of limitations. According to the Soviet press, there are still ex-NKVD members who participated in the killing and now live in retirement in Moscow. The Polish Prosecutor's office passed some names to the Soviet authorities so far without any visible response.

In 1990 a number of ex-NKVD personnel came forward to talk both about the falsification of documents, trying to prove German guilt, and of the execution of the Polish officers which took place in other locations. It became almost certain that the officers imprisoned in the Starobielsk and Ostaszkow camps were executed at the end of the so-called 'Black Road' near Kharkov and in the village of Mednoye. The Soviet KGB officers admitted to the existence of evidence proving this conclusively. In late July and August 1991, a representative of the Soviet Military Attorney General's office, together with the Polish Deputy Attorney General, presided over the exhumation of the graves in two areas.

It is doubtful whether the Soviet war criminals will ever be brought to justice. Throughout 1990 and 1991 the official publication of the Soviet Defence Ministry, *Military Historical Journal*, kept publishing articles signed by various generals in which the blame for the Katyn massacre was once again placed on the Germans. As late as June 1991 the editor of the *Military Historical Journal* General Viktor Filatov said in an interview that 'more and more proof incriminating the Germans was emerging about the Katyn murder.'[31] This was severely criticized by independent publications such as *Argumenti i Fakti*, the most popular Soviet weekly, but brought no official response from the Soviet government, the Communist Party, or President Gorbachev. Almost fifty years on, the Soviet deception continues.

The story of Salomon Slowes is the third book-length account of the terrible months surrounding the Katyn murders written by one of the 448 survivors. This work is a testimony to the human spirit, and brings us one step closer to establishing the details of this horrific crime.

Władysław T. Bartoszewski

Notes

1   Edgar Vincent d'Abernon, *The Eighteenth Decisive Battle of the World: Warsaw 1920*. London, 1931.
2   Jane Degras, *Soviet Documents on Foreign Policy, 1917–1941*. Oxford: OUP, 1953, vol. 3, pp. 374–6.
3   Telegram from Ambassador Schulenburg to the German Ministry for Foreign Affairs, 25 September, 1939, in *Documents on German Foreign Policy, 1918–1945*, vol. VIII, no. 131. London: HMSO, 1956.
4   Degras, *Soviet Documents*, pp. 388–95.
5   *Documents on German Foreign Policy*, vol. VIII, no. 161.
6   Jozef Garlinski, *Poland in the Second World War*. London: Macmillan, 1985, p. 38.
7   Michel Heller and Aleksander Nekrich, *Utopia in Power. A History of the USSR from 1917 to the Present*. London: Hutchinson, 1986, p. 407.
8   Jozef Czapski, *The Inhuman Land*. London: Chatto and Windus, 1951.
9   Janusz Zawodny, *Katyn*. Paris: Editions Spotkania, 1989, pp. 123–5. (First English edition *Death in the Forest*. Indiana: University of Notre Dame Press, 1962.)
10 Telegram from Stalin to Churchill, 21 April, 1943, in *Stalin's Correspondence with Churchill, Attlee, Roosevelt and Truman, 1941–1945*. London: Lawrence and Wishart, 1958, I, no. 150.
11 *Hansard*, 3 October 1939, 351/1910–12.
12 P. M. H. Bell, *John Bull and the Bear. British Public Opinion, Foreign Policy and the Soviet Union 1941–1945*. London: Edward Arnold, 1990.

13 Despatch from O'Malley to Eden, 24 May 1943, in Louis FitzGibbon, *Unpitied and Unknown*. London: Bachman and Turner, 1975, pp. 52–3.

14 Sir Frank Roberts, Enclosure to O'Malley's despatch of 24 May, 1943, in Louis FitzGibbon, *Unpitied and Unknown*, p. 56.

15 Ibid., p. 57.

16 Ibid., pp. 57–8.

17 Warren F. Kimball (ed.), *Churchill and Roosevelt. The Complete Correspondence*. London: Collins, 1984, vol. II, p. 389.

18 P. M. H. Bell, *John Bull and the Bear*, pp. 121–5.

19 See footnote 22 in the main text.

20 Minutes of the conversation between Roosevelt and Stalin at the Teheran Conference, 1 December 1943, in A. Polonsky, *The Great Powers and the Polish Question 1941–1945*. London: London School of Economics and Political Science, 1976, pp. 164–5.

21 Minutes of the conversation between Churchill and Stalin at the Teheran Conference, 28 November, 1943, in A. Polonsky, *The Great Powers*, p. 164.

22 John Colville, *The Fringes of Power. 10 Downing Street Diaries 1939–1955*. New York: W.W. Norton, 1986, p. 473.

23 Martin Gilbert, *The Road to Victory. Winston Churchill 1941–1945*. London: Heinemann, 1986, p. 665.

24 *Hansard*, 5 September 1940, 365/40.

25 *International Military Tribunal. Secretariat*. Nuremburg, 1947, vol. XVII, p. 286.

26 Zawodny, *Katyn*, p. 151.

27 Interim Report of the US Congressional Select Committee, 2 July 1952, quoted in E. FitzGibbon, *Katyn – A Crime Without Parallel*. London: Tom Stacey, 1971, p. 201.

28 Martin Gilbert, *The Road to Victory*, p. 664.

29 The Minister of State, Foreign and Commonwealth Office (Lord Glenarthur). House of Lords, 11 July 1988 and 27 July 1988.

30 Bernard Levin, 'Britain's complicity on a chronicle of shame', *The Times*, 23 April 1990.

31 An interview given by General Filatov to the weekly *Ekonomika i Zhizn*, June 1991.

Acknowledgements

It is my pleasure to express my gratitude to Professor Antony Polonsky and Dr Władysław T. Bartoszewski for their valuable help in publishing the English version of my book.

I am indebted to Mr Rafael M. Scharf for his help in publication. I should like to express my deep appreciation to Mr Samuel Shnitzer for the attention he devoted to the subject of the book and his remarks upon its appearance. Hearty thanks to my friend Daniel Eliram for his remarks in preparing the material for publication. My profound gratitude to Mr Joseph Khroust for preparing the book for print, and to Mr Naftali Greenwood for the devotion he showed in translating the text. It is my pleasant duty to acknowledge with many thanks the support given me by Mrs Łucja Gliksman. Above all, however, thanks to my wife, Dr Miriam Slowes née Czarna. Her patience and encouragement were of inestimable help in completing the manuscript.

Dr Salomon Slowes

Introduction

On the morning of 13 April 1943, Radio Berlin announced the discovery of mass graves in the Katyn Forest near Smolensk. Entombed there were Polish army officers who had been captured by the Soviets in September 1939, after the Soviet army had crossed Poland's eastern border on 17 September. To this day, this has remained one of the most mysterious and controversial episodes of World War II.

At the time, nearly a quarter of a million Polish soldiers, including some 10,000 officers, were taken by the Soviets. As prisoners of war they were confined in three camps: Kozielsk, Ostashkov, and Starobielsk, and letters from their families made it clear that all communication between them and the POWs was broken off in April 1940. The Polish government-in-exile under General Sikorski was first established in France, but moved to London after the fall of France in June 1940. As long as relations between Nazi Germany and the Soviet Union were friendly, the Polish government-in-exile in London had no way of tracing them. This changed when Germany invaded the Soviet Union on 22 June 1941. Then the government-in-exile reached an agreement with the Soviets under which the latter undertook to release all Polish POWs in Soviet captivity for the purpose of enlisting in a Polish military force that would fight the Nazis alongside the Soviets.

A surprise awaited the organizers of the Polish force, General Władysław Anders and his aides: the vast majority of officers did not present themselves for enlistment. Of 14 generals and 300 staff officers taken prisoner of war by the Soviets, only two generals and six officers appeared. All in all, about 15,000 men, including nearly 10,000 officers, had vanished.

All the Polish government's investigations and attempts to discover the fate of these men were fruitless. The only fact that surfaced was that in April 1940, they had been transported in small groups, under heavy NKVD guard, to nearby stations and placed aboard trains. At this point they disappeared.

The Prime Minister of the Polish government-in-exile, General Sikorski,[1] embarked on a special flight to Moscow, had a meeting with Stalin, and was presented with several unconvincing explanations. One example was that all the Polish officers had fled – to Manchuria. According to another, they had been working on fortifications on the border of the German-occupied territories, and were captured by the Germans upon their invasion of the Soviet Union.

Then, in April 1943, the mass graves in the Katyn Forest were discovered. They contained thousands of corpses arrayed face down, in straight rows, several layers deep. All had been shot in the back of the head at close range. Most had their hands tied behind their backs. Many had army greatcoats pulled over their heads. It appeared as if many had tried to defend themselves, for they were studded with bayonet wounds.

In response to Nazi propaganda, various investigatory commissions burst into vigorous activity. At first, three such commissions – comprising German experts in forensic medicine, medical experts from 13 countries, and the Polish Red Cross – were brought to the site by the Germans. All three reached the same conclusions: the victims had been murdered three years before, when the area was under Soviet control, and the trees planted over the mass graves were three years old.

When the Red Army liberated the area in September 1943, the Soviet authorities accused the Germans of having slaughtered the Polish officers. They tried to prove it, and continued in their attempt until 1990.

However, the Katyn affair has a Jewish element, too, which to this day has been mentioned neither in official publications nor even in interviews with the few survivors of the massacre.

Among the victims were about 1,000 Jewish officers, who had been inducted into the Polish army when the war broke out. These were men in their prime. Most were university-trained experts in various fields: medicine, engineering, law. Others were prominent in public and economic life.

By miracle and blind fate, I came out of it alive, one of the few survivors amidst thousands of savaged corpses. Since fate decreed that I drink from this poisoned chalice, it also obliges me, because efforts have been made to blot out the memory of these victims, to disclose long-buried and, in some cases, deliberately concealed details that may help further research into this tragic period.

Spurred by my conscience, I have for years been recording events and dredging up details that form the contents of this memoir. The very idea that important particulars documenting a war tragedy would be banished from recollection over time, and the urge to fight the proclivity to forget are my motives in writing. My intent is to add reliable information on a period relegated to the recesses of history by having been grievously treated by history itself.

These events, half a century after their occurrence, will indeed prove surprising to many people. More profound than this, however, is the sorrow that would afflict me if this important matter is not brought to general knowledge.

This account of events that took place in my proximity, and mention of victims whom I met, may be of informative value to hundreds of victims' offspring and relatives.

I hope this collection of details takes up position as another stone in the symbolic monument atop the mass graves dotting the vast fields and timeless forests of icy Russia.

Background

World War II broke out at dawn on Friday, 1 September 1939, when the German *Wehrmacht* crossed the Polish border with motorized spearheads, overwhelming the country before it could summon its reserves.

With lightning thrusts, armoured advance units penetrated deep into Polish territory, cutting communication between commands and sowing death, panic, and chaos in the civilian public.

The *Luftwaffe*, exploiting its overwhelming supremacy, mercilessly bombarded heavily populated areas, industrial centres, and airfields, and totally paralysed the victim country's air defence capability.

The government ministries fled Warsaw on the fifth day of fierce battles. The next to evacuate the capital were the President, Professor Mościcki,[2] army commander-in-chief Marshal Śmigły-Rydz,[3] and members of the cabinet; they headed for the Romanian border. Despite their inferiority in equipment and inability to communicate between units, the Polish army fought with valiant desperation in the forests, and at rail junctions and seaports, for more than a month, inflicting heavy losses on the Nazi invader.

Thousands of fighters of the routed Polish army were taken prisoner by the Germans as the rear commands retreated to the east, pressed by the advancing enemy. Under a secret clause in an agreement signed by German and Soviet foreign ministers Ribbentrop and Molotov a week before the war, the German army occupied western Poland as far as the Bug and Narew Rivers, leaving the eastern portion of the country to the Soviets.

On 17 September the Polish ambassador to the Kremlin was informed that since his country had no legal government, all pacts between the two countries were null and void. The Red Army marched into eastern Poland that very day, announcing by radio and leaflet: 'The peoples of the Western Ukraine and Belorussia have been liberated from the burden of Polish government repression.'

The Polish army's rear commands, hospital crews, and about 250,000 officers and enlisted men who had retreated from the theatre of battle were taken prisoner by the Soviets and brought to camps in various parts of the Soviet Union. After sorting and repeated interrogation, many ordinary soldiers were sent home; others were consigned to forced labour as miners and road-builders.

In 'their' sector of occupied Poland, the Soviets hunted down those officers and reservists who had succeeded in reaching their homes after the fighting had died down. About 2 million Polish citizens were arrested *en masse*, and they and their families were exiled on freight trains to the Asiatic USSR and camps in the Arctic north.

The prisoners included tens of thousands of Jews, some skilled and others not. Charged with hostile activity and espionage, they were sentenced to years of exile and hard labour in the camps and the timeless forests.

About 10,000 officers, including 12 generals, about 1,000 doctors, approximately 300 professors, hundreds of engineers, attorneys, and other experts, were concentrated in three POW camps: Kozielsk, Starobielsk, and Ostashkov. There they were kept under harsh conditions, behind barbed wire fences, until April 1940.

Then an order was given to wind up the three camps. Work commenced on 3 April 1940, and the job was completed gradually within a month. It was more than a year before the Germans attacked the Soviet Union; the two states were on very friendly terms, and the rumours about the POWs' imminent liberation seemed reasonable.

The procedures for preparing and dispatching the transports were the same in the three camps. The officers were sent out in groups of 100–300, to destinations unknown. From the day they left the camps, all contact with them was broken off. We know only of 394 officers and cadets who were taken from the three camps, first to Pavlishchev-Bor and thence, in seven groups, to Griazowiets. These men, a negligible fraction of the 15,000 POWs, were thus spared their comrades' bitter fate.

The survivors reported in detail on their further sufferings. The last of them, reaching Pavlishchev-Bor in May 1940, mentioned about 20 transports leaving each of the three original camps.

The officers from Griazowiets were among the first members of the Polish army set up on Soviet soil under an agreement concluded in London between General Sikorski and Soviet ambassador Maiski after the German attack on Russia.

General Władysław Anders,[4] liberated from Lubianka Prison in Moscow, was appointed commander of this new force. Multitudes of POWs and other detainees were freed from the camps and prisons throughout the Soviet Union and thronged to enlist. But of the thousands of officers who had been in the three POW camps – Kozielsk, Ostashkov, and Starobielsk – not a man appeared. Recurrent enquiries of the Soviet authorities by the Polish goverment in London, and by Polish army commanders, were treated evasively. Stalin, petitioned personally by Anders during the latter's visit to Moscow, said that the POWs had been sent home before the war with Germany broke out, and had apparently crossed the borders of the USSR in the Far East. According to another Russian explanation, the prisoners had been put to work as roadbuilders in the border zone after the camps were dismantled; when the Germans launched their surprise attack and the Red Army retreated in panic, the men were stranded for lack of transportation, and had been eliminated by the Germans when they reached the area.

Then, in 1943, the *Wehrmacht* discovered the corpses of about 5,000 officers from Kozielsk in a mass grave in the Katyn Forest in the Smolensk district, their skulls perforated with bullets. The precise fate of about 10,000 POWs from the other two camps, Starobielsk and Ostashkov, remains unknown, although there is little doubt that they also were executed. After the Soviet Union and the Polish 'communist' government in Warsaw signed their agreement with respect to repatriation of Polish citizens, thousands of families waited, in vain, for the officers from the POW camps to return.

This book retells the personal experiences of a Jewish officer in the Polish army, who took part in the events of the German blitzkrieg and the hardships of Soviet captivity.

As the chief staff physician, the author, a survivor of the mass slaughter, was close to the persons who helped establish the Polish army in the Soviet Union, organize it in the Middle East, take it into battle in Italy, and conclude its duties on British soil.

1

The Approaching Storm

The peoples of Europe, and especially the Jews, were assailed relentlessly throughout 1939 with horrifying reports. The grey, gloomy clouds dropped earthward and blanketed the Jewish city of Wilno.

Some of the helpless residents gathered in the narrow alleys and the courtyards of the houses. Others refrained from staying outside for any length of time, preferring to be with their families. It was clear to everyone that the noose was being drawn tighter around the necks of Poland's Jews with each passing day.

Fear and dread mounted. The dominant and terrifying sensation was one of a mighty, merciless wave that threatened to engulf all existence, or a mammoth press about to crush, crumble, and consume the universe and all therein.

The news that arrived on 23 August reverberated like a clap of thunder: Nazi Germany and Stalinist Russia, squeezing Poland like a vice, had signed a non-aggression pact. The sword of war was ready to fall, and hopes for peace vanished. In Germany, giant loudspeakers carried Hitler's threatening howls to the masses each day; after Nazi Germany had annexed Austria and occupied Czechoslovakia, there was no doubt as to who the next prey would be.

The Polish government, blinded by Nazi propaganda, failed to take defensive measures while there was still time. An initial call-up was cancelled under influence of Western governments, which proclaimed their willingness to defend Poland while trying to abate Hitler's rage with acts of appeasement. An emergency mobilization was announced only two days before the war broke out, when the engines of the enemy's heavy bombers, his columns of armour, and the muzzles of his cannon were merely waiting for the signal to embark on the slaughter.

It was the morning of a pleasant autumn day. 'Golden autumn', as they call it in Poland, is the country's loveliest season. The Jews of Wilno, however, were not inclined to contemplate the splendour of nature. The sun's rays did not warm the hearts of the families that waited helplessly as the juggernaut closed in on their homes.

The streets of Wilno were increasingly deserted. Mobilized young men rushed to their units; women and children retreated to their homes. Last hopes of a miracle faded.

My own thoughts at the time were melancholy. A chapter of my life was drawing to a close, and another, nebulous and unfathomable in substance and progression, was about to begin. For lack of choice, I resigned myself to the inevitable and surrendered to the verdict of fate that would chart future events. All I could do was to pack a few personal effects into a small suitcase, put on my officer's uniform, belt, and handgun, lace my glistening black riding boots, don my army cap, and head for the unknown.

I had to take a train to the induction centre in Sokółka, a town between Grodno and Białystok. In anything but a clear state of mind, I went to my father's clinic to bid farewell. It was the only time in my life that I dared bother him while he was treating a patient. My father knew what had happened. His face was pale and sad, radiating nothing of his typical smile and good-heartedness. Thus I have remembered him ever since.

My father had gone through great suffering and hardship in his youth. As a young man in the 1890s, he had left his father's home in a farming town near Kamieniec in the Brest-Litovsk district, wandering down the routes of life. As a destitute student he peregrinated through Tsarist Russia, living from hand to mouth and studying by night for matriculation and university entrance exams. To fend off starvation he undertook the bone-breaking task of unloading sacks of grain and cement at the port of Odessa. He also sang in the municipal opera, and taught school.

When the Russian army was defeated in World War I, he and his family were forced to abandon their home on the border of Eastern Prussia. Loading everything he owned on to a peasant's wagon, he headed for Wilno as a refugee. There, as principal of a dental school, he earned his way into the city's highest echelon of experts by means of his professional and organizational abilities. When the Germans occupied Wilno, the thread of his life snapped. Witnesses report that the Nazis murdered him in 1941 in the Kloga forced-labour camp in Estonia. By that time my mother, also a doctor, had been murdered in the Ponary Forest on the outskirts of Wilno.

And now … a last kiss without words, a last glance, penetratingly and deafeningly silent. In the meantime, Mother had come in … kisses on her delicate, tear-stained face. 'There won't be a war; I'll be back in a few days,' I murmured, knowing that the truth was something quite the opposite.

I went down to the street. There my entire life passed before me: my sisters, their husbands and children; my brother in Palestine, relatives, friends, acquaintances. Then and there, at the blink of an eye, a heavy curtain fell on the past, and I yielded in growing surrender to an imponderable distant, and alien fate. I was overtaken with a dull feeling that augured terrible events beyond the control of any one man.

Traffic was light on the main street, although it was noon-time and the lovely autumn sun drenched the air and the city's houses with blinding light. Vigorously I strode out, trying to urge myself to head for the inevitable, immutable future.

The train station was awash with thousands of conscripts en route to their units, all jostling nervously at the steps of the railway cars. I climbed into the first-class car reserved for the officers. The passengers' faces exuded pride and self-confidence. They were sure this passing adventure would end quickly and successfully. Many, it seemed, were looking forward to this chance to rout the enemy once again. Had the Polish not dealt the Germans a severe defeat before, in the times of the Teutonic Knights?[5]

Only a few sat there quietly, introspective and pensive, their faces radiating concern about the future. These were the thoughtful people who understood reality. They kept their views to themselves, nodding whenever anyone pronounced the conventional wisdom and saying nothing that could be construed as hostile and treasonous. It was twilight. Silence reigned in the gloom inside the train. It was behind schedule and the trip dragged on. The frequent stops and lengthy waits attested to the great congestion of rail traffic in the direction of the capital and the country's heartland. Many of the passengers dozed off. An ordinary two-hour journey by daylight lasted deep into the night.

At dawn the train stopped for several hours at the Grodno station. Crowds of soldiers and officers en route to their units ran in every direction, lugging their gear. Groups of young conscripts fortified themselves with traditional folk-songs. Some of the officers, however, looked anxious and were evidently less confident than the enlisted men that the adventure now under way would end quickly and successfully.

Late that evening we reached our destination, a little rail station near a small, poor town on Poland's eastern border. I got off with several other officers, suitcase in hand. We walked down a dirt road to the gate of the army camp. All around was the eerie silence of rustic night, disrupted by the chirping of crickets and the croaking of frogs in a distant marsh. We approached a cluster of towering three-storey barracks pocked with long rows of little square windows. The walls were faded and dirty, indicating many years of neglect since the Tsar's days. The facility looked like a big, mournful prison, abandoned and forsaken at the end of the world.

Our path led to headquarters, a wooden building enveloped in bushes and dry grass. The main door, ajar and totally unguarded, opened on to grey corridors and open, unfurnished rooms. The whole place was deserted. A chilly autumn breeze helped me snap out of my depression and dried the cold sweat on my face. Physically and psychologically spent, I was acutely disappointed with my first encounter with the army in time of emergency. A terrible headache struck me, as if sizzling stones were exploding within my skull. I gathered some straw from a corner of one of the rooms, and, without bothering to remove my clothes and belt, lay down on the wooden floor and fell asleep.

The unbroken night's slumber might as well have been a catnap. I woke up suddenly to find autumn sunbeams filtering in through the branches of the tall oaks in the yard. Some of them found their way through the open window and stoked my face gently, as if it were a silk tassle. I leaped to my feet, shook the grains out of my clothes, brushed off the dust, and ran to the end of the corridor to wash my face. It was the morning of 1 September.

That afternoon we began feverishly to organize the hospital in the nearby village. Residents were evicted from their poor hovels; so were summer vacationers, who were forced to call off the holiday and return to their homes in town. Staff members and doctors busily signed out equipment and medical instruments from the emergency warehouses; horses and carts belonging to the nearby peasants were requisitioned to haul them.

Stacks of padlocked green metal trunks filled with medical paraphernalia, large wooden chests with modern equipment, containers of pesticides and medicines – all were transported to the depot on the rail station platform. Here enlisted men laboriously loaded the gear and spare parts into dozens of boxcars that had arrived along with the passenger cars reserved for the officers and staff members. The train, equipment and all, moved slowly and without forewarning. Tension and nervousness about the future were perceptible in the officers' car. One of the officers, whispering, spread an unsubstantiated rumour about an alleged battle raging on the western front.

No one dared respond, and the unofficial 'news' spread like sheet lightning. The men preferred not to express their views about the state of emergency. The quiet was broken only by the clatter of wheels on rails. It gained in speed and volume, indicating that the train was in headlong flight to the west. None of the doctors knew our unit's destination; only at one of the stations ahead would the secret code be handed over in a sealed envelope.

The hospital commander, Major L., was a grotesque, ageing, irritable mockery of a professional officer. Judging by the impression he made, he had stumbled into army life inadvertently, like many young men who threw their textbooks aside and, in the general fervour surrounding Poland's resurrection at the end of World War I, volunteered for the service.

Rather than attesting to personal ambition, the faded features of his face reflected a man tired of life and chronically depressed. He did not have a happy family life, and had not succeeded in climbing in the army hierarchy. His forehead was thickly creased; he had gone grey at the temples. He was a chain-smoker, never conversing without a glowing cigarette but between his thin lips. He would occasionally gnaw on the butt with motions reminiscent of an infant's suckings, and his false teeth, stiffly shifting this way and that, were readily perceptible. When angry, he would lower his gaze and twitch his right shoulder as a substitute for speaking his mind. He adopted a posture of confusion and helplessness until some sort of decision was handed him. His blue eyes were submissive, half-closed, downcast, and miserable. His expression seemed to indicate weakness of character, and that, to our misfortune, proved to be quite the case within a few days.

It became clear to me at the very outset of the trip that the staff physicians had been recruited from the cities of western Poland. Almost all exuded pride and national hubris, in addition to the feelings of supremacy and anti-semitic hostility implanted in them in early childhood. Thus my physician colleagues proved wholly unwilling to adopt even a reasonably friendly attitude towards the only Jewish officer in the group.

The train stopped at the Białystok station during the night, and the commander disembarked to receive orders for the rest of our trip. He came back puzzled, depressed, and ill at ease, but disclosed no details to the staff of officers that waited tensely for some explanation of the state of affairs. Nobody dared ask too many questions, lest military secrecy be compromised.

In the dead of night, burdened with thoughts and ruminations, almost all the men fell asleep in their seats to the monotonous click-clack of the wheels. The first rays of sun came through the windows at the dawn of Sabbath. Just then the silence was split with the mounting racket of approaching aircraft. The train was racing full-throttle through golden grain fields, and the tired passengers were sure that these were our planes in action.

Like thunder out of the blue, a torrent of automatic machine-gun fire from overhead sent the passengers leaping from their seats. Spurts of shells perforated the train roof like knives. The engineer spurred the locomotive to even greater velocity. Pressing themselves to the windows, the passengers spotted two squadrons, each comprising three black aircraft. They passed rapidly over the locomotive, dropped a few bombs, soared skyward like shrieking arrows, and turned around for another sortie.

The surprise was total. As if propelled by a magic wand, all the men jumped out of the cars, hopping with sublime agility over the deep drainage ditch along the track and vanishing into a nearby grove of trees. In the meantime, the aircraft were spitting relentless machine-gun fire, and the pilots hand-dropped hundreds of bombs on the men as they sought shelter in the woods.

I was stunned. With a hurried glance I saw the cars' open doors and shattered windows, and no one alive all around. I leaped out of the car, hopped over the ditch, and sought shelter at the foot of one of the trees. I fell flat on the thin grass and the soil, which were wet from the night's dew. The smell of gunpowder and soot superimposed on the pleasant, crisp rustic air made my head spin even as death hovered overhead. From the undergrowth I peered at the rail embankment and beheld a terrifying sight: the locomotive, perforated with bullets and ripped open by bombs, was poised vertically on its rear wheels like a horse leaping skyward. The gutted wreck was engulfed in flames and dense smoke. The passenger car windows were shattered and the doors ripped off their hinges. The wrecked boxcars burned madly. Bits of wooden boards, chunks of sooty scrap metal, and disembodied wheels were strewn on either side of the bank. Dozens of shattered corpses of horses rolled in the sand, and the puddles of blood glistening in the rising sun were positively surrealistic.

Nor was this enough to satisfy the bloodthirsty German pilots. Buzzing the grove at low altitude, they continued to strafe murderous machine-gun fire and scatter mouse-sized hand-grenades.

The surprise attack left everyone stunned and unable to grasp what was happening. The self-preservation instinct overwhelmed all logic. Panic-stricken men leaped from one bush to the next, hoping to escape the fragments of the exploding grenades. A cluster of men clung helplessly to the frightened priest, who, clutching his small prayer book, muttered verses of Scripture.

As time passed, the general panic turned into horror. Most of the men had fallen into a state resembling paralysis. No one spoke, no one asked questions; people simply waited for their fate. Then, oblivious to the surrounding chaos and ignoring the fear of death flickering in everyone's eyes, a short, young, be-spectacled little officer with black hair stepped out from among the trees. It was Dr Israel Rubinstein. Barking orders, Rubinstein took over the defence and began to organize the soldiers who were hiding in the adjacent undergrowth and the bushes in the field. His thundering voice drove the surprised men out of their stupor. The new commander ordered the men to open torrential fire on the planes passing overhead. The soldiers obeyed unquestioningly. However, Rubinstein's resourcefulness did not produce the hoped-for results. After the first burst of gunfire, the planes swooped contemptuously low and the men began to mill about, again shocked and frightened, searching for such comrades as remained alive in the undergrowth. No effort was made to sort the men or verify who was present and who not. Now we spotted two hospital staff officers, tottering like drunks past the edge of the grove and into the open field, bareheaded, hair awry, oblivious to the danger of death. Their stumbling gait and the frozen look in their gaping eyes indicated that they had gone insane. The morning's events had cost them their senses. None of the witnesses to the depressing sight could summon the courage to approach the two unfortunates and bring them back to the unit. They headed into the field and finally vanished.

In the meantime the sun had climbed into the blue sky. One by one the men crept out of hiding and began to mill about.

The commander, shaking all over, was the last to spring out of his place of concealment. His plaster-pale face twitched, and his lips moved relentlessly as if in silent prayer. Looking around quickly, he quietly gathered the survivors and, after a brief consultation, ordered them to unload the equipment from the shattered boxcars and reload it on such wagons as remained. We were to continue the trek.

The men worked feverishly throughout the afternoon, pulling equipment damaged in the bombardment out of the wrecked train and loading it on to a lengthy column of peasant wagons hitched to withered horses. The convoy took shape and prepared to set out along the edge of the rail embankment.

The sun began to set slowly into the horizon. The bustle of soldiers around the carts and the harnessing of horses augured the onset of a long, exhausting night's march. Elongated shadows of soldiers striding alongside the miserable wagons stretched the length of the sandy road. Each passing cart sent another cloud of thin dust over the gloomy, purposeless procession. The fine, dry, shifting sand ruined visibility, irritated our skin, obstructed our breathing, and made walking an onerous chore.

At the end of the long convoy there suddenly appeared a coach hitched to two horses. It had been 'requisitioned' from some nearby peasants. Aboard it was the hospital commander, who announced his intention to ride to Warsaw for further orders. The men were to march to the Polish capital and join him there. The wagoner yanked on the reins and whipped the horses, and the coach lurched into motion and disappeared into the night, leaving behind a thick cloud of dust that wafted heavenward in the crisp air. The commander had deserted his unit in time of danger. I never reported it, because it was not particularly unusual.

Our night-time march met with an additional difficulty. The peasant carts were wobbly, their wheels kept slipping off the axles, and the horses were not fit for the load. One by one, five wagons sank into the deep sand, fell apart with their bulky and expensive gear, and blocked the others' advance. Dragging the equipment through the night on the remaining wagons dulled our wits and dissipated our strength. It was a gruelling night for everyone.

Before daybreak we took shelter in a nearby forest in order
to avoid being spotted by the reconnaissance aircraft that seemed
to come up with the sun. It was their job to plot a course for
the heavy bombers that followed in their wake.

We were cut off from the world, out of touch with everyone,
and unaware of anything happening in our vicinity. We verified
our own location on a map of the kind used by schoolchildren,
which one of the officers had packed in his gear by chance. We
were near the city of Pułtusk, in the Warsaw district. Spam and
bread were doled out, water for tea was boiled in a field kitchen,
and the men sat down in groups under the trees for a quick
meal.

Far away in the clear skies we suddenly heard the undulating
roar of aircraft engines. High up in the blue vastness, a dogfight
between two swift assault planes developed before our eyes.
Each of the pilots, displaying combat experience and exemplary
courage, tried to mount his opponent's tail, and occasionally
spit a burst of fire from his machine-gun. Our ears could hardly
pick up the distant rat-a-tat; all we heard were truncated echoes
that sounded like the crying of ravens swooping down on prey
in the field.

From time to time rays of sunlight glinted off the planes'
wings, giving them the appearance of flashing swords engaged
in a duel.

Like a pair of bloodthirsty mosquitoes alternately thrusting
and retreating, stinging and buzzing, the pilots eluded one
another with thrilling spiral manoeuvres that called for agility
and supreme talent. This sublimely desperate contest in the
heavens would last a few minutes only. Neither combatant was
willing to forgo a decisive triumph, and each passing moment
brought one of them closer to his demise. With growing tension
the onlookers thrust their breakfast aside, eyes peeled on the
paramount struggle in the sky. Everyone could sense the rivals'
resourcefulness and reciprocal enmity. Suddenly the noise
stopped. A spot could be seen descending to earth, first slowly
and then rapidly, pursued by a tail of billowing black smoke
that gradually faded into the distant horizon.

The battle was over. No parachute was seen.

The cruel victor sped from the scene of the kill and vanished into the blue void. Tears could be seen in the depressed witnesses' eyes.

In the meantime, I had been ordered to requisition feed for the horses at a nearby country farm. We were in central Poland, where the farms were much better off than in the miserable villages in the country's eastern sector. They had large, modern stables with shingled roofs, well-tended barns and pigsties, and handsome, well-kept residences surrounded with flowering bushes and green lawns. Large purebred dogs milled around with hundreds of geese and chickens. An intoxicating aroma of harvested grain and fresh hay filled us with a sensation of calm and tranquillity, as if we were in a faraway, quiet, happy country at peace. The barn was heaped to its wooden ceiling with fresh grain. As I handed the silent, submissive farmsteader official requisition forms entitling him to State reimbursement, the men loaded two wagons with his bounty.

Neither did the quick-fingered soldiers pass up the opportunity to seize a few chickens in the yard 'for war purposes'. In these cases, no requisition form was presented.

The sun was setting slowly as I returned with the only war booty I would ever procure in my life. I sat down with my comrades for a 'dinner' of hot, fresh chicken soup prepared by soldiers experienced in this craft. It tasted like paradise and warmed our tired bones. The day had passed quickly, with no respite from the previous night's labours.

We were ordered to prepare to march, and the soldiers hurredly hitched up the horses for another night on the move. On the way I occasionally dismounted in favour of a spell on one of the heavily loaded carts. Most of the way, however, I preferred to walk alongside the lurching wagon.

It was a dark night preceding the new moon; only the stars flickered and winked in the eerie, black silence. The air exuded an odour of forest fire with a light, caressing and numbing breeze. The sound of faraway bombardments reached our ears from time to time. The intoxicating silence and exhaustion overwhelmed any attempt to think. My head slumping on to my shoulder, I fell asleep and took leave of reality for a few moments that seemed like forever.

I woke up in the back of the cart as if having suddenly been bitten by a scorpion. The wagon was standing there. Its withered horse was motionless, its head bent at the neck and almost touching the ground. The convoy, I realized, had gone ahead and vanished into the gloom, and we stood at a fork in the dirt road. The wagons behind me, too, stood as if fossilized; their drivers had fallen asleep. I felt as if darkness had swamped my world. Flushed and dizzy, I was seized with fear of isolation and a sense of responsibility for the fate of the rest of the convoy. The men were indeed counting on me to choose the right path. Any hesitation or delay in making the decision would act against me and leave us even further behind the others.

Aware that we were at risk of capture by enemy patrols, I punched the driver in the shoulder and ordered him to advance quickly on the path leading to the right. My jubilation knew no limit when, after several minutes of walking in nerve-wracking tension and fear, I made out the wagons moving slowly in front of us in the haze. Dizzy and weak-kneed, I summoned the last of my strength and mounted one of the wagons that now rejoined the convoy, grabbing a brief nap in order to recover from the threat of separation that I had miraculously avoided.

On the distant horizon, the sky began to glow with the first rays of dawn. Approaching us on the dirt road were convoys of army wagons and terrified refugees. The latter spoke of heavy bombardments in the area, wreaking devastation and destruction. They regarded our pointless advance to the battlefield as the height of illogic. Our men disregarded the rumours and decided to carry on as our commander, now waiting for us in Warsaw, had ordered.

The trail led to the town of Wyszków. We reached the town after surviving some artillery shelling and heavy aerial bombardment meant to soften any resistance. Tongues of fire still flickered on either side of the main street; pillars of dense smoke ascended from the houses, which had been reduced to splinters under the shattering force of the bombs. Flames flickered heavenward as the blazing wooden houses and furniture popped and crackled. Although it was late evening by now, the town radiated the blinding light one associates with a sunny day.

Peering into the burning rooms, we saw paintings, crosses, and statues of Jesus that had tumbled from the walls on to the sizzling floors. Sabbath candles and candelabra still sat on tables under the charred beams of several houses, awaiting the all-consuming flames.

Riding past on horseback, I was forced at times to bend over in order to evade the tongues of fire that reached for me from either side of the street. It was Friday night, eve of the Jewish Sabbath – now a night of terror auguring the devastation of a world.

Then, as if in an apocalyptic vision, I came face to face with a white-bearded Jew in a black Hassidic coat, who had stumbled purposelessly from one of the burning houses. From my rucksack I withdrew a postcard addressed to my parents and bearing four words: I'm OK. See you. 'Put it in the nearest postbox,' I told him.

In its eighth day of bloody, hopeless combat, the war was in full swing. We did not imagine at the time that the government had already left Warsaw.[6] The enemy, flooding Poland with his armoured vehicles, had smashed and routed our army. In the middle of the juggernaut's path stood the capital, Warsaw, which girded up for a protracted defence of the last remnants of the people's dignity.

The sun began to rise. The dirt road twisted its way up a hill that dominated the surroundings and afforded a view of placid, smouldering Wyszków. In the distance a few white chimneys and stone walls stood erect – tombstones on the residents' graves. Far away, in the open field, one could see the remains of destroyed military equipment, burnt-out field kitchens, pill-boxes, wheels, and piles of junk. The mighty wave of destruction and devastation had been a performance worthy of the devil. It was hard to imagine that ordinary lives had ever been lived here, that peasants had ever walked quietly behind their ploughs. Light gathered over the horizon, auguring the beginning of another day and new disappointments.

The convoy slid down the hill and sought refuge from the enemy pilots' line of vision in a nearby grove of trees. Some of the soldiers milled around the wagons and gave water to the thirsty horses; others walked into the woods and sprawled out for a nap.

As the day passed, increasing numbers of people approached us from the front. They were survivors, refugees of the slaughter. All were thirsty; all were bitter. Their tattered clothes and dirty faces attested to the magnitude of the defeat. The soldiers among them described the chaos and general disarray of the army.

With each passing hour, lengthy bursts of automatic weapon fire and the thunder of explosions grew in volume, indicating that the front was closing in. A few stray aircraft and squadrons passed overhead, and no one doubted to whom they belonged.

Protruding from the ground of the open field, which stretched from the edge of the grove to the distant horizon, was the gutted wing of a small airplane bearing traces of red and white markings. A few of us went over to the site of the disaster. In the shattered cockpit was the crumpled body of a young pilot in junior officer's uniform. With the convoy's priest looking on, we lifted the casualty from his seat and buried him in a trench beside the aircraft. To the accompaniment of silent prayer, an improvised, unmarked cross made of two boards held together with a rusty nail was planted in the earth.

Again we met with a train of deserters and civilians, escaping from the battle zone with their personal effects. Their gloomy reports failed to dissuade the men from continuing to head for Warsaw as they had resolved, and reporting to the commander for orders as they had agreed. The horses were hitched up at sunset, and the convoy, with such equipment as remained, gathered along the dirt road that twisted up a nearby hill. As evening fell, the column of wagons embarked on a slow ascent. The heavy wheels sank into sand, and we were forced at times to push them to help the exhausted horses keep the bone-breaking procession on the move. From the top of the hill, the path plunged on to a broad field bordering a thick oak forest. To the left was a valley which extended almost as far as the distant horizon.

Here we came upon a horrifying sight: dozens of corpses – human and horse – along with overturned wagons, crates, rifles, piles of metal pylons, junk, a burned-out tank, and cars lying on their sides.

Exhausted casualties and refugees who came our way told us about the cruel battle that had taken place here the night before. A cavalry formation, displaying self-sacrifice and supreme, illogical courage, had stormed an enemy armoured column. One of the fighters charged at an enemy tank, lobbed a hand-grenade into its open muzzle, and wiped out its crew. The sight of this vale of terror, together with the eyewitness reports, convinced our men once and for all to abandon the plan of joining up with our commander. We decided to retreat to the south-east, towards the Soviet and Romanian borders.

The night-time retreat was exceedingly dangerous. The enemy's motorized patrols, crossing far into territory still held by Polish forces, were sowing panic and chaos in the rear. In the dead of night we sometimes noticed the flickering lanterns of spies and collaborators, marking targets for enemy aerial bombardment. It was clear that we had to get out of there quickly and avoid any engagement with enemy combat units.

Again we had to gear up for a march – this time a retreat in broad daylight. Discovery by the enemy would place us in immediate and obvious danger. Spam, bread, and tea were hastily apportioned. It was a clear, sunny day. The sun-drenched road was swathed in clouds of dust as we followed in the wake of a convoy of large wagons, harnessed to pairs of horses, which had been requisitioned from the affluent farms. It was a hospital that had beaten a retreat from the battle zone. Its staff disclosed gloomy details about how our army had been routed in the general collapse of the front.

Because these reports were provided by our comrades at arms, our men regarded them as reliable and thus came away all the more frustrated and hopeless. Our column of miserable carts crept toward the outskirts of the town of Kowel. Fortunately for us, air attacks were rare; the enemy had more important targets to aim at.

Before dawn, two weeks after the war broke out and following a gruelling day-and-night march, we reached an army camp. There we met thousands of soldiers and officers of various ranks, clustered in the spacious yard of a barracks dating from the Tsar's time. It was a ragtag multitude of exhausted men at wits' end, despondent at the absence of any news about developments at the front and their families' well-being.

The rows of tall, rundown grey buildings pocked with square windows left one with the intimidating impression of a maximum-security prison. Every poor man clung, as to a lifebuoy, to any rumour that might bring some respite to his personal suffering.

The echoes of short-range gunfire could be heard at times over the noise and commotion of the rabble. Walking towards the gunfire, I came upon a ditch behind one of the buildings and found several military police arguing with each other. Someone let me in on the secret: Ukrainian spies caught loitering in the area were brought here, taken before a randomly manned emergency field court, 'tried', and executed without appeal. Miserable indeed was the fate of the individual who, in those times of terror, fell into the clutches of 'judges' who represented the distraught rabble and attempted to clothe their caprices in a mantle of righteousness.

Chaos reigned supreme in the camp yard. Irritability grew, and various rumours spread through the crowd. More than a few became convulsed with panic. Soldiers broke into the warehouses that contained the worn clothing of army recruits, and hastily dragged off bits of civilian attire 'just in case'. The shelves were quickly emptied; all that remained were scraps of tattered clothes and dirty underwear reeking of faeces and mould.

Exhausted by the long day and its events, I sprawled out on a wooden bench in a large empty room and fell asleep. I could not expunge from memory the sight of the ditch where those Ukrainians were arbitrarily executed.

As the new day's sun climbed slowly into the summer-clear skies, the commotion in the barracks yard intensified. Everyone pressed forward for his spoonful of coffee and slice of bread. The sensation of overcrowding, however, was gone. Many had fled in the civilian clothes they had pilfered the previous night. There was a town nearby; relatives and friends were ever-ready to provide shelter in time of trouble. I, too, was bitten by the temptation and eager to break away from the confused rabble of soldiers and put an end to the pointless peregrinations.

A new rumour spread through the chaotic yard: Colonel Koc was organizing a fighting unit made up of local men.[7] Hundreds of soldiers and officers leaped into motion. The war was not over yet! They found weapons and ammunition in the emergency stores. A lengthy line of volunteers took shape.

I noticed about a dozen stalwart thoroughbred horses in the field across the road. Their long legs and forward-thrusting narrow necks attested to their having been pampered. They were an intriguing, extraordinary sight. As I approached the horses, several men stepped toward me. They wore uniforms of green and blue, with glittering epaulette medallions, red stripes down the trousers, and gold-striped berets. They looked like something out of a travelling circus or a zoo. The leader of the group, bedecked in a blue dress jacket with gleaming buttons, informed me politely that the men and beasts came from Count Poniatowski's thoroughbred horse farm in western Poland, now retreating from the front. Without waiting for further questions on my part, he went on to describe how the *Wehrmacht* had been routed in the last few days, and how our air force had been bombing Berlin. After Hitler had been killed, he said, his army commanders begged for a ceasefire.

So persuasively elegant was this man in his impressive livery that no one could doubt the veracity of his gospel. The general despondency, together with the tendency to look for redeeming news when in distress, worked their spell; for a fleeting moment it seemed as if a miracle had occurred.

I came back to my senses with no further ado when a squadron of enemy bombers passed deafeningly overhead. Sober now, if somewhat perplexed, I strode toward the convoy of pitiful carts and companies of exhausted soldiers that were gearing up to march into war under Colonel Koc.

As the convoy began to move, a little aircraft burst into view. Swooping devilishly low, the pilot dumped candies wrapped in coloured foil. Hungrily the soldiers snatched up the treat. A few minutes later, three of our soldiers doubled over with stomach convulsions and, despite medical help, died in agony. The cunning enemy's lethal poison had gone to work.

The military column marched vigorously through the town of Kowel. Despite the summer sun, the windows and shutters in the homes were shut, the streets were deserted, and no one was in sight.

From one man to the next, persistent rumours spread through the column about organized gangs of criminals and thugs who waylaid individual soldiers on the desolate roads, stripping them of weapons, money, and uniforms. Many of those who defended themselves were murdered.

As the sun slowly set, the convoy headed for the woods. A quiet day had passed – no gunfire, no strafing – and the suspicious silence surprised us all. Cut off from the world, we did not imagine that Poland's fate had long since been decided.

The wagoners tended to their horses, and the tired men spread out for a night's sleep in the dark, eerily silent forest. The air grew hazy, exuding the intoxicating aromas of pine and wild flowers.

I lay down beside a tree moist with dew. Suddenly the wagoner turned to me: 'Doctor, it's the eve of Yom Kippur.'

Something like a massive electric shock jolted me from head to toe. My family members appeared on the black mask of the night; above them all, gazing down, were my father's sad eyes. A heavy pressure gripped my forehead, and I dried my moist cheeks with trembling hands. Ruminations from the past flew by helter-skelter. Then, gradually, the pictures faded and I was left there, suspended in the vastness of space. Bursts of gunfire and intermittent explosions could be heard in the dark. As dawn broke, we found that a battle had taken place at the edge of the forest between Polish formations and a Red Army unit that had crossed the frontier. Nearby, we found two gutted Soviet halftracks, witnesses to this engagement with the saviour force. First morning rays of pink light appeared on the horizon beyond the treetops. We were near the village of Werba.

From the east came a sudden roar of heavy aircraft. As the planes swooped low, they scattered piles of leaflets that the wind carried in every direction. Gathering them, our soldiers found a mimeographed appeal by the Soviet commander of this front, Marshal Timoshenko,[8] typed in Russian and halting Polish:

'You are to bring all pointless resistance to a halt. The war is over; the friendly Red Army has arrived to liberate the people from the oppression of the Polish tyrants.'

The men in the woods were thunderstruck. Palpable relief was mixed with profound anxiety about the future. Our purposeless migration and flight from capture and death had been a burden to us all, an impediment to any logical thought.

The last of the men came out of the forest. Eerie silence and overwhelming tension set in – the kind of atmosphere that marks the seam between two parts of a lengthy campaign. Disappointed, the men huddled in the surrounding void and began to ponder their next move. Several of them soundlessly stepped away from the group and vanished down the dirt road.

2

Trapped

A squad of armed Soviet guards approached us from the other side of the street and, with restrained politeness, announced that we were POWs. We asked a Russian officer if we might keep our personal weapons; he agreed. Then additional officers appeared and confiscated them, disregarding the previous promise. Soviet soldiers surrounded our group and ordered us to advance towards the rail station.

Stooped and crestfallen, we marched down the main street of the town of Włodzimierz-Wołyński. Four senior officers strode at the head of the group of nearly 100 tightly bunched, tense men. One of them was Colonel Koc – tall, impeccably dressed, chest bedecked with medals of honour. Under heavy guard in the gleaming autumn sun, we moved down the road that bisected the town. Polish women in flowery summer dresses strolled by, taunting us in unmistakable terms: 'We won't give up an inch of our land!' It was the slogan our leaders and people bandied about before the war. In our present downcast state, the words were knives in our backs and salt on our wounds.

Across the street, a woman in black wiped her flowing tears with trembling hands.

As we reached the station, a freight train clattered into slow motion and we leaped on to one of the flatcars. After a short distance, we realized that the armed guards had vanished. Jubilant at having slipped out of the noose, three of us (my friends Dr Antoni Łagun, the pharmacist Józef Żołnierowicz, and myself) fled the railway area, packs and all, and plunged into the adjacent forest, to take shelter in the thick undergrowth. Peering between the trees, we saw convoys of Soviet tanks and trucks moving west. The young, narrow-eyed soldiers with their thick moustaches smiled innocently as if on an outing. Cut off from the world, we perceived the danger that lurked in every corner and were gripped with the depressing sensation of being beasts of prey. Circumventing villages and asking no help of the civilians we encountered on the way, we headed north, home-ward, using the trees' shadows as a compass.

The days were enchantingly beautiful. Fortunately for us, Indian summer was in full swing and clear skies accompanied us in our wanderings. After having shaken off every kind of forced dependency, our feeling of freedom was both pleasant and threatening. By night, we slept under twinkling stars on a bed of grass that exuded a fresh, living aroma. The crisp air drugged our senses, and we awakened to sunbeams bursting through the morning haze.

After an improvised meal from the remnants of our battle rations, we resumed our march toward the longed-for destina-tion – home.

When we had spent several days thus, we were exhausted and utterly alone. For lack of choice we trusted our fate to the mercies of a peasant, purchasing a short trip in his cart for items of clothing that we would not need on our way to freedom.

Total silence reigned. The absence of explosions and roaring engines hinted at the end of the campaign. The illusions of victories had been dispelled, and we were anxious about the uncertain future we faced after the two neighbouring powers had divided up our country. Our exhausting peregrinations and irregular, fitful sleep had dulled our wits; the sensation of freedom thwarted any judicious thought. Our peasant escort informed us that we were close to Baranowicze, en route to Wilno.

Tempted at the thought of being reunited with our families, and anticipating relief from the pent-up burden, we dropped our guard. Like moths drawn into fatal fire, we strode spell-bound towards the rail station, disregarding the peril that threatened us from every direction.

Thousands of soldiers and civilians milled about noisily on a platform at which a long train stood. Its freight cars were filled with army men, and hundreds of curious eyes expressed one and only one desire – home.

An ancient locomotive spat dense smoke from its huge stack and steam from superheated boilers. Intermittent sharp blasts of its whistle augured an imminent departure. The three of us approached the engineer and asked where he was headed. At first he said nothing; only when we repeated the question did he confirm hesitantly that the train was going to Wilno. Hastily we leaped aboard one of the boxcars. Because we were officers, the soldiers pressed against each other in an effort to make room for us. Packed like sardines they stood, reeking of sweat and filth in the gloom of the boxcar.

The train suddenly jerked forward, and a short, deafening whistle blast split the air. An unseen hand outside the car slammed the heavy sliding door shut with a grating shriek, and a sharp clank of latches indicated that we were locked inside.

The train immediately gained speed and left the station behind. A few seconds passed. The soldiers began to tremble unexpectedly. A barely audible, sceptical mutter was heard: 'The train's going east. To Russia. *Not to Wilno.*' Waves of horror reverberated through the thick air, followed by shock.

In a split second I realized that a fateful disaster had overtaken us. 'We fell for it,' my two comrades muttered. Indeed, I sensed, we had stumbled into a cul-de-sac.

My world collapsed. I became dizzy and broke out in gooseflesh. In the dull light that penetrated through the narrow boxcar grating I observed my two comrades, standing silently and deathly pale. Overhead was a skylight; through its bars appeared the tip of a bayonet. *We had been taken prisoner.*

It was as if the ravings of a sick imagination had become horrifyingly real. My heart throbbed strangely. I felt as if embarking on a new and terrible episode in my life. The captives' desperate calls and cries were to no avail. No reaction came from outside. Surprise was total; all was lost. We were overwhelmed with the feeling that the bowels of the earth had opened and that we were descending into an abyss.

We were smilter with an indescribable pain of disgraceful, irreversible failure and irrevocable defeat. After our hardships and suffering, hunger and distress, we had obviously been humiliatingly ambushed. The captives' faces reflected wrath and bitterness at having been so cunningly deceived.

The soldiers near the grating had dislodged the bars. One of them worked himself free and, with agility of a cat, leaped out. A second man slipped out after him. outside, gunshots could be heard. The results of the daring breakaway could not be verified.

The train, with its cargo of helpless, hopeless creatures, continued to race eastward to destinations unknown. The shouts and curses of the anguished captives went unanswered. In the meantime, the train crossed into the Soviet Union at the border town of Negoreloje, and stopped in a vast field near Orsza.

With a screeching of latches, the sliding doors were thrown open, flooding the car with blinding sunlight. From the semi-illuminated cars we leaped on to the rail embankment, where an uncommon sight awaited us: thousands of people crouching in the open field.

A rabble of men of various ages, brought together by bitter fate, wandered about in confusion and lay on the ground in shameless positions. The embankment was covered with faeces and filth left behind by tens of thousands of men on their way east. Having enjoyed the glory of freedom and the intoxicating aroma of forest and fresh fields only a few hours before, we found the sight repulsive and embarrassing.

Boxcars loaded with men, women, and children awaiting transport to the Russian interior stretched endlessly to the horizon.

The train suddenly jerked forward. The confused rabble frantically scrambled aboard; better that than to be left behind in the terror of the present inferno.

After a short trip, we stopped at the edge of an earth bank lined with improvised field kitchens. Large metal pots on wooden fires emitted steam, and cooks stirred boiling soup with wooden poles. The hungry prisoners, grabbing bowls and heavy wooden spoons, shoved their way into a lengthy queue for their portion. Evidently experienced, the cooks plunged large ladles into the boiling soup and filled the bowls pushed under their noses by the jostling people in line. Examining the concoction, I found it to be a thin liquid enriched with a few bits of fish and potatoes.

One of the petty officials doled out slices of black bread. It was flat and sour, apparently because something added to the flour had prevented the yeast from fermenting. Tasteless as it was, the soup warmed and filled our stomachs, which had been empty for days. After the hasty meal in the open field, the bowls were thrown into basins of water for reuse by the next trainload of POWs.

A long whistle from the locomotive augured the next stage of our trip, and the thousands of unfortunates leaped aboard the cars. A new malady had overcome the mob: stomach convulsions. Here and there men threw up in the crowded car, to their neighbours' dismay.

Rail traffic was relentlessly heavy in both directions. Our train occasionally pulled on to sidings to let other trains, laden with field guns and army trucks, race westward towards occupied Poland.

The sun set slowly, and the despondent travellers hunkered sardine-like for their night's sleep. Only a few successfully dozed off, snoring wildly and frighteningly. The gloom of the boxcar magnified the stench of their sweat, permeating through clothes that had not been taken off for quite some time.

A few happy souls had found positions near the narrow grating near the ceiling. They clung to their places, imbibing the crisp air penetrating from outside. Observing the shadows of the cars in the setting sun's light, they reported the direction in which we were heading. Some time later, in the darkness of night, the clickety-clack of the train wheels ceased and we stopped in an open field. In the eerie silence all around, those with initiative put the empty hours to use, steadily carving slits in the wooden boxcar walls to admit air. Others, using primitive tools in their possession, drilled a hole in the boxcar floor with which they might tend to their bodily needs. This was carried out efficiently, since the guards treated with deaf ears the prisoners' howling, obscene pleas to open the doors.

The grating near the ceiling had long since been stripped of its bars, and the prisoners eagerly peered through the slits in the walls. The yellowing fields and green groves that passed by their eyes put thoughts of longed-for freedom into their minds.

The younger men began to concoct escape plans and communicate them in whispers. Fuelled by their imagination, they were nevertheless deterred by the barrier of fear and the magnitude of the effort this dangerous operation entailed. Cold logic argued against any sensible chance of success. After leaping through the narrow opening in the boxcar, which was racing at full speed, they would have to wander, hungry and without identifying documents, in a hostile environment where their fate could be sealed either by the authorities or by residents ever-sensitive to the presence of spies.

Logic notwithstanding, the boxcar gradually became less crowded; sitting on the floor became more comfortable.

We stopped near the Viaz'ma rail station, and one of the passengers who knew the area announced that we were approaching Moscow. In the meantime we were ordered out of the cars; they wanted to record our particulars. It was an overcast late-September day.

Two Soviet officers sat on wooden stools at a small table in an empty field. Large hand-guns clipped to wide cloth belts dangled casually from their hips, and a stack of papers lay before them on the table.

In a lengthy queue our men approached the table and reported name, rank, and serial number. This went quickly for the enlisted men, less so for the officers. It was almost my turn. In front of me were two Poles, about thirty years of age. They leaned over the registration table, and, in a whisper, asked the Soviet officers to inform their superiors of the presence of two Polish Communist activists among the prisoners.

One of the Soviet officers looked up with pronounced suspicion. With a penetrating, hostile glare, he answered firmly: 'Cut it out. We've wiped out more important Communists than you.' With this, he nonchalantly continued recording the details of the next men in line.

The two dumbfounded Poles tore along to the cluster of officers who had already been recorded. Perceptibly confused

and profoundly disappointed, they knew their hopes for a glittering future in their dreamland had been dashed.

At the end of the painstaking head-count, about two dozen
officers remained out of the hundreds of men registered. These
were led to a dark, filthy boxcar, under heavier armed guard
than the norm. By contrast, the dozens of cars set aside for the
enlisted men were open and unguarded. Among the officers I
met Colonel Marynowski, a senior physician and head of the
internal medicine department of a military hospital in Wilno. I
had known of him as an intellectual whose lofty status imbued
him with self-confidence, and who used to be handsome. Now
I was anguished at the sight of his face – furrowed, sheet-pale,
deeply despairing. His clear, frightened eyes could hardly be
seen behind their swollen lids. Confused and helpless, he moved
about with a bag over his shoulder. Tied with a thick length of
rope, it contained his personal effects.

Another officer stepped out of the group and approached
me: Dr Merenlender, a physician from Warsaw and head of the
dermatology department in the well-known Chista Hospital in
the Polish capital. Over his shoulder, too, was a tattered sack
with everything he owned. I gathered from his desire to converse that he had long been out of the company of friends. He
spoke of his wife and daughter, whose fate concerned him
greatly and left him sleepless at night. As we talked, we were
joined by Dr Arcichowski, a handsome, fastidiously dressed man
in his forties. Arcichowski spoke of his membership in Warsaw's
B'nai B'rith lodge and described in detail the treachery by which
the Soviets had captured him.

This convocation of partners in misery provided some small
consolation for our suffering and a little relief from our overbearing melancholy. The sliding doors of the officers' car were
slammed shut, and with a shriek of the locomotive the train
again advanced towards its secret destination. We lay down
side by side on the damp floorboards, our few remaining possessions at our heads.

In the gloom of night, a cold wind penetrated through the
cracks in the boxcar walls, producing sounds reminiscent of a
wailing baby. From time to time the older men, sunk in drowsy,

gloomy thoughts about their future and their families, emitted heavy sighs.

As dawn broke, we stopped at the train station at Oriol, near Moscow. Here we leaped on to the platform for a hasty 'breakfast': herring dry as a board, poor-quality black bread with the consistency of moist mortar, and hot water from the station spigot or the locomotive's boiler. There was hardly time even for this, and everyone rushed back to his place in the boxcar.

The train went on by daylight. The men began to grow more familiar with one another, and were willing to help procure hot drinks and make each other more comfortable.

As the trip progressed, it became apparent that ours was a well-educated group including doctors, teachers, standing army officers, and white-collar workers. Only one man in the group, a village mayor, was uneducated; he stood out for his tattered clothing and careless personal hygiene.

A favourably conspicuous member of our group was Dr Marynowski. A distinguished-looking, well-dressed colonel in his late fifties, blond and balding, he was a gentleman by nature and a well-known, broadly educated physician well versed in the arts and literature. Fluent in Russian, he was notably and intimately familiar with the history of this people. His extensive travel throughout the world had equipped him with talent in human relations and ability to understand others.

To the monotonous clickety-clack of the boxcar wheels, Marynowski began to describe the historical battle that had taken place at the outskirts of Moscow, as depicted by Tolstoy in his great novel *War and Peace*. In that very month, September, in the year 1812, Napoleon stood on one of the hills flashing past us now, waiting for the men he had sent to the besieged city's leaders. They would return, he was sure, with the city's surrender agreement in hand.

Napoleon's confidence was premature, and his expectations of entering the capital as victor proved false. His emissaries reported that Moscow had been evacuated and was going up in flames. The venerable Russian commander, Marshal Kutuzov, declared a holy war for the salvation of Russia and, in the battle of Borodino, determined the progression of history.

The listeners soaked up the fascinating story-teller's every word. With his eloquence and vivid style, Marynowski had succeeded in averting the depression of the men, prostrate on the wooden floor of the blacked-out boxcar.

No one imagined that the gifted story-teller of the POW boxcar would be taken on his last journey to the Katyn Forest six months later. Two years afterwards, the hobnail boots of the Thousand-Year Reich would meet with their historic defeat in the same area. An eerie calm overtook the boxcar, and weak beams of light came through the narrow aperture near the ceiling. The train slowed down gradually, and the increasingly frequent clickety-clack of wheels on switches showed that we were approaching a large station.

We stopped with a protracted screech. After the doors were slid open, we were ordered to climb down to the platform. It was Moscow. Far away we could see buildings and warehouses bedecked in banners bearing portraits of Stalin, Lenin, and Marx. They carried giant slogans calling for the triumph of socialism and liberation of the peoples. We approached a workers' restaurant in columns, two abreast. Bowls of hot soup and portions of black bread were doled out through a kitchen window installed in the restaurant's spacious interior. For the first time in our travels, we ate at tables.

As we marched back to the boxcar, the rays of the setting sun bounced off the golden domes of the city's churches. Powerful loudspeakers boomed folk-songs and stirring military marches from every direction. Labourers and clerks bustled this way and that and vanished from sight. Only a few glanced at the strange uniforms.

As we walked, those among us with quick fingers were able change money with some old women and swap worn-out shirts or pants. They procured sweet Russian pastries and even a few hard-boiled eggs.

As we returned, full of impressions, we were surprised to find that some of the heavy platform boards had been dislodged, revealing a deep pit. Climbing out of it was a white-faced rail worker. For lack of housing in the crowded Russian capital, he lived right there, in harsh conditions.

The train began to move, we peppered our guards with

questions about where we were headed. They ignored our queries. Peering through the skylight, our men reported that we were heading north.

We continued guessing about what awaited us. The pessimists among us recalled what the guards had said: we would come out alive but would never see our families again.

When the crisis struck us, Dr Marynowski opened his pack, pulled out a last piece of dried Polish sausage, and in uplifted spirit divided it equally among those present. It was a symbol of everything that was gone forever. Fatigued from the long day's hardships, we sprawled out late that night for sleep.

At daybreak the train was still galloping across a monotonous landscape of desolate fields. A few tundra bushes and withered trees were visible on the horizon, and patches of snow could be seen in the valleys. At dusk we stopped in a field alongside a village enveloped in deathly silence. No cackling roosters, barking dogs, or lowing cows were heard. The hamlet was built of wooden cabins with rotting straw roofs. Dark smoke spiralled from one of the chimneys: evidence of life. An old woman in a black woollen kerchief, clutching a wooden pail, peered curiously from around a corner and quickly took shelter behind the shack. Everything was quiet and grey.

The sun set and eerie darkness overtook the crowded boxcar. Disquiet gripped the men as they contemplated their future. The temporary silence was suddenly shattered by the approaching sound of barked orders, accompanied by yapping dogs and the sharp pounding of soldiers' boots around the train.

The latches of the car doors were thrown aside, the sliding doors were flung open, and we were ordered to get out. The gloom of night was pierced with burning torches mounted on long poles, clutched by guards armed with bayoneted rifles and machine-guns. Many of them came along with large, undomesticated wolfhounds, straining on metal chains that clattered in the chilly air. The beasts barked gratingly and lunged furiously at our men, their presumed prey.

The commander of the operation produced a hand-held megaphone and, bellowing at an ear-shattering volume, warned that anyone who stepped out of the column would meet his end.

3

The POW Camps

Griazoviets

Our living nightmare caught us off guard, left us stunned, and boded ill for the future.

The frightened men silently obeyed the orders and gathered into ranks of four for the night march. As we advanced, armed guards with fierce dogs ran about.

Attrition grew as the men, clutching their belongings, trod over sharp protrusions of frozen mud on the dirt road. The older ones plodded on with their stooped gait and had to slow down from time to time, the guards' howls notwithstanding. In the darkness I turned and noticed the man next to me, Dr Merenlender. With difficulty he advanced, pace by faltering pace, his trembling lips murmuring unintelligible words of despair. He was nearly spent and on the verge of collapse. Without hesitation, I lifted his pack off his back; we continued the gruelling march arm in arm.

The night-time trek lasted about three hours, to the relentless accompaniment of the guards, prodding us with crude warnings produced at the top of their lungs. On the way we passed a deserted village of miserable wooden shacks. The shutters were down, and the abandoned yards were sullied with piles of rotting garbage. Where living souls should have been, there was silence and sadness all around.

At chilly daybreak we took fate in our hands by striding across a rickety little bridge without a handrail. Below, a frozen river lined with desiccated bushes meandered across the desolate plain. Now we passed an abandoned residential house, with the ruins of a destroyed church and heaps of shattered stones alongside. The vast territory was not fenced in. It was 3 October 1939; we had reached the Griazoviets camp in the Vologda district, about half way to the Arctic port of Archangel.

The fourteen officers in our group were housed in an isolated hut at the end of the path, far from the camp's large residential structure. Outside, day and night, we were guarded by a sentry with a large rifle, a greatcoat, and a fur hat with flaps that covered his entire face, punctuated only with narrow slits for his indifferent eyes.

Trying to keep himself warm, the guard engaged in agile jumping jacks and other vigorous calisthenics to the loud pounding of his heavy boots.

Our hut was across from camp headquarters. Even as they feigned disregard for our existence and conspicuously avoided all contact with us, the Soviets observed us carefully. We felt as if left to our own devices, banished in our distress, and bereft of any hopes of improvement in our situation.

No one was spared the afflictions of hunger and cold, least of all the unfortunates who had been taken prisoner of war while dressed in summer uniform. In the evening gloom we occasionally succeeded in eluding the sentry's alert eyes, and gathered bits of boards and sticks, which we burned in a clay pit dug out for this purpose.

Transports with thousands of POWs pulled into the camp around the clock. Many were packed into the large building and little wooden structures along the dirt road. Overcrowding there was terrible. Multitudes of men milled to and fro in the camp, unguarded.

The embittered soldiers grumbled, cursed, and blamed their commanders for the miserable circumstances brought upon them by their defeat in war. Soldiers belonging to Poland's ethnic minorities – Ukrainians, Russians, and Lithuanians – hated Poland and the overbearing Polish officer corps. In their frustration, the enlisted men would inform on their officers, who were trying to hide from the Soviets, and sometimes shoved them out of the trains while in full motion.

Such officers as were discovered in the transports were added to our group, whose number grew to thirty. One of these was Lawrinowicz, from Wilno. He reached Griazoviets in a torn bath robe and worn underwear, barefoot, and trembling with cold. While walking home, the poor man told us, he had been attacked by a gang of armed bandits and forced to part with his weapon, clothes, and shoes. He was released stark naked; the rags in which he was taken prisoner by the Soviets had been miraculously procured from villagers. Tall and thin as a skeleton, he was reclothed with garments contributed by other members of the group.

Late in the evening we received our daily ration of dry herring and black bread. We complained, and one of the staff officers promised to do something about it. This promise, like others, was never kept.

The room was not wide enough for sleep in any normal posture; we had to lie down shoulder to shoulder, rolling over only with our neighbours' consent. This caused serious friction even among friends.

Only a few managed to fall asleep the first night. The rats and fleas ran absolutely wild after waiting so long for prey. As we were awakened in the morning, we discovered multitudes of insects under the worn and peeling plaster of the room's walls. To keep a distance from this infestation, we had to forgo some of our cramped living quarters.

The enlisted men were liberated gradually; some time later it became known that only a few ever got home. Most were put to forced labour – paving roads, building fortifications – or were sent to coal-mines in the heavy industrial area of Donbass.

The days were beautiful, even though it was October in the far north. The afternoon sun warmed the permafrost, but the fierce cold of night penetrated the men's bones to the marrow and caused intolerable suffering.

Increasingly anxious about spending the long winter in my thin officer's uniform, I slipped out of the officers' shack one day and blended into the mass of POWs milling about unsupervised in the camp.

By chance I noticed a huge artilleryman striding about in large felt-lined winter boots. 'Let's exchange boots.' I suggested. The strapping villager eyed my gleaming leather officer's boots, and the rare temptation was irresistible. Immediately he whipped off his heavy boots. To secure the transaction, I pulled two 100-zloty banknotes from my pocket and handed them to the peasant.

So tight were my boots that the artilleryman could hardly pull them over his muscular calves. He looked at me as if doubting my sanity and, after convincing himself that the deal was for real, swiftly stepped away and vanished into the crowd like a fish into deep water.

The large, heavy boots kept me healthy during my years of captivity in the far north, where the mercury fell to −60° Celsius in the winter and blizzards blanketed the frozen ground for months on end. So large were the boots that I could even insert rags to keep my feet warm.

That night I pulled one of the boots apart, and stuffed my personal papers between the outer leather layer and the thick felt inside. Thus they were safe from discovery by the Soviet security men during their frequent searches. The documents survived the war period, which went more easily for me for this reason.

The thousands of soldiers were transported out of the camp a few days later, and our group was transferred to the two-storey residential structure that stood alongside a magnificent church that had been reduced to rubble by an explosion during the Revolution. All that remained of it were heaps of shattered basalt stones, fragments of marble pillars bearing prayers in ancient Cyrillic characters coated with glittering gold, and remnants of multicoloured medieval mosaic floors.

Inside the spacious rooms of the surviving house, three tiers of bunks reached the ceiling. The men in our group organized their affairs for a protracted stay and hoped that the hardship of our wanderings had come to a quick end. The camp kitchen was on the ground floor; once a day, sometimes at midnight, a warm meal of malodorous herring soup and a quarter-loaf of black bread was doled out. Once a week we were given a packet of *makhorka* – a ersatz tobacco smoked in Russia. To heat our quarters, we secretly and gradually dismantled wooden benches in the empty rooms.

After we organized ourselves in our new quarters, a few quiet days sped by. Then, to our profound dismay, we were suddenly ordered on the afternoon of 18 October to gather our belongings. Surrounded by a column of armed soldiers, we were forced to march to the rail station.

Beside the deserted platform stood an open, wet boxcar. Everything around us was desolate; biting cold and strong wind penetrated our bones. The mouldy boxcar was furnished with dirty wooden benches and scraps of food left behind by previous occupants.

Our men, begrimed and chilled, sat down shoulder to shoulder, bundled in their coats and trembling with cold. In the middle of the boxcar stood a rusted iron stove equipped with a sooty chimney. Nowhere was there any wood for a fire with which we might warm our frozen bones. Late that night, a locomotive came by and we resumed our wanderings. After herring was doled out, our men began to shout for drinking water, and the guards had to open the boxcar at the depots to dispense it.

The conditions of protracted crowding, isolation, and frustration intensified fraternal feelings among the occupants of the darkened car. Yearnings for family were alleviated with recollections of the past and willingness to help one another in our hopeless reality.

After weeks of peregrination, differences of age, social class, and ethnic extraction gave way to first indications of devotion to others. The intellectuals in our group found common language and exchanged views on problems that had concerned them before the war. The group included white-collar workers, teachers, and standing army officers, who did not flinch from taking an anti-semitic tone when arguing about the causes of the war and Poland's defeat.

Some of the men were silent, introspective types who retreated in their solitude to the corners of the boxcar and kept themselves out of the conversations. Eyes half-shut, they followed what was going on around them indifferently. One of these men was a dentist, Dr Winograd. Another, dressed in filthy, reeking rags, had been the mayor of a ramshackle village. Yet another was a withered, pale, and frightened teacher.

Dr Marynowski, a perspicacious man bursting with ideas, spared no effort to raise the company's morale. Summoning his descriptive vocabulary and poetical rhetoric, he told of his travels throughout the world, and with rare talent fanned flickers of hope of rescue from the abyss into which we had fallen.

In the middle of the night of 20 October the train stopped in a field. Deafeningly barking dogs and shouting guards roused the slumbering passengers. A heavy contingent of armed soldiers surrounded our group. We were informed that any attempt to lag behind or slip out of line would be met with gunfire.

In an ambience of gloom and fury, we embarked on a march in an unknown direction. For the first time the despairing men whispered to one another about the possibility of having reached the end of the road – execution.

In heavy fog, biting cold, and knife-like wind, we advanced on a path paved with nerve-wracking frozen mud. The older members of the group, although stumbling from time to time, had no choice but to summon the last of their strength and keep going.

Vologda

After a lengthy trek we reached a high wall encased all along with multiple banks of barbed wire and soaring observation posts. The latter were manned with alert guards armed with automatic rifles and powerful searchlights that illuminated the surroundings.

An iron gate was pulled open, revealing a vast courtyard flanked by contiguous buildings along the wall. At the edge of the yard was a towering, magnificent church. Its belfries and elegant narrow windows with their splendid stained glass, preserved for many years, had survived.

The church gave out a dull light, and, although silence reigned, the presence of a large numbers of people at the site was evident.

Our group was ordered into one of the empty buildings, which was equipped with wooden benches. Without orders, we let our belongings fall to earth and, exhausted, sprawled out on the boards.

The following morning we found that we were in Orthodox, a large medieval monastery near the city of Vologda, about halfway between Moscow and the Arctic port of Archangel. The buildings, flush against the camp wall, had once accommodated friars and nuns who had retreated from social life, preferring to commune in isolation far from any human settlement.

With the sun's first rays, the camp began to hum like a beehive. Thousands of soldiers, pale and shivering in tattered clothing, burst out of the church as if out of a giant pressure cooker, and gathered into groups in the yard.

The church entrance with its broad stairs was graced with an iron gate lavishly adorned with stylized laurel leaves and flowers. The massive structure lay in timeless semi-darkness, and the few electric bulbs merely cast weak light in the cavernous interior.

White marble columns with Corinthian capitals separated the high-ceilinged nave *chapel* from the side chapels. Six tiers of roughly cut wooden bunks filled the void to the vaulted ceiling, on which mural paintings of the Holy Trinity, the Apostles, and smiling angels with golden haloes survived.

Thousands of soldiers were packed into the space under terrible conditions; many clung to the pillars supporting the bunk tiers as they ascended and descended the scaffold-like tier structure. Damp socks, dressing-gowns, and other articles of clothing were piled in disorder at the edges of the boards. The air inside was heavy, mouldy, and malodorous. Those who had taken up position on the upper tiers sweated in the suffocating dampness, while those on the lower levels shivered in the piercing cold that came in through the open door and unglazed windows. Neighbouring soldiers argued to the extent of shouting and fisticuffs about closing or opening the main door.

Kitchen boilers in the square yard abutting the church turned out noodle soup around the clock. Water was drawn from a deep well in the main camp yard. After a few days of intensive drawing, bone fragments began to appear in the turgid water. The well was declared out of commission, and water was now trucked in by the barrel from outside the camp. An old Russian with a long beard, employed as a servant at the Soviet camp headquarters, explained this latest mystery: the residents of the monastery had been killed during the Revolution, and their corpses had been thrown into the well.

The dozens of officers who turned up among the multitudes of enlisted men in the transports were added to our group, which now numbered about sixty. Our original Griazoviets contingent stayed on good terms, even though the general atmosphere took an ugly turn after some of the newcomers missed no opportunity to vent their nationalism.

In our first days in the camp, we alerted the Russian woman doctor to our presence and helped with her work in the clinic. Most of the soldiers suffered from skin conditions, weakened vision, and bleeding gums because of malnutrition and infections caused by poor hygiene and no baths.

The doctors in our group were put to work inoculating the men against smallpox and administering doses of 'bacteriophage', the conventional Russian remedy for typhus and dysentery.

The inoculation certificates bore a rubber stamp: 'General Kiev Camp of the NKVD'. The Russian doctor explained to us that the camp had taken over one of the old monasteries that punctuated the tundra from the Arctic coast to the Ural Mountains. The timeless forests and desolate expanses of the area, referred to as 'not very distant places', became the homes in exile of Pushkin, Lermontov, and other freedom-lovers who opposed the Tsar's regime. ('Distant places', by contrast, included the Vorkuta and Piechora tundra regions bordering the Ural Mountains. The long-term detainees were sent to the Kolyma and Kamchatka areas in the Far East, from which people seldom returned.) After the Revolution, administration of the monasteries was entrusted to the 'Popular Commisariat for Internal Affairs' – the NKVD – for use as prisoners' transit camps.

Within ten days we accustomed ourselves to the conditions and began to hope that our stay would be a long one. We were wrong again: we were suddenly ordered to gather up our belongings and get ready to march.

We quit the monastery with its sardine-like multitudes of soldiers undergoing investigation, and marched to the village rail station under heavy guard. Waiting for us at a considerable distance from the station were the filthy boxcars we had known in the past.

Now and then the train progressed in various directions, but it spent most of the time standing on the desolate tundra waiting for a locomotive. Each time we switched engines, there came a deafening screech of brakes and repeated smashing of couplings that jolted the despondent men out of their languor.

This time, the doors of the cars were open and we were less stringently watched. During the lengthy stops, we raided other trains for coal and wood to stoke our rusty stove. Daring souls among us slipped away at the stops to draw boiling water from the locomotive spigot; the diet of herring and dry bread left us chronically thirsty.

En route, we encountered passing freight trains packed with people, mostly young women, pressed closely together. Their round faces and protruding cheeks attested to their Central Asian extraction. The women vented their urges without inhibition, behaved crudely, and sang vulgar folk-songs at full volume. The audacious among them pushed themselves against the car windows and, gesturing and making faces at us, cursed in ridicule, stuck out their tongues, and, at times, shamelessly exposed their buttocks.

By chance, we found out what these strange reactions were all about, when at one of the stops we found an inscription in white chalk on our boxcar wall: 'Dog Car'. The trains that passed by as we watched were carrying multitudes of civilians from all parts of the USSR to the festive parades marking the anniversary of the Bolshevik Revolution, celebrated on 7 November at Moscow's Red Square.

Skit

On the night of 6 November, the clicking of the wheels and the frequent thunder of passing locomotives fell silent. After waiting irritably for hours, we were given the order we had expected: to vacate the cars.

We debarked on to an unpopulated tundra covered with deep snow. The grating shouts of the guards' officers came as no surprise this time, and the men, experienced by now, were more indifferent than fearful of the future.

After more than three hours of marching in Stygian darkness, skipping over trenches and obstacles, we reached a camp abutting a forest, ringed with high barbed-wire fences.

The Griazoviets inmates flopped down in exhaustion, clothes and all, on the floor of the structure at the camp entrance. Hordes of fleas kept us awake. Notwithstanding our fatigue, however, we burst into the camp yard at daybreak.

All around were towering observation huts, manned with guards with heavy sheepskin coats and machine-guns. Skit was a small, square camp, each side about 200 metres to a side, surrounded with primeval thick oak forest whose branches no axe had ever touched. In the distant past it had accommodated monks craving solitude and roving priests.

Now some 700 officers were packed on to bench-bunks in little summer houses with shingled roofs and porches at the entrances. Alongside the houses were lawns and withered, long-untended fruit trees. Skit was being used as temporary quarters for low-ranking officers awaiting transfer to the main POW camp, Kozielsk.

In the middle of the yard stood the mess hall; beside it was a storage area for large metal barrels full of small salted fish compressed into a frozen mass.

The daily fish soup was a thin gruel with a miserable supplement of bits of potato. While doling out the portions, the cooks did not bother to stir the brew, thus reserving the thick material at the bottom for their buddies.

On this diet of tasteless soup of little nutritional value, and lacking major nutrients in general, the prisoners suffered from pus-filled skin eruptions, gum infections, and vision disorders.

The officers fell into existing groups of comrades-in-arms. Most of the cavalry officers and pilots came from affluent families, and they segregated themselves as they believed superior specimens should. Furthermore, some of them pointedly avoided the Jews – except when they needed first aid. The estrangement was so pronounced as to verge at times on a subtle, agreed-upon boycott, consistently applied despite the conditions of imprisonment and humiliation we all shared.

One of the buildings was set aside as the crowded quarters of Jewish doctors from various cities of Poland. Some of the best-known of them were Dr Fryszberg, Dr Levinson, Dr Lipes, Dr Owczarek of Warsaw, Dr Epstein of Krakow, Dr Goldstein, Dr Zwykielski, Dr Tanenbaum, Dr Frischman, Dr Weinreich, and others. This encounter with partners in misery was exciting; it helped improve our mood as frustrated Jews in an ambience of ostracism.

A group of officers belonging to the Polish aristocracy stood out in the camp. According to rumours, they included Prince Lubomirski, Prince Radziwiłł, and two Counts Tyszkiewicz. The names of others were also mentioned at times.

The members of this stand-offish group strolled down the camp paths with pronounced self-confidence, disregarding the anxious men all around. Prince Lubomirski, about 25, tall, strapping and fat, stood out for his exceptional appearance and behaviour. He would stalk about ramrod-straight and proud, dressed in leather fur-lined clothes and high, gleaming tan hunting boots.

This elite vanished about two weeks later; we learned from the Soviets that they had been taken abroad with the Germans' consent through intervention of the Italian royal house. Indeed, equality in the Soviet paradise knows the prerequisites of the more equal.

The hundreds of officers hummed with conflicting guesses and groundless rumours about the Soviets' plans. Many mentioned the Geneva Convention rules for POW officers and the possibility of our repatriation. Others whispered despairingly about years of exile in the far north. All the secrets seemed to be based on talks with Soviet officers or overheard conversations in camp headquarters; most were pointless and reflected their disseminators' wishful thinking.

Swings in mood from hope to disappointment led to irritation, anxiety, and frustration. Many wandered about in despair and stupor. One of the officers hanged himself on a tree in the camp. At that, the men lost much of whatever hope they still had of witnessing any improvement in their situation.

About a week after reaching Skit, we marched under the winter sun to the bathhouse at the main camp, Kozielsk. We were warned neither to step out of line nor to converse with anyone outside.

A surprise awaited us upon entering the camp. On both sides of our path thousands of officers jostled and shoved, waving and calling jubilantly in our direction. Some of them were old friends, many were acquaintances. It was the first reunion of long-time comrades since the war broke out. At a great distance I spotted my colleagues Drs Berlinerblau, Prujanski, Leon Kapliński, and many friends from my university days. The meeting left its mark on all of us, and kindled hopes for the future and a feeling that we had not been abandoned to our loneliness in a forgotten world.

At the entrance of the spacious bathhouse shack, we were handed towels, soap, and thick linen underwear. Inside there were hot showers. For the first time in months, we were given a golden opportunity to wash and change underwear. The happy men launched into joyous renditions of songs of the motherland. Sorrowfully we returned to Skit, hoping for another encounter with our comrades.

A few days later they marched us to Kozielsk for a movie: *Battleship Potemkin*, a film on the Revolution directed by Eisenstein. The film was biased; its whole purpose was to glorify the Revolution. The critical audience reacted coldly, and the film's emphasis on propaganda overshadowed its artistic value.

Visits to the movies gradually became routine, and the guards were slightly less stringent than before. The arrangements made in the camp attested to the possibility of a protracted stay there.

Diarrhoea, colds, and skin conditions were rife among the POWs because of malnutrition and inadequate hygiene. In response, a clinic and a two-room emergency ward were set up in one of the structures, and several Jewish doctors were placed in charge. My role in this affair was that of patient. An insect bite on my hip became infected, resulting in a build-up of pus, high fever, and fierce pain. I called on Dr Lipes, a surgeon, who was forced to operate on me under makeshift conditions with local anaesthetic only. In agony and generally exhausted, I had to spend several days in the infirmary.

Barely recovered, I staggered, weak-kneed, dizzy, and white as a sheet, back to my room. To my surprise, my place on the bunk had been claimed by a standing army officer. The resulting dispute developed into a fist-fight accompanied with vociferous profanity and anti-semitic slurs.

Stunned as my veteran comrades were, none, unfortunately, summoned the courage to intervene on my behalf. I was particularly disappointed by two of my erstwhile friends, Józef and Antoni; the camaraderie we had developed during our wanderings under hardship in the forest proved to have been false.

Other neighbours stepped in and resolved the incident, but the well had been poisoned, and my expectations of loyalty from my friends were proved a will-of-the-wisp.

To our good fortune, we were transferred to the main camp of Kozielsk two days later, and my fair-weather friends vanished into the crowd of 5,000 POWs. I never saw them again. The corpses of all the Griazoviets veterans, with the exception of Dr Merenlender, were discovered three years later in the mass grave in Katyn.

Kozielsk

On 30 December 1939, we were ordered to move into the main camp, Kozielsk. The men in our group waited happily if impatiently for the moment we could join our comrades after having been isolated and separated from most of the POWs. The event made our men feel as if they had attained parity with thousands of men in similar circumstances.

The guards vanished at the camp entrance, and we found ourselves on a path bisecting the camp interior. Both sides of the path were lined with buildings, wooden structures, and shacks. Throngs of POWs congregated along the path to reunite with relatives and pre-war acquaintances. Our group quickly dispersed, and many joined their long-time friends.

Together with my own friends, Drs Merenlender and Mieczysław Arcichowski, I strode in puzzlement down the path, each of us carrying a sack of belongings from the various peregrinations. Suddenly someone called out. It was Dr Berlinerblau, with whom I had worked at the university hospital in Wilno. He was an older and more experienced man, having served as an aide to Professor Szmurlo, the ear, nose, and throat specialist. Stooped, face furrowed and sad-eyed, he approached and embraced me as if expecting succour from an emissary of Fate.

It was a very exciting reunion. Both of us had been seriously troubled by feelings of loneliness and guilt for having been taken prisoner by letting our guard down.

In an uplifted mood, I chose a place on the rough boards of a bunk in the corner of a cavernous monastery hall. Hundreds of officers were packed on to four tiers of bunks, each allotted two boards. The three of us joined our neighbours and formed a group of ten; together we would receive half a pail of soup every day and a weekly ration of bread, sugar, and ersatz tobacco. Because I had chosen a place at the edge of the bunk, my neighbours would not be pushing me, and I could breathe fresh air through a nearby window.

The upper bunks were less crowded, but by establishing quarters there I would have bothered the neighbours and endangered lives as I clambered up and down the wobbly scaffolds. The younger men preferred the hot, suffocating upper tiers; the older men chose the lower bunks and had to accommodate themselves to the cold and wind that blasted in throught the open door and the unglazed windows. In the chill of night we had to sleep in our clothes, bundled in our coats, our packs and shoes at our heads.

We selected Captain Wilk, a quiet, melancholy officer, as the head of our group of ten. His major duty was setting our rotation in the lengthy queue for hot water. Before sunrise we stood in the bitter cold, switching over every hour, in the line at the spigot in the camp yard. Water from the spigot would trickle on to the frozen ground and create an icy slope which endangered the irritable, jostling men. Exhausted from what had amounted to a catnap instead of a night's rest, the men would engage in disputes, at times accompanied by fisticuffs; slipping on the ice, they would break arms and legs. Patience was ever-necessary in the constant squabbling, always accompanied by insults and epithets.

From the day I was reunited with my friend from Wilno, we spent hours strolling on the camp paths, apart from the surrounding multitude, sunk in thoughts of the past and dread for the future. Profoundly embittered, Berlinerblau described his difficult wanderings after the defeat of the army, and his misfortune upon reaching home.

After the Red Army had entered the Wilno area, the streets of the city proliferated with posters calling on army officers to sign up at town command headquarters. While taking a walk with his wife one fine day, he innocently decided to enter the registration building near the city park. After presenting his personal details, he was taken through a back door into a courtyard, and, together with dozens of other men in similar situation, was loaded on to an army truck and driven to the rail station. Following a journey of great suffering and despair, all the men were impounded in the POW camp. The demonic way in which he was taken prisoner of war, in broad daylight in the centre of town, was reminiscent of the way I had been captured at the Baronowicze rail station. His wife, still outside the registration building, waited for him several hours and, as night fell, walked away in anguish.

Dr Berlinerblau, once a superb surgeon and still a handsome man, now comported himself sloppily and oddly. Divorced from reality, he took every opportunity to distance himself from the group; he wandered about at the edge of the camp dressed in a filthy *fufaika*, ignoring the jeers of the Gentiles all around.

After we had spent a few weeks in Kozielsk, a rumour broke out of our imminent release and transfer to a 'classification centre' in the border town of Brest-Litovsk. There we were supposed to appear before a committee representing the three occupying powers, which would decide on our disposition. My friend was painfully uncertain about which destination to choose – Warsaw, where his family was living under German control; Lwow, where his wife was staying, newly annexed to the Soviet Ukraine; or Wilno, newly reinstated as the capital of Lithuania.

His complicated problem was resolved without any need to choose. On 15 April, he and about 150 officers of various ranks were ordered to report for the long-awaited transport. We parted in hopes of meeting again in the near future as free men. My gaze followed him until he vanished through the wicket-shaped opening in the camp wall. I saw him no more.

Two days later, I parted from my bunkmate, Dr Arcichowski, who was ordered to join a large transport of some 300 officers and cadets. Thereafter he vanished. The sadness of his gaze expressed his feelings at his departure on a lengthy trip, after which we would probably not see each other again.

The corpses of my two close friends were disinterred about three years later in a mass grave in the Katyn Forest.

The POW Camp

The Kozielsk camp was about 250 kilometres south-east of the district city of Smolensk. Before the Revolution, the land in this area had been owned by two families of the Polish aristocracy, Puzyna and Ogiński, by virtue of whose generosity the magnificent church was built. The large monastery was well known throughout Tsarist Russia; according to local peasants, Rasputin, who exerted such mysterious influence over members of Nicholas II's family, had once lived there.

After the Bolshevik Revolution, all the monasteries were handed over to the People's Commissariat for Internal Affairs (NKVD). Kozielsk was put to use as a resort and hostel, officially known as 'Gorki Vacation Home, Recipient of Three Orders of Lenin'.

Packed into the square kilometre of the Kozielsk camp were dozens of two-storey buildings, several churches, some residential structures, and various shacks.

The monastery sat behind a high wall of fortifications including firing slits, and at its corners were soaring stone towers manned by armed guards who illuminated the entire area with blinding searchlights.

On the other side of the wall was a steep bank leading to a river, along which were thick mounds of earth and barbed-wire fences rooted in the ground. The entire camp was encircled with ranks of wooden scaffolds with observation posts manned by jailers and camp guards in a duty rota around the clock.

Built into the wall towers were storage rooms and isolation cells. Selected POWs and prisoners brought in from other camps for interrogation before transport to destinations unknown were temporarily housed here.

Rabbi Steinberg, chief rabbi of the Polish army, and several priests were locked up in one of the towers on Christmas Eve, 1939. This group of notables, with the exception of the venerable priest Professor Kantak, rector of the Catholic Seminary in Pińsk, were taken out of the camp at dead of night, never to be seen again.

A pack of wild wolfhounds was kept in a special tower. Their barking and grating howls, accompanied by the pounding of the guards' jackboots during their relentless patrols, echoed into the distance and shattered the silence of the night.

A large, magnificent church loomed skyward in the centre of the camp. Its entrance staircase, flanked by marble pillars, led to an iron gate adorned with flower and bird ornamentation, the work of a master artist. A bulky concrete statue of Marshal Voroshilov, clad in a long military greatcoat and high boots, stood in the church square. A large hand-gun protruded from a holster on his hip; one hand clutched a field glass and the other pointed to the west.

The statue served as the butt of jokes for those so inclined, as they and their comrades 'bargained' with the Marshal for his greatcoat and winter boots.

The church interior was punctuated with two rows of exceedingly graceful marble pillars. The vaulted ceiling had arches bordered with frescos of saints; a set of stained-glass panes graced the upper windows.

Wooden scaffolds stood in the grand sanctuary, supporting six tiers of bunks that reached the ceiling. By day, the church was a picture of gloom and coldness; only a few electric bulbs cast a dull light on the thousands of densely packed prisoners who twisted to and fro on the wobbly planks of the scaffolds. The prisoners called the place 'Monkey Valley'. The air in the church was suffocating and drenched with humidity from the damp rags and clothes that were hung to dry on the scaffolds. The lower bunks were bitterly cold; their elderly occupants had to sleep in their clothes. The upper levels, by contrast, were hot and muggy because of the condensation generated by the breath and sweat of thousands of men.

The younger men packed themselves into the upper tiers, almost naked. Some of them had the effrontery to attend to their bodily needs without bothering to come down. Emissions of water and urine froze on the walls, creating a layer of filthy ice beside the lower bunks.

The pale faces and feet of thousands of prisoners protruded in the gloom over the edges of the six tiers of bunks. Broadcasts from Radio Moscow – orchestral and operatic works – entertained the embittered multitudes for hours on end. Among the operas, the Soviets went out of their way to play Glinka's *Ivan Susanin* and Mussorgsky's *Boris Godunov*, which portray the Poles' putative treachery against the Tsar's regime in the seventeenth century.

The disconcerting admixture of pure art and gloomy reality was used as a means of brainwashing the unfortunate men, who were driven into an even deeper state of depression.

I was overtaken by a feeling of hell on earth whenever I found myself in that place, and flickers of dancing fire in the gloom would conjure, Dante's words: 'Abandon all hope, ye who enter here.'

Next to 'Monkey Valley' was a hut used as a cinema; behind it were the bathhouse and kitchen.

The monastery structures with their chapels and confessionals, lined with three-tier wooden scaffolds, towered over the camp's main path. At the end of the camp were a large number of wooden houses tenanted shoulder to shoulder with two-tier bunks. Nearly 200 Jewish doctors and intellectuals established their quarters here, apart from the masses of prisoners, and additional hundreds of POWs were dispersed among the many structures in the area.

Some of the most prominent doctors were Professor Szepelski, Mogilnicki, Edelman, Landsberg, and Pajewski of Łódź, Goldstein of Kraków, Luxemburg of Warsaw, Wojdenfeld, Weinbach, and others. While in the camp I met friends from my student days at the University of Wilno, Drs Bunim Prujanski and Leon Kapliński, and several civilians: Józef Talerman, Hersh Halpern, and David Godel.

The senior and high-ranking POWs were housed in two renovated residential buildings at the edge of the path that bisected the camp. These included the senior officer in our group, Dr Marynowski, who was transferred to more comfortable conditions upon our arrival at the main camp.

In the well-kept two-man rooms of the 'first block' lived four generals, an admiral, a naval commander, and about 100 colonels. These rooms had beds with mattresses, and tables on which the inhabitants were served hot meals from the kitchen. They enjoyed larger rations of bread, sugar, and ersatz tobacco. Nor were these exalted personages in the habit of appearing before the masses of prisoners in the camp. On occasion they could be seen marching, all alone, along the side paths or towards the building at the edge of the camp where the senior Soviet interrogators worked.

There was also a 'majors' block' with about 300 regular officers and a few low-ranking reserve officers who had public or scientific positions. The latter included Professor Komarnicki, who taught international law at the University of Wilno, the well-known paediatrician Dr Kopeć, who treated the camp commander's children, and several Polish cabinet ministers.

The generality of POWs was not allowed to enter the two blocks.

Talks and interrogations

Kozielsk was not a POW camp in the customary Western sense of the term. In addition to Soviet personnel in charge of administration, physical plant, and guard duty, the camp had a special senior team of NKVD investigators. These officers were professionally well-trained; their duties spilled into general fields and their authority was exceedingly broad.

National Security General 'Kombrig' Zarubin, was at the head of this team. He was a tall, strong, and heavy-set man in his fifties, steeped in Western manners and fluent in European languages. Rumours circulated about his diplomatic past as an ambassador. His word was law. He worked with a team of investigators at the rank of major. Zarubin was a mysterious figure; he showed his face in public only to mark special events – receiving new prisoner transports or transferring groups of officers from the camp to destinations unknown.

The tenants of the privileged blocks, and POWs whom the investigation staff found especially intriguing, were summoned to an isolated building at the far edge of camp near the wall. There, in rooms branching off a long corridor, sat the senior investigative officers: Elman, Lebediev, Kadishev, and Dymidovich.

These were well-educated men. Several knew foreign languages, and during their intimate talks they made a point of being polite in an effort to earn their guests' trust. One of the purposes of the talks was to identify such officers as were inclined to collaborate with the Soviets. Also of concern were the senior officers' military activities and political views. The matter of their participation in the Legionnaires' War under Marshal Piłsudski against the Red Army in 1920 was of special interest.[9]

The high-ranking POWs were summoned to General 'Kombrig' Zarubin's personal quarters, seated in padded armchairs, and offered prestige cigarettes or a glass of tea. The ambience of the talks was congenial but secretive, and it had the effect of promoting whatever rumours the Soviets felt like floating. The overall goal was to keep the POWs lethargic and quiet, while allowing them a regular dash of expectations of positive imminent change. The atmosphere was meant to dissipate the tension and keep the prisoners from organizing for exceptional purposes.

A special status was reserved for Major Alexandrovich, a handsome, habitually polite Soviet officer always willing to act on the prisoners' behalf. From time to time he attended to deliveries of books in various languages from the camp library or the nearby town. For the German-reading prisoners, a copy of Hitler's *Mein Kampf* was provided. Alexandrovich himself was fluent in German, French, and English.

The erudite officer accompanied us in our future travels, sometimes accidentally disclosing random details about what awaited us. He joined the party of officers who survived the journey to the next two camps, and was present upon our liberation. When the new Polish army was established on Soviet soil, he parted with us as we set out for Persia.

Command headquarters and the rooms of the junior investigative staff were next to the main gate. The thousands of POWs were summoned to command head-quarters near the camp gate for investigation, usually at night. Most of the junior investigators were poorly educated; some of them were laughably ignorant. Prisoners' personal details, educational background, and occupational standing were recorded during the protracted interrogations. The investigators traced the POWs' military past and their duties while Marshal Piłsudski's legions were battling against the Bolsheviks and establishing the Polish state in 1920.

Of special concern was the prisoners' involvement in political and public life; details concerning their friends and neighbours were also gathered.

The questions were sometimes presented bluntly and caustically, especially when subjects tried to conceal information the investigators already had. At the end, the prisoner had to sign a lengthy, detailed protocol. In accordance with the outcome of the investigation, he might be summoned to the senior investigators for further talks on political matters, attitudes toward the Soviet regime, and various social problems.

The investigators were wont to mark their records with comments such as 'former Polish army officer' beside the subject's name. This elicited chronic anger and fierce protests from the prisoners. During one of my investigations, I was asked about my party activity. My negative reply was greeted with a panel of snarling faces. Jerking his head, the interrogator peered self-confidently into his desk drawer and snarled 'So what is

"Jordania"?' Unbeknownst to me, the Soviets had dredged up detailed information on my activity in Wilno's first Zionist college fraternity.

With great difficulty, I tried to explain that Jordania's activity was neither political nor anti-socialist; it was meant to prevent the assimilation of Jewish students into Polish social circles. At this, the investigator's disgust with anything related to Poland convinced him of my bona fides; a light, hesitant smile spread across his face.

The course and results of the investigations were not widely revealed and were usually kept secret. Prisoners leaked a few details: some mentioned having been threatened with a pistol that lay on the table during the interrogation; others spoke of collaboration by several investigators, who took turns working on the subjects through the night.

The investigators' poor education gave rise to funny anecdotes. One POW was asked about his relations with President Roosevelt. When he denied any such relations, the Russian ignoramus grew furious. As the two argued, the origin of the misunderstanding became clear: the POW had received a letter from the United States with a stamp bearing the President's picture, thus arousing the investigator's suspicions about the subject's association with international capitalism. In another case, a POW answering questions about relatives abroad mentioned a brother in Jerusalem. The investigator fumed, believing that Jerusalem was not abroad. Once convinced of his error, he corrected himself by saying that the city would one day fall within the borders of the Soviet Union.

Camp celebrities

The group of 400 senior officers, housed in the two special blocks, was a negligible minority against the 5,000 junior officers of various ranks.

The vast majority of the POWs were reserve officers, including about 20 professors and university lecturers, 300 doctors, experts in various disciplines, and hundreds of lawyers, engineers, authors, and well-known journalists.

The junior officers had been serving in rear and service units that retreated to the east as the front approached. Most of the combat officers had been killed or captured by the Germans; only a few had been captured by the Red Army when it entered eastern Poland.

One individual revered by both the POWs and the Soviet command was Professor Bolesław Szarecki. I became acquainted with him in the camp clinic, and found him to be a broadly knowledgeable physician and a superb surgeon, who exuded paternal warmth and projected a hearty bedside manner.

Before the war, he had been commander of the army's medical instruction and training centre, and head of the surgical department of the military hospital in Warsaw. Notwithstanding his 70 years, he was sturdy, erect, clear of mind, and strong of character.

Szarecki was the son of a rail worker in Mińsk, Belorussia. In his youth he had worked as a hospital orderly, and embarked on medical studies in his thirties. He was a 'Renaissance man' – honest, a lover of science, steeped in Russian culture, and devoid of anti-semitic feelings. He spoke Polish with a Russian accent and a smattering of Russian words. Although a devout Christian, he harboured no illusions and contemptuously rejected the affectations of clergy.

As a senior physician in the camp, he was asked by the authorities to instruct and help the Russian woman doctor who ran the hospital. With his status and vast experience, he did much toward keeping the camp clean and improving the prisoners' conditions and nutrition.

We also became friends as we worked together; this served me well during my years as a POW and may have decided my fate during and after the war years.

By virtue of the Soviets' special regard for the great physician, he remained alive despite his senior rank and position before the war. When the Polish army was re-established under General Anders on Russian soil, he was promoted to the rank of General and appointed head of the Medical Corps. He saw action in the Middle East and later on the Italian front, where, taking his life in his hands, he himself operated on wounded soldiers on the advance battle line. After Anders' Army was disbanded in Great Britain, he was one of the first to return to Poland – much to his colleagues' displeasure. There he was appointed head of the new Polish army's medical corps. Szarecki earned the people's admiration. This man of high principle died in Warsaw at a ripe old age.

The camp hospital was housed in a two-storey wooden structure. On the ground floor was a miserably equipped clinic. Upstairs, packed side to side and end to end in three poorly lit rooms, were creaking iron beds with mouldy straw mattresses and thin army blankets.

The infirmary food was no different from that served in the camp, but the patients did have access to a hot water boiler throughout the day. Most of the patients were elderly POWs suffering from exhaustion, chronic heart disease, or dysentery, which was rife in the camp. The young were hospitalized for lung infections, arthritis, and malnutrition. Medicines were insufficient in both quantity and quality. With bandages in short supply, gauze and cotton wool had to be reused.

In a few rare instances, the Russian doctor was authorized to provide patients upon release with a note addressed to the warehouse, recommending the issue of crude winter *fufaika* made of two layers of thin fabric with cotton wool between them.

While I was working in the clinic, the Soviet doctor gave me a book called *How the Steel Was Tempered*, by one Ostrovski, about the beginning of the Revolution. Between its pages was a photograph of the doctor and her sister, taken from outside the monastery walls with the camp in the background. After reading the book, I could not resist the sudden temptation to keep the photo, which I considered an important piece of documentation. Late one night I sewed it between the thick leather layers of one of my heavy boots, where it would not be discovered during the frequent searches in which POWs' personal certificates and documents were confiscated. Later I returned the book, without the photograph. This original photo of the camp is an exceptionally rare document, especially when possessed by someone outside the Iron Curtain.

As a clinic physician, I had an opportunity to enter the senior officers' quarters for a game of chess with Admiral Czernicki, an engineer by profession and a builder of submarines in the Italian port of Monfalcone. An intriguing man, this senior officer was held in special esteem by the Soviets.

I met him one day as he marched erectly and regally toward command headquarters in a blue dress uniform with glittering buttons, stiff epaulettes, and a navy hat with a gold-embroidered rim. General Zarubin appeared on the steps of the building to greet his guest. Advancing, he shook hands warmly, held out a letter that had arrived from Czernicki's family in Warsaw, and said briefly, with a polite smile: 'I welcome you, Admiral.' The two then went into command headquarters for a long talk.

Visiting the admiral's room by chance, I noticed his four large suitcases, made of expensive burnished leather. Czernicki had been taken prisoner of war in his car, and the Soviet authorities displayed their special attitude towards him by letting him bring his suitcases to the camp. His corpse, and those of the four generals, were found later in the Katyn Forest.

Quartered next door to Czernicki were Generals Minkiewicz, Smorawiński, and Bohaterewicz. They kept to themselves, appearing only in the evenings, when they would march in dress uniform to headquarters for lengthy talks to which they had been summoned by 'Kombrig'.

A unique character was General Wołkowicki. Elderly, tall and skinny, he had a bit of blonde hair atop a balding pate, and a desiccated face. Although he was retired, the Soviets treated him with pronounced respect because of the special privileges he had accrued in Tsarist Russia.

At the beginning of the century, Wołkowicki had been a junior officer on a Russian battleship in the Baltic fleet. When the Russo-Japanesse War broke out, this fleet was dispatched to the Far East to smash the Japanese navy. After sailing thousands of miles under poor supply conditions, the Tsar's ships were trounced in a brutal engagement near the island of Tsushima. Of the entire crew of his ship, only young Wołkowicki desperately resisted surrender to the Japanese. The Russian people adulated him. The young officer's courage became the very emblem of valour, and was described by the Russian author Novikov-Priboj in his best-seller, *Tsushima*.

This exploit of young adulthood still served the venerable general well when the fate of the thousands of POWs was decided. Of the 12 senior officers imprisoned in Kozielsk, only he survived. The corpses of all the others were discovered three years later in the mass grave in the Katyn Forest.

On the towering scaffold structure opposite my bunk was Antoni Eiger, an officer and an engineer from Warsaw. He was the grandson of Rabbi Akiva Eiger, chief rabbi of the Poznań community about a century ago. A tall, blond, masculine type of about 40, he wore his officer's uniform in a painstakingly correct manner that befitted his appearance. Many of his family members were assimilated and had intermarried.

He had been head of the Polish anti-Hitlerite league, and made a name for himself as an international bridge referee. In one of their night-time searches, the Soviets confiscated some of his valuables, including a precious watch, a gold cigarette case, and an ancient ring that was a family heirloom.

In our talks, he revealed that he had reached the Starobielsk POW camp about two weeks previously, where about 5,000 officers including generals, professors, and many scientists were being held. Conditions there were similar to ours, although the bread was doled out more generously. There, too, POWs vanished in the dead of night, and new groups of officers arrived from time to time.

We struck up a friendship after I told him about his uncle – Professor Marian Eiger, one of my great teachers in the University of Wilno, an assimilated Jew, and a member of the Jewish Agency Executive. His lectures on physiology, accompanied with fascinating experiments on the effects of electric currents on animals, attracted throngs of students from other departments. He covered his institute's expenses out of his own pocket. The unforgettable lecturer died as a Jew before the war.

Anton Eiger, my comrade in captivity, was prudent by nature and treated his neighbours like a gentleman. He helped them obtain sundry items, which he kept in good order in his suitcases. In our talks on the stacked bunks, he did not repudiate his Jewishness but knew little about his people. At the same time, he was well-versed in world affairs and stressed his absolute allegiance to the Polish motherland.

Eiger's bunkmate had once been Poland's ambassador to a Latin American country. He was a lively, effervescent man, exuding self-confidence, broadly educated in the arts and world literature. Now reduced to misery, he described how he had been lured into the Soviet snare while enjoying a brief vacation at home.

My two neighbours' corpses were unearthed in the Katyn Forest.

One of the officers who reached us from Starobielsk was an acquaintance of mine: Professor Godłowski, a lecturer in psychiatry at the University of Wilno. He had succeeded the late Professor Maximilian Rose, the great and world-renowned researcher on the human brain.

Godłowski, about 38, made no strong outward impression. He was introverted by nature and refrained from striking up friendships with the people around him. In our talks, he surprised me with his grim opinion on our dangerous situation, countering the optimism that had pervaded the camp in the wake of secretive, whispered rumours about our imminent release. His iconoclastic pessimism proved to be fully justified three years later in the Katyn Forest.

Strolling along the camp paths one bitterly cold day, to take in some fresh air after the stench in the bunk building, I encountered Dr Gołyński, a major in the standing army and head of the ear, nose, and-throat department in the military hospital at Antokol, Wilno. A long-time friend of my father's, Gołyński had agreed to admit me into his department for advanced training. As we discussed what might be happening in Soviet-occupied Wilno, I repeated a sad rumour I had heard about how zealous things had engaged in pogroms and looting among the Jews just before the Red Army entered the city. My interlocutor stood perplexed for a moment. Then, furiously condemning me for spreading malicious gossip, he stalked away snarling, without saying goodbye.

On one of the overcast winter days at twilight, while queuing at the kitchen door with a multitude of shoving men, clutching the pail that I would fill for ten of my neighbours, I caught a quick glance of Dr Israel Rubinstein. This friend, conspicuously resourceful and valorous during the aerial attack on our hospital near Małkinia, now stood there, clearly overwhelmed, crestfallen and pale. He had nothing to say about how he had been captured. I sensed that he, like others, had been cunningly trapped after going home when the front collapsed. He tortured himself for the shameful failure that had reduced him to misery. Depressed, he poured his heart out in the bitterness that he had developed after absorbing the venom aimed at the Jews by those who shared our humiliation. He, too, met his end in the Katyn Forest.

A group of Jews, mostly university-trained, with well- formed leftist views and sympathies for the Communist regime, were profoundly despondent and disappointed. Several of them had been friends of mine at university. Now they spent hours and days, under nerve-wracking tension, in the corridors of the Soviet interrogators' building. Relentlessly they tried to find someone who would listen to their demand for liberation as Soviet sympathizers. Nor were they finicky about the ways they used to attain their goal. They shunned long-time friends and refused to divulge the contents of their talks with the authorities, lest this adversely affect their efforts.

In the sad jostling and queue-jumping for an additional interview with the Soviet interrogators, they would spend hours on end in the bitter cold until the Soviets appeared at the door. The cynical investigators advised them to present requests for release to the camp commander, the President of the Supreme Soviet, and Stalin himself. They occasionally did so. The investigators' promises had no real backing, and the requests apparently remained in their authors' files. The corpses of these men were found in the forest where they were murdered.

A woman in the camp

Among the thousands of POWs was woman in an air force officer's uniform. I caught sight of her by chance during a friendly visit to the rickety barbershop shack. There, together with some others, I was offered a modest piece of fresh herring which, considering our conditions, was like a luxury out of the past. Its pleasant taste lingered in my mouth for weeks.

The air force woman lived next to the barbershop in a ramshackle wooden cabin set by itself, far from the churches, the sardine-can bunk buildings, and the noise of the rabble.

Once in a while she put in brief appearances, in the company of two young air officers. A tall, athletic young woman in her early twenties, she cut an elegant figure and had a beautiful, delicate face that expressed noble tranquillity. Her carefully tended blond curls spilled over the epaulettes of her blue uniform and bounced with the graceful movements of her head. Supple as a cat, she strolled down the camp's side paths on those occasions, which she apparently kept to a minimum on order to avoid curious onlookers' excessive attention and interest.

Rumours had it that she was the daughter of the famous General Dowbór-Muśnicki, and the wife of a senior air force officer.

This exceptional character presented an impresive sight – a young, pretty woman in trousers, with air force wings on her chest, amidst the cold reality of isolation from the outside world. The perplexed onlookers came away with the feeling that Jeanne d'Arc had been reincarnated in their midst.

The camp authorities did not allow the intrigued men clustering in the area to enjoy the uncommon sight for long. After a brief stay in the camp, the woman vanished one winter night. Her name appeared on the list of victims in the Katyn Forest.

Religion, culture, and art in the camp

The Soviet authorities enforced a total ban on mass assemblies and encounters, including public prayer and group talks.

Suspicious security officers patrolled the camp regularly. To thwart questionable activities, they roused people in the middle of the night with powerful searchlights, and peered into the corners of the buildings and behind the garden shrubbery. By day, command officers talked with our men, who eagerly grasped at news from the outside world and sought advice on their personal affairs. When groups of POWs engaged in argument, Soviet officers would suddenly materialize and try to win their trust by disclosing 'secrets' pertaining to our future.

The prisoners were interested in the possibility of liberation for health reasons and to receive news about their families. Their enquiries were usually answered with the same solemn pronouncement: 'Present a reasoned request to the camp command.' Then, smiling, they threw in a well-known Russian saying: 'Butter does not ruin porridge' ('It can't hurt'). In fact, all these requests were consigned either to the garbage can or the writer's personal files; they were never met with any response.

The younger men, mostly cadets from military academies, attempted various tricks to circumvent the prohibition against organizing, with guidance by standing army officers. Every evening the POWs would retreat to their bunks in order to escape from the cold outside. At a predetermined time, someone in one of the corners of the packed hall would suddenly announce two minutes of 'communion'. This was a call to public prayer, accompanied by whispered song – a symbol of general unity and resistance to the authorities.

Catholic religious consciousness was deeply entrenched among the prisoners. Officers could be seen strolling along the camp's winding paths with priests, whispering confession (fortunately for them, the priests were not identified by the authorities). Others would hide between the shacks, praying and crossing themselves in spiritual ecstasy.

Many of the thousands of POWs had artistic talents which, in their yearning for a release from depression and an escape from harsh reality, they were motivated to practise. Soon the POW quarters abounded with exquisite carved reproductions of Mary and Jesus in various sizes, pipes for smoking, and cigarette cases with delicate artistic covers. The camp commander paid 2,000 roubles for a splendid, complete chess set. As raw material for all these, they used chips of wood and branches of the few fruit trees that survived in the camp garden.

One of the POW artists, displaying sublime patience and impressive persistence, created a model of the Belweder Palace in Warsaw. Everything – the grand palace and its surrounding gardens, the ponds with their swans and little bridges – was fashioned out of used matches and bits of wood gathered on the ground and stuck together with bread dough.

For tools, the men gathered bits of scrap metal in the camp yard, which, with toil and persistence, they smoothed and sharpened on flagstones. The tools were kept out of sight of the camp guards in their frequent searches, usually undertaken at night.

Painters had to settle for pencil stubs or burned match- heads. For 'canvases' they used sheets of yellowed paper picked up around the camp offices, or blank propaganda sheets that were handed out to those interested. Pamphlets containing the Soviet constitution and the history of the Russian Communist Party WKP(B) were put to especially extensive use.

A group of journalists, actors, and singers succeeded in building a little stage with some boards that had been laid in a passageway between the two sets of bunks in the monastery chamber. At sunset, the day's news, as heard on the radio, was read. Jokes and riddles were told, and bits of song performed, sometimes superbly. The audience responded with appreciation and applause.

As time passed, the camp authorities began to develop an increasingly tolerant attitude towards the cultural activities. This helped maintain the calm and release the tension that occasionally built up among the disgruntled young prisoners.

The camp command, too, initiated certain cultural events. We were shown documentary films on the Revolution and the development of Soviet industry and agriculture. One of the films had an anti-Catholic bias, which provoked a spate of loud booing. Some men went so far as to stalk out of the room.

On several occasions professionals from Moscow showed up to deliver lectures on the values of life in the socialist state, the Soviet constitution, and the brotherhood of the peoples in the Soviet community.

The pianist Zbigniew Grzybowski, winner of an international competition, gave us a recital of Chopin that was greeted with vociferous appreciation.

Representatives of the government diamond trade agency appeared in the camp one day, in order to buy gold, silver, and various valuables from the prisoners. Fountain pens commanded twenty roubles. The prisoners needed the money for purchases in the mobile canteen that showed up twice with an inventory of buttons, shoelaces, thread, and, to our surprise, lipstick.

Postal service

About two months into our stay at Kozielsk, the camp command announced that we would be able to send letters and receive mail parcels from families once a month. This was more than satisfying news; it aroused hopes that conditions would improve in the future. A large postbox was installed in the camp, and demand for paper and envelopes grew. It was met in part by the limited supplies in our own possession, and in small part by command headquarters.

The first letters came from the cities of eastern Poland, which had been annexed to the Soviet Union. The camp's official address was Gorki Rest Home, Moscow, PO Box 12. This gave the POWs' wives the idea that their husbands were living in high style in a vacation centre in Moscow, while they and their families suffered through a harsh winter with insufficient food and clothing for their children.

While strolling among the rickety shacks and the few withered fruit trees that survived in the camp garden, I came across a ramshackle wooden structure hidden in a mantle of vines. Inside was a rotting bench. Etched into the rickety posts were the names of Soviet 'vacationers' and snide remarks about the rundown, flea-infested 'vacation home'. They evidently saw through the misleading address.

The letters from my family in Wilno were jubilant; it was rumoured that I had been killed in the war. In the meantime, Wilno had been declared the capital of Lithuania, and I had the privilege of getting a food parcel from home. I shared the canned meat and fish with my neighbours, and used the empty tins as teacups and storage containers.

Letters from the towns of German-occupied western Poland

began to arrive in March 1940. The camp authorities posted long lists of letter recipients, and hundreds of men crowded and pushed in hopes of finding themselves among them.

To my Jewish comrades' distress, letters for them were few and sad. Almost all reported changes of address, indications of great suffering, and dread of the future.

The Polish POWs received letters of different content, including gripes about the food rationing and the hardships of the winter cold. The letters to the German and *Volksdeutsch* (ethnic German) POWs exuded joy and high spirits, and were signed off with 'Heil Hitler'. Their recipients waved the slogan in their neighbours' faces. This little detail proved to be significant in the course of future events.

While waiting for letters, I saw on many occasions tears flowing from the eyes of my comrades as they read the distressing news from their families.

In March, it was widely rumoured in Kozielsk that the camp would be dismantled and that we would be transferred to 'classification centres' (*razpredelitelnyje punkty*) for repatriation. Of three such centres, one in the city of Brest-Litovsk was mentioned. There, on the new border between the countries, we were told that a joint German, Russian, and Lithuanian committee would approve the destinations selected by the liberated men.

These reports originated in the camp commander's talks with Admiral Czernicki and other generals. Command officers confirmed them, as did the janitors in the camp shower room. Even as the rumours about our imminent liberation proliferated, some 400 inmates of the camp were separated and transferred to the neighbouring camp, Skit. Before the war, they had lived in parts of eastern Poland that were now annexed to the Soviet Union ('Western Ukraine' and 'Western Belorussia'); this made them Soviet citizens. By this time Wilno was reinstated as the capital of independent Lithuania; at this time Lithuania had not yet been annexed to the Soviet Union, so its residents, as foreign nationals, were not segregated from the general POW population in Kozielsk.

Clear evidence of the senior Soviet leadership's ponderings

and indecision in its policy on the POWs' future emerged when the men sent to Skit were brought back to Kozielsk about two weeks later. In 1943, most of them were found in the mass graves in the Katyn Forest.

4

Through the 'Gate of Freedom' – to Katyn

On the afternoon of Wednesday, 3 April 1940, the sentry Kopiejkin, a ridiculous nonentity whom we called 'Parrot', walked past several of the building and shacks reading out names from a printed list. Every man on that list was to report with his belongings to the cinema hut.

Like lightning the news spread between the camp buildings and the residential quarters. Tremendously agitated and excited, an electrified crowd gathered in nervous anticipation. The camp buzzed like a beehive as the thousands of POWs leaped out of their bunks and streamed to the cinema shack to witness the first happy men as they went free.

A larger-than-usual detail of armed sentries perched on the wooden steps leading to the cinema. At the door, erect and exuding self-confidence, stood 'Kombrig' Zarubin. Alongside him were Major Alexandrovich and Commissar Dymidovich, who carefully checked the names of the men as they entered.

After painstaking examination, the happy men bounded down the entrance stairs, beaming from ear to ear and clutching portions of bread and dry herring wrapped in white paper. This latter was considered a luxury in the camp. Observing the precautions taken and the way the men were examined, we were more convinced than ever that the rumours were true, and that our comrades were about to be repatriated. To the onlookers' surprise, however, the camp gate was still locked, and the guards' routine continued unchanged.

Then, unexpectedly, the line of men awaiting liberation was

ordered to march down a narrow side path past some out-
houses. They came to a stout, wooden wicket-shaped opening
in the camp wall, of whose existence we had not known. One
by one the men ducked as they passed under the lintel. After
the last of the men had gone through, one of the guards abruptly
slammed the little gate shut. Our comrades vanished, and we
heard nothing more of them.

The thousands of witnesses to this extraordinary event stood
in shock, as if rooted in the ground. We had succeeded in
counting 62 men who had gone free. They included a number
of young cadets and elderly officers of various ranks.

We tried to guess the key to their selection, but all our efforts
and reckonings – for this group and future ones – were in vain.
Tension among the multitudes of onlookers remained high.What
would happen next? The next afernoon the process repeated
itself; about 300 officers were summoned to the cinema shack
and then passed through the secret aperture in the camp wall.

Command officers amplified the tension by floating various
hints and utterances, which fuelled innumerable animated conversations and arguments between doomsayers and more hopeful
men. Some were dubious; the departing men were given so
little food that they could not have embarked on as long a trip
as that required by repatriation.

The men in the infirmary were ecstatic. War casualties,
amputees, and men stricken with fever pleaded with the Russian
doctor to move them up on the list for transport. Their ailments
would surely be more conveniently treated near their homes.

About 280 men were sent on their way on the third day.
Curious observers crowded around command headquaters.
Through the open window they heard the names of the candi-
dates being read over the phone from Moscow.

An impressive list of senior officers was read out on 7 April.
Among the 90 men were three generals, about ten colonels
(including Marshal Piłsudski's former personal physician, Dr
Stefanowski), and several Jewish professors and doctors.

The entire process – reporting to the cinema, marching
through the aperture in the monastery wall, etc. – was re-
enacted, down to the last detail, four or five days each week.

The riddle that intrigued all the POWs was why these men, in their transfer to freedom, were being taken down the narrow, twisting side path to the little wicket behind the buildings and shacks – while the main gate was shut and the guards pursued their duties as usual.

My recurrent attempts to talk the guards into revealing the transports' destination were in vain; their duty, they said, was to escort the group as far as the rail station and no farther. Every prisoner received a first hint of the answer as he passed through the little gate, on his way to what he thought was liberation.

On the afternoon of Friday, 26 April 1940, I was summoned to the cinema with my friend Dr Merenlender. This transport, the sixteeth, included 96 officers. Among them were Professor Szarecki, General Wołkowicki, and Colonels Bolesławicz, Grobicki, Mara-Meyer, and Prokop. Also in the group were the elderly priest Professor Kantak, the pianist Grzybowski, a journalist named Ginsbert, and Drs Mucho and Sadowski. In the cinema, the names were painstakingly rechecked and the portions of black bread and herring in their white paper were doled out. We marched in pairs towards the hole in the wall that we all knew so well.

Passing through, I came upon a terrifying and unexpected scene. Our column was caught between two solid lines of vicious, snarling soldiers. Their rifles were fitted with bayonets, and hand guns protruded from their belts. With unbridled gall they plundered our belongings, contemptuously confiscating anything made of metal, any mirror, any piece of glass, and any fountain pen. From me they appropriated a small thermometer, even though I protested I was a doctor. It was evident that they were obeying strict orders from their superiors on how to treat persons who had no way of complaining against them.

Their atrocity finished, the soldiers backed off and we saw three army trucks, motors revving impatiently, several paces away. The junior officer in charge of the guard detail, in a grating and martially curt tone, ordered us to remain silent, board the trucks without a sound, and sit down. At the end, he cautioned: anyone who moved would be killed without warning.

The senior officers in our group, all middle-aged men, complied in catatonic silence. As if finding movement difficult, they climbed into the large trucks and sat down hip to hip, resting their elbows on their knees and the balls of their feet on the metal trunk.

Receiving a pre-arranged signal, the armed sentries leaped aboard the trucks and surrounded our men, rifles cocked. With a deafening roar of engines and creaking of wheels, the convoy fled the scene at dizzying speed. None of the passengers dared open his mouth or turn his head in the direction of the frozen general and colonels. Everyone was stunned and tongue-tied at the unexpected development. Our expectations of liberation vanished in a trice. It was clear to all of us that any hopes of seeing home again had vanished.

The soldiers' atrocious comportment during their search, the effrontery of the guard detail, and the sight of the drawn bayonets put paid to all the Soviets' promises and rumours. Their deceitfulness had come into full view once again.

The living cargo, even with its now-vast experience in disappointment, was shell-shocked and tuned into a silent, frozen mass. Events succeeded one another with whirlwind speed, and no one harbourd any doubt as to what awaited us.

The heavy truck advanced headlong, as if trying to shake off its cargo. Now and then it would hit bumps in the frozen soil at full force. As the wheels, which had no shock absorbers, struck these protrusions, the spent, depressed passengers were tossed mercilessly into the air. For me the wild trip seemed to last forever, and the passengers all around, packed like so many sardines, wallowed in the stench that wafted from the truck cabin.

After about half an hour's travel through desolate, snow-patched fields, we caught sight of six green rail cars at a considerable distance from a village station. The convoy screeched to a halt on an earthen platform next to the tracks, and the soldiers jumped out and surrounded us in an impenetrable human chain. With a shout meant to humiliate, their commander ordered us to dismount and advance silently to the train.

Like my comrades, I understood that the march of afflictions was not yet over, but had reached a new and decisive stage.

Trains in the War

My chess partner, an engineer and transportation expert, was impressed with the way the Soviets made full use of their freight trains. In this respect they vastly outperformed the West. In addition to the normal hauling of freight and livestock, these trains made a great contribution to the mass transport of human beings.

From the day we were taken prisoner of war, we were dragged on lengthy treks to this camp and that, using whatever means of transport forced upon us. As we travelled, we beheld trains passing by at all hours of day and night, comprising dozens of bulky, filthy boxcars that reeked with the stench of horses and sheep.

When the Red Army marched into eastern Poland, each of these motorized crates, with their faded brown paint, became the quarters of 60–70 people – old men, young men, women, children, and infants – who, suffocating and packed together, had been uprooted and exiled to the Soviet Union.

When we reached the Kozielsk rail station in the trucks, and before we could recover from our shock upon the guards' astonishingly rabid behaviour, we were ordered to line up in front of the cars. These were not the familiar brown boxcars; they were green and quite out of the ordinary. Submissively obeying the officer's orders, we climbed down from the trucks, and marched, perplexed, towards the new means of transportation.

Two technical inventions were introduced in rail transport at the end of the nineteenth century. In the United States, George Pullman designed the first sleepers and diners, thus making long trips in North America much more comfortable. In Tsarist Russia, the prime minister, Piotr Stolypin, introduced the prisoner car, in which multitudes of participants in the 1905 insurrection were exiled to the northern reaches of Siberia. The Soviet regime put this secure means of transport to extensive use, and 'Stolypin cars' were part and parcel of most of the trains that plied the vast expanses of Soviet Russia[10].

Prisoners' cars were shorter than the ordinary passenger model. An iron mesh ran the length of the narrow corridor inside; built into it were steel doors opening on to the compartments. The compartment walls had little openings, also with grilles, through which food might be passed. There were neither windows in the compartment walls nor electric lights in the vaulted ceiling. Weak light filtered through from the opaque corridor windows and in turn through the lattice-like grille, so that the compartments were in semi-darkness throughout the day. The compartment walls were lined with two bulky wooden benches seating four; overhead were shelves for luggage.

The older officers and their younger colleagues mounted the high steps of the steel cars and followed the narrow corridor into the compartments. Sixteen men were pushed into each compartment, eight of whom had to seat themselves on the overhead shelves. Personal effects were shoved under the benches. The crowding in the compartment was terrible. Eight men sat hip-to-hip on the benches, and the feet of the other eight, doubled over on the shelves, dangled in their faces. To alleviate matters somewhat, two men climbed on to an additional set of luggage shelves directly under the vaulted ceiling.

Although the impact of the last few hours' events had left us all terribly fatigued, the conditions of the trip were such that any rest was impossible. Armed guards patrolled the narrow corridor heavily and relentlessly, peering at us through the slits in the door as if observing beasts of prey in the steel cages of a zoo. For the first few minutes the men sat there as if fossilized, deep in soundless rumination about their situation.

In the dead of night after long hours of pounding guards' footsteps, shouts, and orders from without, we suddenly felt the powerful jolt of a locomotive being coupled. A few moments later, the train moved. Yet more boring hours passed in depressing silence. Only on rare occasions did neighbours whisper audibly or rustle about in an effort to find a better position in the exhausting, shoulder-to-shoulder accommodation.

Towards dawn, the shock wore off. The passengers began picking through their belongings and exchanging views about the situation and what the group might expect. Cautiously knocking on the wooden partitions between the compartments, we established communications with our neighbours despite the guards' warning. The older men told us of the history of our unique rail cars.

Our train progressed only under cover of night. At daybreak it stopped and waited at length, far from any populated settlement. The daily food ration – dried herring and dry black bread – was handed us through the grilled aperture.

On the third day of our trip, one of the passengers on the uppermost shelf noticed a inscription in pencil on the wall: 'We don't know where we're heading.' Then another: 'We're leaving the cars and armed soldiers are waiting out side.' Other unintelligible words had been scribbled in a hasty, trembling hand. They were the last writings of the members of the previous transports.

As the trip continued, similar inscriptions were found in the neighbouring compartment, too; the men, already depressed, descended even more deeply into gloom. In the corner of the half-lit compartment sat Professor Szarecki, despondent and deep in thought. The latest news had cast a shadow over his smooth face, which usually exuded hope and good cheer.

We passed the time by ceaselessly consulting the guards and asserting ourselves; all we really wanted was some water, after having downed the herring.

After about an hour of rapid travel westward, we heard the screeching of brakes and the grinding of train wheels lurching on to a siding. Outside, we detected commanders' voices and the thud of running soldiers' boots. In faraway compartments, the sounds of pounding and slamming doors were audible. The train inched forward and everything became silent.

The somnolent passengers returned to their ruminations; no one sensed how fateful the passing moments were. Only by reconstructing the events years later can one reasonably surmise that the train had stopped at the Gniezdovo station, from which thousands of POW officers were taken into the nearby Katyn Forest for execution.

The great surprise

On the fifth day of the exhausting journey, the prisoners' train stopped in a field drenched in winter sunlight. Through cracks in the sealed window of the car's corridor, the men on the uppermost shelf noticed a sign with large letters: Babynino Station. Colonel Mara-Meyer, in the next compartment, recalled having been here when first taken prisoner of war about half a year before. The place had been known as the Pavlishchev-Bor camp, near the town of Yukhnovo in the Smolensk district.

Ordered to vacate the cars, we were surrounded by a contingent of armed soldiers. Three army trucks stood on a sandy surface near the station, with throngs of soldiers milling about.

By order of the guard officers, we boarded the trucks, this time embarking on our trip standing up and with a small escort contingent. A few minutes later the convoy plunged into a dense forest of towering oaks and pines, whose crowns converged and blocked out the sun. Tense, we continued travelling in near-darkness on a winding dirt road enveloped in secrecy and mystery.

About half an hour later we stopped in front of a wooden gate. Barbed-wire fences branched off in either direction. Behind them we saw rooftops.

We marched two-abreast on a paved lane between lawns, a row of trees and green, well-tended shrubs, towards a deserted camp. Everything was clean, and there was a tranquil, pleasant country silence all around. All this contrasted with everything to which we had grown accustomed. We were amazed.

The men were ordered to stop next to a wooden cabin which, to judge by its aroma of freshly cut boards, had been erected in anticipation of our arrival. It was in fact a spacious bathhouse. Inside were benches and towel hooks. We were handed clean linen underwear and blocks of laundry soap. Hastily we stripped, tearing away the shreds of our worn, sweaty underwear which we threw into a pile. Naked, the men burst into the adjacent shower stalls with a commotion and cries of joy.

The young bodies were skinny and pale, and the faces, tanned and exhausted, looked like masks on tall skeletons. The older men were spent, and the folds of their dry skin hung loosely on their necks and abdomens. They moved slowly, precariously maintaining their balance on the wet boards as the water cascaded on to their heads. The men exploited the rare opportunity and eagerly scrubbed away, singing and whistling lustily, oblivious to their surroundings.

Refreshed, we walked out of the bathhouse and marched, still two-abreast, past the row of shrubs. We were increasingly suspicious about what awaited us and what further surprises we might face. We came to a large wooden structure at the end of the camp. Passing through a high doorway, we entered a spacious round hall. We had been brought to an estate; the building had previously been used as exercise grounds for the owners' horse.

The chain of surprises – beginning with the humiliating trip in the criminals' train under the threat of bayonets, followed by the mysterious trip through the forest, and finishing with the delightful hot shower – left us puzzled and increasingly anxious about the future.

The senior officers' melancholy faces expressed dulled senses and forced indifference as to their surroundings. Submissively and passively they obeyed the Soviet sentries. Every man's heart pulsed with the sensation of having been swept from a bottomless pit to a mountaintop flooded with light and hope. As stunningly contrasting as the events were, we could hardly believe they were real. They might as well have been magicians' tricks. The contrasts were so eerie that they left no room for logical thought.

The next surprise came when we looked about the spacious hall. There stood a long row of tables covered with crisp, clean sheets and decked with bowls of fresh, sliced, carefully arranged white bread. Beside the tables were heavy wooden benches on which, very hesitantly and silently, we seated ourselves. Sentries in clean aprons politely dispensed hot vegetable soup, brought straight from the kitchen next door. At first the men stared in wonder at the dream come true; then they began to gorge themselves on the delicious bread and on the soup with its chunks of meat and potatoes. Those who dreaded the morrow hastily shoved leftover bread into their pockets.

Satiated for the first time in about half a year, we marched in pairs toward the residential hut. There a long corridor opened on to rooms with large windows. A loudspeaker blared music and regular news reports from Radio Moscow.

The prisoners selected Colonel Mara-Meyer, who knew the procedures here from his previous stay, as their representative with the camp command.

Showcase prisoners

The Pavlishchev-Bor estate, in the forest of the same name, had been owned before the Revolution by the Koziell-Poklewski family, members of the Polish aristocracy. Parcels of fertile land bordered a timeless forest of thick oaks and pines. The buildings were enveloped in greenery, fruit trees, and flowery shrubs, well tended by professional gardeners.

Next to the camp gate was a three-storey red-brick structure in Gothic style. It had been the residence of the estate's owners. Its miniature towers with high flagpoles soared over the sloping tiled roof. Steps between marble columns led to the entrance, and the windows, shaped like elongated arches with decorative stained-glass panes, gave the building an ambience of fable. Now the original house served as headquarters for a POW camp command; guards and servants lived in the cellars. In the middle of the camp yard was a large two-storey structure erected after the estate's owners had left, when because of the area's temperate, healthy climate, Pavlishchev-Bor had served as a recuperation home for people with pulmonary diseases. After staying in shacks for a week, we were moved to this building. Its long corridors led to spacious, sunny rooms furnished with large metal beds with bedside tables alongside. The beds had been made.

The surprising reception during our first two days in the camp was short-lived. Thereafter we stood in lengthy queues at the kitchen door for rations of soup and black bread. Severely limited portions of sugar and ersatz tobacco were doled out each week. Still, the command personnel treated us reasonably, and it was our impression that things would settle down now.

The day after we reached the camp, a group of 63 officers arrived. Most of them were doctors originally quartered in the Starobielsk camp in the Kharkov district. The newcomers described the Starobielsk POW population: about 5,000 men including high-ranking officers, professors, doctors, and lecturers in various disciplines. Transports of officers began to leave the camp in early April 1940, and nothing was heard of them thereafter. Life was easier there than in Kozielsk. Just the same, men would vanish suddenly, and new arrivals were brought in for recurrent night-time interrogations and annoying searches. Lately, correspondence with families had been permitted.

Several days later, a new transport arrived from the Ostashkov camp, about half-way between Moscow and Leningrad. These men reported that Ostashkov had been reserved for members of the civilian police, military police, and the border patrol. The camp was situated on an island in a large lake that was frozen solid throughout almost all of their stay. Living and housing conditions were harsh, and so was the authorities' attitude toward the POWs – especially those who had been Polish officers or intelligence men before the war.

On 14 May 1940, a second transport from Kozielsk arrived with 95 officers, followed by another group of 16 officers from Starobielsk. The latter group included my long-time acquaintance Lieutenant Izaak Shapiro, who brought me up to date on friends from Wilno, Drs Hanac-Bloch, I. Gopenheim, Leon Papp, and others. In the last transport from Ostashkov were another two friends from Wilno, Drs Michael Rom and M. Lewin.

A total of 394 POWs reached Pavlishchev-Bor in seven transports: two from Kozielsk with 191 prisoners, two from Starobielsk with 79, and three from Ostashkov with 124.

All the men were obsessed with the unfathomable strangeness of it all: why this combination of repression, intimidation, and sympathy on the authorities' part? Even as we enjoyed our surprisingly comfortable conditions, we were still concerned for our thousands of comrades in the three camps, whose fate was shrouded in mystery.

Many of us believed that they, too, had been taken to little camps and were being treated as required under the Geneva Convention. What really happened was totally different, as we subsequently learned. After renewing contact with our families, we found that all communication with members of the other transports had been severed, and we feared for their fate. Repeatedly we petitioned the camp officers for information, and were given evasive answers, which changed each time as if to confirm our worst fears.

Commissar Alexandrovich, in charge of us, went to considerable lengths to improve our conditions. Another contingent of investigative officers reached our camp and attempted in various ways to elicit our comments on political matters, economic problems, and personal attitudes toward the Soviet regime.

Headquarters entrusted us with routine camp administration. Professor Szarecki was chosen to run the infirmary, and he put me to work there. The Gentiles were furious and jealous at the sight of a Jew as an infirmary physician; only the esteemed professor's unchallenged stature stopped them from reacting.

The warm, sunny days of spring prompted the men to start up a prison farm. Tools were handed out, and organized groups began drawing furrows and planting peas, beans, cucumbers, and lettuce. The men worked eagerly and very devotedly. Painstaking care and good irrigation caused the seeds to sprout quickly, and the furrows filled with fresh greenery. By evening the men gathered in the corridor to hear the radio news, translated by Captain Ginsbert, a journalist who had belonged to the editorial board of a monthly journal put out by the Maritime League in Warsaw before the war. When mandolins and guitars were found in the camp warehouses, inmate musicians geared up to organize a band.

Reading matter in several languages was sent to us from the Kozielsk camp library. Our men were in charge of the kitchen, and they took action to improve the flavour of the soup. The fact that the camp command acceded to our proposals indicated that the authorities meant to leave us there for a long time.

One day, Professor Szarecki was summoned to the nearby town of Yukhnovo for a medical consultation and examination of a high-ranking security officer who had fallen ill. Because some of the older people in the camp had problems with glasses and false teeth, I was asked to come along in order to establish working relations with the town clinic.

Contact with our families had been broken off after our transfer to Pavlishchev-Bor, and our men became despondent for lack of word from their loved ones. I had the idea that my trip could be a rare opportunity to restore communication with my family in Wilno. Thus, before the trip, I prepared two postcards. One was brief and did not bear the camp address. The other was packed with details about my life and that of my comrades.

On the appointed day we seated ourselves with Commissar Alexandrovich in the back seat of a spacious, black Zil automobile. Our taciturn driver took us down a broad, deserted dirt road at great speed. No one said a word. Then I noticed a green postbox alongside a fence at the edge of the road. Obtaining our escort's agreement to send the terse postcard, I hopped out and quickly mailed it – and the other one, too. Fifteen minutes later, we reached the town clinic and met the doctors. My ruse had worked. The postcards were the first information my parents had received from me since the Kozielsk camp had been wound up in April 1940, and the POW transports to destinations unknown had begun.

It had been an audacious and risky thing to do, but the tremendous urge and challenge of it overcame my apprehensions. Ultimately, luck was on my side. Shortly thereafter, the camp authorities permitted all the men to resume contact with their families, and I was the first to receive word from home. Indeed, my postcards had been among the few that reached Wilno after the POW camps were liquidated, and they were quite the talk of the town. The letters from home were full of concern over the fate of my comrades in the POW camps. The questions proliferated as time passed, and families of the thousands of POWs grew increasingly anxious about their loved ones' fate and whereabouts.

After arrangements in the town clinic were completed, the Commissar invited Professor Szarecki and me to his private residence. Notwithstanding his senior status of security officer, his home was small and simply furnished. On the walls of the guest room hung cheap prints of landscapes and pictures of Stalin and Beria.[11] Alongside a wooden counter stood a set of bookshelves crammed with novels and volumes on art. A small table and a set of cheap armchairs stood in the centre of the room. We were served tea in thick cups, sweet biscuits, and top-grade cigarettes. During our talk we did not succeed in extracting any hint about our future and our comrades' fate. We brought our impressions back to the camp, where we were greeted with a barrage of questions about our stay on the 'outside'. The experience had indeed affected us, and the illusion of longed-for freedom lingered.

Even though the inmate population was small and the conditions reasonable, anti-semitic discrimination and hatred were no less intense. The young cadets were especially hostile incited by two senior officers whom we had known long before. They found an opportunity to demonstrate their enmity after one of the young Jewish officers came down with a headache at the end of the meal, and stepped out of the column of marchers to hurry to lie down in his room. The cadets went wild and began to hunt down the unfortunate officer. They could not find him, and vented their rage with vociferous epithets. Their blatant hostility actually took the command officers by surprise.

Because of the estrangement or lack of friendship with these erstwhile comrades-in-arms, in conditions of captivity, the Jews in Pavlishchev-Bor had to segregate themselves, keeping to separate rooms to avoid hostility and tension.

Of the 400 officers in the camp, many displayed a higher level of thought than that of their comrades, demonstrating notably liberal opinions toward their Jewish neighbours. One extraordinary personality of this kind, radiating innocence and warmth, was Captain, Józef Czapski – a man of about 40, a cavalry officer, and a member of a veteran aristocratic family.[12] He was tall and thin as a rake, and his pinched face was punctuated by deep-set blue eyes that expressed suffering and empathy with others in their hardships. During one of our talks he reached into his pack and pulled out a photograph of himself with his five sisters, all tall and slim like him. Together, with their stature and innocence, they looked like six holy candles.

Czapski was a man of devout Catholic persuasion, artistic talent, and deeply rooted liberal views. Educated in St Petersburg, he was steeped from early youth in Russian culture, under the privileged conditions of a vastly wealthy family extensively married into various royal houses. Before the war he studied art in Paris and spent time in England, Spain and Switzerland. He was fluent in most European languages and at home with the French intellectuals. On top of this he was an author, journalist, and painter. His vast erudition and easy-going nature were to serve him when appointed as General Anders' agent in Anders' efforts to trace the thousands of officers who had vanished from the three POW camps.

This noble soul refrained from using his title of Graf von Hutten-Czapski; indeed, he disparaged his pedigreed origins. One of his confidants in the camp was a young doctor, Joachim Cohn, from the town of Horodenka in eastern Galicia. The two found common ground for interminable conversations on art and literature.

Another nobleman with a notably fair-minded attitude was Captain Ślizeń, who became General Anders' adjutant when Arders' Army was set up. A further senior officer with liberal views was Colonel Bolesławicz, cousin of Professor Michejda of the University of Wilno, my teacher of surgery. Yet another was Colonel Tyszyński, a relative of General Anders. Several junior officers, too, objected to their comrades' extreme views and steered clear of arguments with their opponents.

Our farmers were not fated to bring in their bountiful harvest, which they had produced with so much toil and care. Nor were the strains of the mandolin and guitar band ever heard. These were like other promises that were not kept.

The period of calm and lessening of tension in the camp was not long-lived. After six weeks at ease, we were suddenly ordered on the morning of 12 June 1940 to gather up our effects and prepare to move on. This time our belongings were not searched, and the guard contingent treated the POWs politely.

In orderly pairs we marched to the Babynino station, where a long train of familiar green prisoners' cars waited. Packed only 12 to a compartment this time, we embarked on a boring, week-long trip. We were crowded nevertheless, but free of the psychological tension that had accompanied us on our last journey.

The command officers announced that we were going over

to 'comfortable conditions' because the camp was required for vital, urgent needs. Some time later this message was put into context: Lithuania had been annexed to the Soviet Union, and the camp we had vacated was being retenanted by thousands of new prisoners.

My partners in the narrow compartment included three long-time friends, the lawyer Izaak Szapiro and Drs Lewin and Rom. We assumed sardine-like positions on the upper shelves, with our shared loaf of bread alongside. Our discomfort and gloomy thoughts were ameliorated by the friendly atmosphere and awareness of common fate. On the lower benches sat Professor Szarecki, the Rev. Professor Kantak, a pilot named Czyż, and five middle-aged high-ranking officers.

Standard transport procedures for prisoners were strictly maintained. A short sentry with a round face and Mongolian eyes, armed with a large, old-fashioned rifle, patrolled the car's narrow corridor. Now and then he would peer curiously through the grille at our wristwatches, puzzled as if day-dreaming. The innocent soldier profoundly coveted this item, the most sought-after in Russia. My comrades egged him on, repeatedly and deliberately sticking out their palms to show off their glittering watches as the spellbound sentry, who looked like a dwarf out of an animated cartoon, gaped.

The older men sat on the lower benches, saying little. Father Kantak, pale, thin and short, cringed in a corner and kept to himself, totally silent. He spent most of time deep in his own thoughts, his lips delicately murmuring a silent prayer.

Professor Szarecki, too, had little to say. His features had lost their colour under the shoulder-to-shoulder conditions, and his blue, worried eyes gazed into the distance through the compartment's grille. His rare comments during the lengthy trip had to do with his anti-German feelings. Steeped in admiration of the civilization of his Russian homeland, he harboured a natural disgust for the German lust for violence and conquest.

The shadows of the electric poles and the few trees we passed on our way indicated that we were heading north. As the wheels clicked, we occasionally ventured various and sundry guesses about our new destination.

5

Full Circle

On 18 June 1940, at twilight, the prisoners' train stopped beside a rickety shelter far from any station. Facing a brisk northern wind, we stepped down into a field and marched along a path of sand still moist from the long winter. On the horizon we saw a few tottering cabins, capped with straw roofs. After walking for about half an hour, we approached a rickety little wooden bridge with traces of a handrail. Under it, a narrow river plied a chasm lined with green shrubs.

I knew where I was. It was the camp to which I had been taken nine months ago on the train from Baranowicze, where I had been snared.

This time the camp was ringed with several closely laid banks of barbed wire, along which observation posts manned with armed guards in scaffold-like towers. Blinding search lights illuminated the territory around the clock. Only my friend Dr Merenlender and I remained of the original Griazoviets group. The traces of the other thousands of POWs had vanished as if they had never existed.

The Griazoviets camp was near the town of the same name, some 20 kilometres from the district city of Vologda, about half-way between Moscow and the Arctic port of Archangel. Within the camp, on a hill near the brook, were the ruins of an Orthodox church; beside them was a two-storey residence meant for the priest and his servants. The believing Christians among us retreated to the ruins and, inspired by the place, engaged in silent prayer.

The yard was deserted. All that remained there were some indications of farm activity, piles of junk, a stable, and some rickety shacks. Our men set up quarters on the wooden bunks in the spacious room of the half-destroyed stone building, whose doors had long since been torn away and whose walls were peeling. The Finnish names of POWs who had preceded us were carved into the window lintels. Two blonde, blue-eyed Finnish secretaries, who spoke halting Russian, occasionally appeared among the Soviets who ran the camp.

On the ground floor was a kitchen with a set of boilers. These were used for heating water and cooking a malodorous, tasteless soup made of frozen sea sprat supplemented with barley, chunks of potatoes, and, at times, bits of bone of unidentified animals.

On rare occasions the diet was augmented with large frozen fish from the sea or from the Russian rivers Lena, Ob, or Yenisei. These fish – *Syomga* or *Byeluga* – were about two metres long, and their spines were almost as big as a man's. *Byeluga* means 'white belly'; it has to do with the white sediment on the river's bottom.

Frozen chunks of little and big fish were packed in salt and kept in huge metal barrels that sat for months on end in the camp stores. To make the tasteless soup, chunks were hacked out with a hatchet and thrown into boiling water.

As time passed, our cooks began to innovate by smoking the fish in an improvised stone oven. Even the fussy eaters among us regarded this smoked fish as a delicacy. We used the fat that gathered at the bottom of the oven, for frying and to improve the flavour of the daily soup, of which everyone was sick. One large chunk of fish made eight servings. It was a refreshing luxury on the monotonous menu.

As the camp commander, Colonel Volkov, toured the Gria-zoviets camp one day, someone in his party noticed the new structure in the yard. The aroma of the smoked fish whetted Volkov's appetite, and the brown colour of the chunks of fish was evidently a feast to his eyes. 'The Polish invention', as he called it, made quite an impact in camp command circles. Word of the important culinary improvement spread past the barbed wire fences. Several days later, a committee representing the authorities in Vologda reached the camp. The officials were impressed with the way we improved the food, of which suitable use had not been made throughout the country.

Twice a week we were allotted rations of black bread, sugar cubes, and *makhorka*. The latter, made of a blend of ground vegetable roots, was widely used for smoking, especially by villagers and labourers. Wrapped in a 'cup' of folded newspaper, it produced dense, dark smoke with an aroma of its own. Smoking *makhorka* was a veritable ritual in camps and other places of detention. The smoking addicts among us would trade their bread for *makhorka*.

A row of wooden houses lined the other side of the stream that partitioned the camp. One of them served as quarters for the senior officers, another housed the lower-ranking officers, and a third was used as an infirmary. On the ground floor of the infirmary building was a poorly equipped dental clinic, comprising an old wooden chair with a wobbly headrest, a leg-powered, pulley-driven drill of nineteenth-century vintage, two sets of pliers for pulling teeth, a few random assorted instruments, and some bottles of medicine. Upstairs were two treatment rooms and an infirmary. The primitive equipment was quite satisfactory in view of the circumstances, and permitted first aid and vital treatment for the inmates.

Captain Czapski found himself in an embarrassing situation one day, when he broke a front tooth while biting into a piece of bread. The rest of his teeth were so weak that he could neither chew nor speak. When he presented himself in the clinic, helpless and depressed, the sight of his crestfallen, pale features provoked both compassion and a smile, since the damage could not be repaired under the camp conditions.

Always resolutely willing to help a man in distress, I procured the bone of an unidentified animal from the kitchen, and, after carving and sharpening it as needed, installed the tooth in the happy man's mouth. It worked, and was replaced with a 'real' false tooth several years later under better conditions. The patient commemorated the operation with a letter of thanks, and mentioned it in the memoirs he published in Paris after the war.

The clinic's doings were brought to the attention of the Soviet doctor, on whose recommendation camp commander Colonel Volkov himself showed up for treatment. As the clinic's reputation spread beyond the barbed-wire fences, a number of senior district officials, too, made use of it.

Such 'outpatients' occasionally expressed their appreciation by giving handfuls of rock candy or little bottles of strong Russian vodka. The senior patients had to conceal their gifts when being searched as they entered the camp. The tough guards' uncompromising suspicion made no exception for power and rank.

After months of monotonous, insufficient nutrition, the men suffered from deficiencies of vital nutrients, resulting in diarrhoea, skin rashes, and eye infections. The soup was so low in food value that it was imbibed only to fend off starvation; even then, its poor flavour and nauseating stench were noted. As time passed, the younger inmates began to rebel, and one day they decided to turn down the menu altogether. The camp authorities were sensitive to any organized initiative towards group resistance, and knew where the food-refuseniks' thoughts were leading.

The camp commander, visiting our clinic for dental work, pleaded with me to ask my comrades to rescind their rash decisions in view of the situation outside the barbed-wire fences. Subsequently we found out what he meant: tens of thousands of people had been put to forced labour, chopping down thick pines in the nearby woods. Men, women, and children were languishing in subhuman conditions and near-starvation in the timeless forests that covered the vast expanse from our location to the shores of the White Sea and the Arctic port of Archangel. Multitudes had been exiled to the area for having been regarded by the regime as 'bourgeois and anti-socialist elements'. Thousands starved or froze to death.

In reaction to the flickerings of rebellion among the younger men, Soviet command officers showed up and tried to verify the leaders' identities by interrogation. The camp menu was not improved, and the disgruntlement ebbed by itself.

Civilian prisoners

Among the 400 POWs in the camp was a group of civilians, thrown in among the army officers by tricks of fate.

Seventy-year-old Jakub Kleinman, from a town near the city of Kovel in Wołyń district, was a quiet Jew and a quick-witted, respected lumber merchant. A short man with a desiccated, creased face framed in a white goatee, he would retreat every morning to the back of the camp or a corner of the building, put on his *tallis* and *tefillin*,[13] and recite the morning prayers. His tumble into Soviet captivity was a sad story which ended with his miraculous rescue – a descent into an abyss of misery for the purpose of salvation by Divine mercy.

While walking home from synagogue one day in early September after the war broke out, he chanced to pass the rail station, which was bustling with crowds of soldiers and civilians. When a soldier escaped from one of the boxcars taking 60 Polish prisoners into the Russian heartland, the Soviet officer responsible for the car and its contents seized the elderly Kleinman, who, curious, had paused near the scene, and shoved him in with the soldiers. The train reached the POW camp, and all the old man's requests and supplications for release at the transit stations were in vain. Promises to check into the matter at subsequent stops proved false, and the old man was stuck in the camp for Polish officer POWs.

This Orthodox man, a noted anomaly in the Christian environment, conducted himself with nobility and exemplary discipline, and earned the admiration of his intrinsically hostile young neighbours. Several senior officers, including General Wołkowicki, treated him with pronounced respect and occasionally walked about in his company, discussing matters of economics and policy in lively tones.

Old Kleinman was liberated with the rest of the POWs about two years later, thanks to the Sikorski agreement. The army and Captain Czapski went to great lengths to locate his relatives, who had been uprooted with multitude of Poles into the heart of Asia. Kleinman joined his family, which had been saved from the Nazi Holocaust by being exiled to Kazakhstan. Indeed, the twists of fate!

Another civilian who found his way into the POW camp was Józef Blumenstok, a likeable man who stood out for his general erudition and perfect command of most European languages. He had been the official translator in Warsaw's international airport, and had worked in conferences as an expert simultaneous interpreter. He had been arrested by the Russians as a suspected spy, thus escaping the Nazis' clutches in their blitz of Poland.

The Soviets treated his command of foreign languages as sufficient reason to bounce him from prison to prison until he reached the POW camp. His cultured and gentlemanly behaviour earned him the regard and respect of the senior officers, many of whom enlisted with him for language instruction. After liberation from the camp, he died in a typhus epidemic that claimed tens of thousands of civilian victims in southern Russia.

Also tossed into the camp were two Russian farmers who owned land in southern Poland. They had been seized after being spotted in the chance company of several officers at the time POW transports were being sent east after the Red Army entered Poland. The camp guards were especially alert in the presence of these two representatives of Western-style landed gentry. Both were suspected of being intelligence officers in disguise, and were interrogated night after night by the camp commanders.

A real oddity to fall in with the officer group was a Ukrainian murderer named Jan M. a macho type of about 26, mentally retarded and a lifelong criminal. He had fled prison from one of the outlying cities during a German aerial bombardment. He was a stubby dwarf of a man, broad-shouldered and thickly built, muscles overlaying his bones like steel rails. His face was fat and pink, his forehead low. Blonde hair spilled on to his short neck. His cheekbones were high and his eyes thin as slits, with heavy earlobes protruding on either side. He went about with his large mouth gaping open and his thick tongue lolling on his lower lip.

He wore an unbuttoned shirt with a flower pattern, and a worn jacket with sleeves too short for him. Fleshy palms dangled to the vicinity of his knees. A forced, murderous, frozen smile plastered across his face concealed indifference to his surroundings.

He strode about slowly and confidently like a predatory Neanderthal, giant shoes protecting stubby feet. Always hungry and ready to consume anything at hand, he would fume in rage as the bread rations were doled out. His eyebrows would furrow angrily behind a furious glare, and one could sense a repressed brutality that augered a sudden outburst of violence.

One day it was his turn to carry the pail of fish soup. As he walked along, he consumed the portions of his ten neighbours and quietly returned the empty pail to the kitchen. Bunkmates kept their distance from him because of his questionable personal hygiene, and the camp command stuck him in an isolated room in the attic because of his toughness.

However moronic, he was nevertheless a skilled lumberman who wielded an axe with perfect control. A glint of sweetness would flicker in his eyes as he rolled heavy metal barrels of frozen fish from the warehouse to the kitchen, where it would be cooked as soup. Liberated from the camp with the rest of the prisoners, he was handed over to those who would be sure to exploit his physical prowess to the hilt.

Another civilian who found his way into the POW camp was an innocent youth of 15. According to Soviet occupation army orders, his father, Captain S. had enlisted at his city's command headquarters, where he was arrested. His only son refused to part with him, and was promptly attached to the transport of POW officers en route to the camp.

For months the teenager stumbled around among the elderly officers, idle and depressed. Then, for his own comfort, he was reassigned to the attic together with the moron M. They did not make for good neighbours. The young prisoner grew up unusually fast in captivity; liberated two years later, he joined the Polish army and was seriously wounded as a private in Italy, alongside his father.

The Germans

Following an initiative by several officers, camp command set up a POW barbershop in one of the wooden huts. Its management was entrusted to a group of officers headed by one Gerhard. The barbershop quickly became a German-speaking nationalist club, and the Nazi salute became customary upon entering. The Jews disgustedly declared the barbershop off-limits.

After postal communication with families was restored, members of the barbershop clique would receive encouraging letters in German, full of Nazi slogans. The select group's next step was to order – and receive – an embellished edition of *Mein Kampf* with an expensive leather binding.

Volksdeutsch officers joined the club, hoping to exploit Soviet–German relations – amicable at the time – to secure early liberation. Indeed, several officers of German origin who belonged to the group were liberated and repatriated, in part for this very reason. Their comrades were arrested after the German surprise attack on the USSR, and were handed over for special treatment commensurate with the circumstances. Their revered commander hanged himself on a tree as we marched out of the camp after joining Anders' Army.

POW university

Extensive cultural activity went on in the camp. Among its inmates were numerous top intellectuals and professionals in diverse disciplines. Their presence helped create an ambience of culture and promoted the establishment of study groups and expert lectures on various fields of research.

Professor Aleksandrowicz, rector of the University of Lwów, spoke on the achievements of medicine and the secrets of biological research. The erudite lecturer, steeped in European culture and a scientist of broad horizons, had taught me medicine at the University of Wilno. Professor Sienicki of the Warsaw Polytechnic department of architecture, gave an illuminating series of lectures accompanied with splendid sketches of royal palaces, churches, and fortresses belonging to various styles of previous centuries. With great skill and astonishing powers of recall, he would use bits of chalk and an improvised blackboard to reproduce grand halls, citadel towers, turrets of medieval castles, and the domes of famous European churches. An engineer named Kaminski, a well-known expert on motor vehicles, discussed auto mechanics and engines with the help of fascinating models made of bits of pipe and metal wire gathered in the camp yard.

A doctor from Lwów and an assimilated Jew, lectured on general literature. Displaying an uncommon memory, he quoted excerpts from the finest works of world literature. This Renaissance man abounded in talents and knew many languages. He avoided the company of Jews and occasionally was the butt of ridicule and anti-semitic slurs from his friends. Despite his proud proclamations of his Polishness, he was occasionally heckled during his illuminating lectures. The insulting reactions did not change his subserrient ways. The eccentric Doctor could not find his place in society, and converted to Christianity in England at the end of the war.

Professor Czarnowski, an expert on ear, nose, and throat diseases at the University of Wilno, gave a series of travelogue talks on Scandinavia, about which he had once published a fascinating book. He was a delicate, liberal man devoid of extreme views, a pleasant conversationalist and a gentleman by nature.

I struck up an interesting acquaintance with the son of Emil Młynarski, the well-known Polish composer and director of the Warsaw Philharmonic. Lying on the camp lawn one day in the summer of 1940 with my fellow inmates, I described an interesting excursion I had taken to the Norwegian fiords a few days before the war. One of the men listening was a handsome, blonde officer in his thirties, who indentified himself as the manager of the governement shipping company that had organized the outing. After we had become friends, he told me who his famous father was, and how, as the conductor of famous orchestras, he had taken him around the world in first-class conditions.

In greatest secrecy, he informed me that his sister had married the Jewish pianist Artur Rubinstein. He revealed fascinating details about the early career of the short, slender young man with the dreamy eyes in the grand halls of Polish aristocracy in turn-of-the-century Warsaw. It was a fetching story about daring and hopeless love of the young genius' for the proud and wealthy composer's beautiful daughter. Firmly set on making the most of his talents, Rubinstein rented an empty garage near the Warsaw Airport and locked himself inside, spending most of the day practising the piano undisturbed. His relentless efforts gave rise to a virtuoso, happily married to his heart's beloved.

All this was confided to me guardedly. Attitudes in the camp being what they were, my interlocutor was apprehensive lest the intriguing details become known. This invasion of exclusive Polish aristocracy by the young Jew was not in keeping with the spirit of the times. I kept the secret.

Our lowly standard of living left us totally dissociated from the 'other' reality, with its workaday luxuries. In one of our conversations, Młynarski asked me whether there were still people in the world who drank tea out of glasses. Living in a protracted state of deprivation in the camp, we valued every empty tin of preserves.

Two years later, to our good fortune, we recalled our talks when we met by chance in Cairo's famous Groppi café. Allied military intelligence in Egypt was making good use of my friend's command of most European languages. At that time, Cairo was the espionage centre of all the warring forces. This was shortly after Rommel's forces had been trounced at the approaches to Cairo. Most people in Cairo had been expecting the Germans to enter the Egyptian capital en route to conquest of Palestine and the Middle East.

Anti-semitism in the camp

In contrast to the intellectuals and academicians, the camp had a contingent of regular army officers and cadets many of whom had been brought up from early childhood on anti-semitism. These men recoiled from any contact with Jews and treated them as if not there at all. This cohesive, nationally extremist clique was under the guidance of several senior officers. The group held separate meetings for lectures and advanced military training by experts in the various disciplines of warfare. Few members of this group were interested in the talks on artistic and literary themes. Occasionally they gave vent to crude eruptions of extreme nationalism.

One day as we queued for soup, a quarrel fuelled by exchanges of profanity broke out. During the fisticuffs, someone spread the rumour that a young physician named Gurwitz had insulted a former police officer. A short time later, dozens of agitated young men appeared with clubs, knives, and belts that had been concealed from the guards. One of them even waved a hatchet in his zeal to avenge the honour of the Polish police. After great effort and a threat to turn to the authorities, Captain Czerny, the Polish commander, succeeded in persuading the wild rabble to call off their lynch.

The Soviets launched an investigation, after which the chief inciter was jailed for several days. The incident added fuel to the sizzling flame of enmity.

One of the officers had been commander of a cavalry division in Poland. In national consciousness, the cavalry had worn a halo ever since the glorious era of the Crusader wars. Its horsemen were recruited from village youth, and its officers were selected from the aristocracy, who often volunteered with their horses and were looked upon as the knights of Poland. The officer was a tough, massive man, tipping the scales at twice an average man's weight. Officers who had been under his command described the especially large horse he rode, and the two servants who helped their commander mount it.

After two years in the camp, I came face to face with the haughty colonel in the bathhouse. His sagging countenance was full of creases; his eyes were sunk in their sockets. The skin of his once-bulging abdomen now sagged over his hips and thighs in a long fold down to his knees, like a chef's apron. The proud, unbending officer refused to accept the circumstances of his confinement, and was perpetually disgruntled and angry about everything surrounding him. Anti-semitism was in his very blood, and he reserved special rage for those Jews who, he believed, lay at the root of all the world's evil.

Among the extremists were a dentist, a pilot, and a cook. These men clustered with other young men who formed a clique that stood apart from everyone else in the camp, interminably discussing the nature of future nationalist Poland.

One thoroughly corrupt individual was a standing army officer. Dissatisfied with the camp menu, he made efforts to diversify it with the flesh of the few starlings that frequented the northern skies. He hunted them down with a slingshot that he had nailed together with junk in the camp warehouses. The intrepid hunter and his cronies would sneak far from the camp buildings, kindle an improvised bonfire in the shade of the withered bushes, and fry their victims on skewers. His perverse cruelty and his lust for poultry rid the area of the last of its birds. Thus their chirping, perceived by the prisoners as a symbol of freedom beyond the barbed-wire fences in the desolate north, was no more.

A rare and extraordinary event took place at Griazoviets in the summer of 1941: a POW officer was liberated. With no forewarning, my friend Dr Michael Rom was ordered to report to the command headquarters prior to repatriation. Sceptical about the Soviets' bona fides, we undertook the sophisticated ruse of throwing in a pair of trousers with Rom's personal effects; before his release, the happy man was to return the garment.

It worked. We got the trousers back, and Dr Rom reached Wilno in good health. This rare event came about thanks to intervention in Moscow by the famous Soviet author and stage director Mikhail Rom, our friend's cousin.

Unfortunately, Rom's happiness was short-lived; several months later, he perished when the Wilno ghetto was liquidated.

'Villa of Bliss'

The deliberate selection of men from Griazoviets, when there were three POW camps to choose from, was an act on the part of the central Soviet authorities that reflected precise awareness of the realities of Polish demography. The 400 camp inmates included officers belonging to the minority groups – Lithuanians, Russians, Ukrainians, and about 40 Jews – whose numbers corresponded to their percentages of the pre-war population. Despite national contrasts and differences in attitude toward the Polish authorities, all but a few who harboured extreme leftist views were far from sympathetic to the Soviet regime and values.

The Soviet officers' personal talks with the prisoners, lectures by professionals who came in from Moscow, and pro-paganda films fell on deaf ears at best. At worst, they fortified the feeling of total rejection reserved by most of the officers, especially the younger men in the standing army, for the Soviet system.

Following an initiative by the camp authorities, about ten leftist officers started up a 'Red Corner' for sympathizers of the regime. The 'Corner' had occasional lectures and a supply of newspapers and propaganda sheets. The group's accomplish-ments and influence were scanty, and the authorities did nothing to back or encourage it. The other inmates were hostile to the 'Red' officers, which resulted in friction and charges of treason. Only a few Poles visited the Red Corner, and they, too, did so irregularly.

One day in October, four senior officers were summarily called to camp headquarters on the other side of the barbed-wire fence.[14] Three were colonels – Berling, Tyszyński, and Buko-jemski – and one, Lis, was a major. About two weeks later, another three colonels joined them: Gorczyński, Morawski, and Künstler. None of the dignified officers returned from the visit, and no explanation for the mysterious event – extraordinary under POW circumstances – was offered.

Guesses and rumours about the officers' fate became the topic of routine talk for quite some time. Their friends were

genuinely worried. Because no reliable information was forth-
coming from anyone in the group, spirits sank gradually – as
if by hint from on high – and the mystery slipped off the
agenda.

About half a year later, just before Germany and the USSR
went to war, all the vanished men except for Colonel Berling
reappeared in the camp. No details of their adventure were
disclosed. The mystery of the colonels was kept under wraps for
months; only fragments of rumours gradually surfaced.

The officers had been transported to Moscow with dignity
and pleasantness, by first-class rail, and were quartered in a
grand villa on the outskirts of the capital. There they enjoyed
the polite services of well-trained Soviet young ladies, especially
luxurious living conditions, and select meals washed down with
champagne. This done, senior Soviet officers then tried delicately to convince the guests of the national value of political
collaboration with the Soviet Union.

The chosen officers attended special lectures and were shown
well-formulated plans for the establishment of a Polish army
that would fight the German occupation until their homeland
was liberated.

Enticed by the Soviets' promises, the officers fell into stormy
dispute and reciprocal accusations. As time passed, we heard
that they had come to harsh verbal exchanges, threatening their
continued stay in their pleasure villa.

After spurning the Soviet proposals for good, the officers
were sent back to the camp, where they disclosed nothing about
what had transpired. The Moscow authorities, in turn, despaired
of the possibility of collaborating with Polish officers.

The details of the senior colonels' activities under luxurious
conditions were scrupulously buried in the cellars of Moscow
and the archives of the Polish government-in-exile in London.

Damming the river

The summer of 1940 was unusually brief. The soil in and around
the camp was a blanket of mud with splashes of green grass and

miniature wild flowers. The fields outside the camp were deserted and uncultivated; some were barren. The nearby village had been abandoned, and its miserable shacks emitted none of the normal sounds of peasants, barking dogs, and cackling chickens.

The nights were clear for several weeks, and at midnight the aurora borealis bathed the area in faint light. Exploiting the warm, sunny days, the POWs swam in the cold water of the stream that tumbled frantically along the edge of the camp; others tried their hands at amateurish and futile fishing.

Bored at length, and bereft of hope for a change in the situation, the men were increasingly beset by feelings of disappointment and despair. Camp headquarters, aware that ferment was on the rise, sponsored a lecture for all the POWs by a professional summoned especially from Moscow. Softly and descriptively, the orator explained the world political situation that had come about as a result of the war in the west, making note of the Allied forces' defeat and Europe's speedy acquiescence to Nazi occupation. Thus, the speaker concluded, the listeners would do well to snap out of their depression, believe in the future, and keep their uniforms in good trim; they might be needed in due course. All this was true, and became even truer about a year later.

To keep the idle POWs occupied, the camp commander sponsored a vegetable garden on the camp grounds. Volunteers were provided with hoses, rakes, and irrigation tools. In short order a large, previously parched area behind the residential quarters had been ploughed and planted with enthusiasm and exemplary order. Under the POWs' devoted care, green onions, lettuce, peas, and potatoes quickly sprouted. The men eagerly looked forward to this supplement to their monotonous diet; furthermore, it gave the farmers the joy of having created something.

Then a group of POW engineers came up with a plan of their own, which would offer POWs interesting work and help develop the desolate area. The difference in elevation in the river that flowed through the camp, they suggested, made this a good place to build a dam. The structure would regulate the harmful spring floods and impound substantial quantities of water with which the fields could be irrigated during the rainless months of summer. The sponsors also proposed a hydro-electric plant that would electrify the nearby town.

After surveying the area, the engineers succeeded in infecting the camp commander, Colonel Volkov, with enthusiasm for their treasured notion. When the appointed authorities in the district capital of Vologda agreed, the go-ahead was given. There was a reason for the quick approval. After the previous fish-smoking initiative and other culinary improvements, the central authorities had become impressed with Polish know-how.

Several days later, trucks carrying construction material, boards, wooden poles, and work tools began arriving at the camp. After promises of handsome pay for the effort they would expend in establishing this enterprise, many men joined in with the work. The first step was to dig deep holes into the soil and build frames and fillers for the dam. Work proceeded at a pace that surpised camp headquarters, and continued steadily through the summer. Thus the dam was completed on time – before rainy autumn set in.

As quantities of water backed up behind the dam, as expected, a special committee arrived from Vologda to confirm that the job had been completed and to take official possession of the enterprise. The members of the committee were sincerely appreciative, noting the potential it represented for the area's development.

Autumn, with its thunder and lightning, came early that year. One overcast, cold night after a few severe rainstorms, a deafening explosion was heard. The camp inmates and commanders leaped as if facing an earthquake. Water surged over the river's banks, flooding much of the camp including the site of the disaster.

We awoke the next overcast morning to a terrifying sight: the dam had burst along its entire width. Shattered remnants, uprooted poles, and disembodied boards floated in the turbulent waters. The wreckage swept away chunks of earth and stones, which gathered speed and slammed into the barbed wire fence at the edge of the camp. The fence, not made to withstand such pressure, was about to rupture. The miserable remnants of the dam, protruding from the flooded riverbanks and the surging water, looked like the ruins of a terrible aerial bombardment.

Two days later the rain died down, the torrent of water began to ebb, and the full extent of the devastation became apparent. The dam's sponsors and builders faced the embarrassing spectacle helplessly. The camp commander, Colonel Volkov, disappeared on the day of the disaster; we never saw him again. Other camp officers told us that he had been summarily court-martialled for sabotage and was executed. A few of his close assistants also vanished.

The miserable adventure was quickly forgotten when the winter cold that had settled over the area brought more urgent, immediate concerns to the fore. More and more men fell sick with high fever, severe colds, and pneumonia. Lacking warm clothes, the inmates holed themselves up in the crowded rooms and spent their time reading or pursuing various improvised hobbies.

When the mercury dropped to −60° Celsius, the pipes froze. Water for drinking and cooking was brought in a wooden barrel on a country sleigh hitched to a pitiful, starving horse. Early risers had the privilege of watching this vehicle put into the camp in the pre-dawn gloom, horse and barrel covered with a thick layer of ice. In all that transparent armour, only fissures over the knees of the exhausted beast permitted it to navigate in the deep snow and tow the cargo to the camp kitchen. The wagoner, an elderly, stooped man wearing a filthy but warm greatcoat with a creased hood shoved over his forehead, marched heavily alongside his horse, with a crust of ice formations covering his white beard, moustache, and eyebrows.

The second winter in confinement dragged on and exhausted the depressed men's strength. The men were forced to sleep through the long nights bundled in what remained of their sweaty, damp clothes, in the musty atmosphere of their crowded, unheated quarters.

Work went on in the camp infirmary, with sparing use made of the medicines and bandages, which were qualitatively and quantitatively poor. Inmates who happened to be specialist physicians were called to the infirmary from time to time for consultation: Dr Unger for eye diseases, Dr Merenlender for dermatology, and others for digestive and pulmonary ailments.

Although gloom and irritability still reigned, the men sensed a change in the authorities' attitude. A new spirit emanated from headquarters; there were signs that the Soviet officers were interested in effecting a rapprochement with us. It was rumoured that the Soviets were about to establish a Polish army to fight the Nazi enemy.

Command began to allot the men an allowance – twenty roubles a month for officers, ten for enlisted men and civilians. The money could be spent at a mobile canteen that visited the camp only twice. Its severely limited selection included stationery, needles and thread, colourful buttons, and shoelaces.

Surgery in the 'Kremlin'

The spring of 1941 came late. Finally, though, the sunny, clear days became more frequent, and the fiercely cold nights that sapped the POWs' strength, less so.

One day in April, Professor Szarecki was summoned to the camp's new commander, Major Khodas. He was instructed to travel to the district capital of Vologda, where a senior secret police officer had fallen ill several days previously and showed no improvement. My earlier trip from Pavlishchev-Bor to Yukhnovo stood me in good stead. Again I was allowed out of the camp to accompany the professor on his intriguing journey.

In the company of our confidant, the gentlemanly Colonel Alexandrovich, we set out in a black, spacious Ziss sedan, crossing the untamed tundra, still blanketed with thick snow, on frozen roads. The car passed through little villages and low peasant homes with straw roofs. Traces of wooden fences could be seen in the yards, protruding through the snow drifts. Now and then a few women came into sight, wrapped in dark kerchiefs and clutching pails of water. There were no barking dogs, no crowing roosters. The villages were silent, as if frozen in the cold of the protracted winter. Along the road we saw ten old men queuing beside a rickety shack. The hut was an ice cream stand; the Russians, it seems, eat ice cream even in the winter.

Our courteous escort asked us if we wished to stop for some ice cream. We answered in the affirmative, and, with a confidence that attested to our power, the driver stepped directly to the head of the line. The old men, shoved backwards, tried to vent their displeasure on the intruder, who responded with a vigorous: 'You've got to respect the authorities.' Without queuing, he was given three portions of ice cream and went back to the car. The 'ice cream' proved to be a concoction of leftover milk, saccharin, and frozen water. That is how it tasted, too.

In the meantime we had reached the outskirts of the northern district capital, and pulled up to a large iron gate in a towering wall that stretched into the distance. Behind it we could see clusters of buildings and some church steeples. A small door next to the main gate was opened for us, and we entered a vast compound that accommodated the regional secret police headquarters.

Rows of multi-storey buildings rose along paved roads and paths in various directions. In the centre of the compound towered a grand Byzantine-style cathedral. Its belfries and steeples, with their golden domes, glittered in the winter sun.

The place was called the 'Kremlin of the North,' a namesake of Soviet government's citadel in Moscow. The church's mosaic walls formed an arcade punctuated with stained-glass windows. Marble columns flanked broad staircases leading to the sanctuary, in which no trace of a cross could be seen. Nothing moved all about. An eerie and threatening silence hovered over the grey stone masses with their closed windows. Probing the gloom past the corners of the houses, we could make out a few soldiers, armed with machine guns and identifiable as security police by the red ribbons on their caps.

Led by Colonel Alexandrovich, we entered a spacious hall on the ground floor of one of the buildings. It was being used as a restaurant, and was furnished with long wooden tables parallel to the walls, with heavy chairs alongside. Together with our escort we took an elevator to the fourth floor of the local hospital. In one of its rooms we found a man of about 60 writhing in severe abdominal pain.

Pausing in the doorway, the experienced physician observed the patient quickly and whispered his diagnosis in my ear: acute intestinal obstruction. His examination confirmed that such an obstruction was present and had been neglected; the patient would die without immediate surgery. As if by magic, an operating theatre was readied, and a team of nurses meticulously carried out the surgeon's orders. As the operation proceeded, the surgeon described how he had laboured as a young doctor in Russia before World War I. When the electricity suddenly failed, the nurses lit some improvised oil lanterns that had been left in the area, apparently because of previous blackouts. Thus the operation was completed.

Returning to the restaurant on the ground floor, we enjoyed a lunch of lamb chops and a tasty dessert. That evening, we returned to the camp with our impressions of the day's events. We were beset by dozens of curious men, who showered us with innumerable questions about our experiences during those few hours of temporary freedom on the other side of the barbed-wire fence. What mattered most to them was the restaurant menu and the size of the lamb chop. These and other details of our trip became the topic of conversation in the camp for many days.

The elderly professor was known as 'Golden Hands' for the successful operations he had performed in pre-war Warsaw. After word spread that his latest endeavour had succeeded, and that the Soviet officer made a rapid recovery, the great surgeon became widely admired. Partly as a result, our conditions in the camp improved.

Now I had taken two trips with Professor Szarecki and efficiently assisted him in surgery, his trust and friendly attitude toward me became firmer, despite the mutterings from the extremists all around. Although we were far apart in age, social status, and experience, we developed fraternal relations that withstood the test of time and the emergency conditions we would later face in war.

The 'Lithuanians'

In the summer of 1941, after we had spent about a year in Griazoviets, construction workers materialized on the camp lawn and began erecting a large wooden shelter with three tiers of bunks. This done, a transport of about 1,200 variously ranked officers arrived from detention camps in Lithuania. These were men who had crossed the Lithuanian, Latvian, and Estonian borders after the Polish army had been routed, and were placed in detention in those countries.

After the Soviet Union and Nazi Germany signed their non-aggression pact and partitioned Poland, the Baltic countries came under the Soviet sphere of influence and were eventually annexed by the USSR. The Polish officers were then transferred from the Baltic detention camps to Griazoviets.

This massive influx violated the exclusive nature of our little camp. Food rations were cut, and the atmosphere changed unrecognizably. Command headquarters began looking for ways to establish dialogue and communication with the POWs. They embarked on information and propaganda activities, and began plans to prepare military units that would help liberate Poland from Nazi occupation. The Soviets began making efforts to recruit volunteers who would be parachuted into occupied Polish territory. A delegation arrived from Moscow to enlist experts as teachers and lecturers in Soviet universities.

However the Soviets bolstered their proposals with persuasive salesmanship and enticing promises, the POWs disregarded and categorically rejected them. Previous bitter experiences and letdowns had taught them their lesson. The dominant emotions in the camp were tension and expectation of change. Men whispered to one another about the possibility that Germany would instigate hostilities. Many of the men hoped this would occur, believing it was their only chance of liberation.

The prisoners' whisperings about the topic of war with Germany were treated by the Soviet officers, who had limitless trust in the stability of the Third Reich's friendship, with ridicule and contempt. At every opportunity they repeated the well-learned slogan, 'We'll hammer the last nail into Britain's coffin.'

The new inmates were up-to-date on world affairs, and had been able to follow political events while enjoying conditions quite similar to freedom during their detention. Some of the 'Lithuanian' newcomers were senior officers, doctors, professors, and experts in sundry disciplines. Most were standing army men from combat units, who had abandoned the front and crossed Poland's borders.

Conditions in the 'Lithuanian' camp had been reasonable, and despite the offical 'state of detention', the officers enjoyed personal freedom, plenty of food, and regular contact with their families. They arrived in excellent health, with belongings neatly arranged in suitcases. The well-equipped 'Lithuanians' entered into trade and barter with the indigent veterans. In demand were petty luxuries, razor blades, warm clothing, and writing implements.

The POWs maintained lively correspondence with their families, and lengthy lists of letter recipients were posted on bulletin boards. Men would throng around the lists, hoping to find their names there. Towards the end of May I received a parcel of food and books from home. The victuals were immediately snapped up and apportioned among my friends and neighbours. Under POW circumstances, the empty wrappers and containers, too, were put to efficient use.

The Wilno area had been annexed to Lithuania as far back as October 1939; in keeping with its residents' historical wishes, Wilno itself was declared the country's capital. Life in the little Soviet satellite went on placidly, although the Jews there were profoundly anxious about coming events with the war inferno raging west of them.

For the Jews of Nazi-occupied Poland, it was a different world: wave after wave of decrees, expulsions, and brutal repression. My relatives, in their letters, poured out their sorrow and anguish at their inability to extend vital assistance to their downtrodden relatives in Poland, who were dying of hunger and being led to the slaughter. One cannot imagine how agonized the Jewish prisoners would have been had they known precisely how hellish life under the Nazis had become. The families of my Polish neighbours expressed complaints about shortages of food and winter clothing in the Nazi-occupied areas.

Our camp address was as before: Moscow, PO Box 12. A remark had been added: forward to Griazoviets, Vologda District, PO Box 61. The address continued to mislead the naive families as to our whereabouts and conditions in our faraway confinement.

6

Hardships en Route to Freedom

After the surrender of the Western European countries to Nazi occupation, all hopes of our release from the Soviet camps were dashed. The Russians' blind adherence to their non-aggression pact with Germany only substantiated our desperate and hopeless situation.

Two years from the day the Nazi juggernaut invaded Poland, and two years into our stay behind barbed wire in the camps, the first rays of longed-for freedom began to glow in the heavy fog of our lives.

On the morning of 22 June 1941, a clap of thunder resounded in a clear blue sky: we received news of Germany's surprise invasion of the Soviet Union.

Radio Moscow's senior commentator on special affairs, Yuri Levitan, broadcast the news in a deep, trembling voice. Then came Stalin's agitated call for a war to the finish, in order to save the Motherland and eradicate the fascist enemy. The Soviets had been totally taken by surprise. The Soviet officers were in shock, as if hit by an earthquake, and huddled with our men like helpless eccentrics. Many of them tried to trace the origin of the POWs' 'secret information' on the encroaching war; after all, we had warned them about it.

Our men greeted the reports on the German offensive with concealed satisfaction, and the enemy's victories encouraged them to look forward to future events. Deep down, they yearned impatiently for the crucial moment that might determine their fate.

As the hours passed, a gust of fresh air refreshed the inmates, sweeping away their feelings of melancholy. Having lost all hope of escaping the clutches of Soviet security, they now felt that the invader's dizzying thrust into the Russian heartland had changed the progression of developments. The sparse reports that reached us strengthened the view that we had embarked on a new era, and that a road to liberation was being paved.

Excitedly the men plunged into the reports filtering into the camp about the deep penetration of German strike forces into Soviet territory. Obviously the German offensive would change our status in Soviet eyes from hopeless POWs to comrades-in-arms, fighting the Nazi enemy together.

Other disturbing news reached the camp. The Red Army was taking tremendous losses in its retreat, and civilians in the Nazi-occupied areas were being subjected to atrocities and brutal slaughter. This left the command headquarters staff virtually prostrate. As cities and smaller communities near the camp came under heavy aerial bombardment, the Soviets became even more fearful and jittery about the future. The camp commander, Colonel Khodas, was overwhelmed; he took to wandering about in the company of his senior aides. In their talks with the POWs they noted that contacts between Moscow and London, meant to provide the Soviet Union with urgent assistance, were under way. Radio Moscow essentially confirmed this.

It was the growing degree of cooperation between the former rivals that fostered expectations of a radical change in the POWs' status. Stunned Soviet officers began to meander around the camp, openly trying to strike up relations and assess our men's reactions to events. In the course of these talks, we learned that Poland's prime minister in exile, General Sikorski, and Maiski, the Soviet ambassador to London, had agreed on terms for the liberation of Polish citizens from camps and prisons throughout the Soviet Union.

As the fascinating reports followed one another, an air of festivity and jubilation infected the POWs. The camp buzzed like a beehive, and preparations for long-awaited liberation were made. Many of the men laboured feverishly to sew up their uniforms, fix their belts, and polish the copper buttons with their eagle emblem.

Officers and cadets strutted about with expressions of arrogance on their faces. Anti-semitism, somewhat restrained under the conditions of confinement, now surfaced in full force. Effrontery mounted every time an argument broke out, and some Jews, especially members of the Red Corner clique, were threatened with revenge upon repatriation for their behaviour as POWs.

General Anders

The general excitement and expectation of liberation intensified when word came through of the agreement to establish a Polish army on Soviet soil under General Władysław Anders. The revered commander had been arrested by the Red Army in southern Poland during the last stages of the battles against the Germans. Seriously wounded and bleeding heavily, he was interrogated and jounced from one Soviet field headquarters to the next. After a bit of first aid in a hospital in Lwów, he was taken directly to Lubianka Prison in Moscow.

The agitation reached a new peak when reports came through that Anders himself was about to visit the camp. Hastily the men began preparing an enthusiastic welcome for the beloved general, who symbolized more than anything else the leap from hopelessness to expectation of freedom.

The camp command took the initiative to hand each officer, commensurate with rank, between 2,000 and 10,000 roubles – symbolic compensation for the suffering they had endured as Soviet POWs.

Two days before Anders' visit, the men began to rehearse a military parade for the general and his entourage. The red and white flag of Poland was raised over the main building. The armed guards at the gate stopped body-searching persons entering and leaving the camp.

General Anders, accompanied by General Szyszko-Bohusz and their Soviet host, General Zhukov, entered the camp on the afternoon of 25 August 1941. General Anders had been liberated from the Moscow prison three weeks earlier. After two years in solitary confinement, he had been given some hasty treatment, handed his uniform, and put aboard a special flight for a meeting with his officers in the Griazoviets POW camp.

All the POWs perceived that a sacred, exalted moment was at hand. The young zealots had to reconcile themselves to the unfortunate fact that their Jewish neighbours, too, benefited from this miracle. Within minutes the hundreds of POWs formed two lengthy columns behind their highest-ranking officer, General Wołkowicki, on the lawn next to their residential shacks. Heading the columns were the colonels, followed by other officers according to rank.

Many of the men were pale as ghosts and were so agitated by the surrealistic scene as to look confused. For the excited older men, it was a rare occasion of a dream of redemption come true; their tears of joy were plainly visible. As the fairy-tale scene was enacted before their eyes, a tremor passed through the ranks. Some of the men, taut and waiting with bated breath, swooned as if hit by electric shock. Wondrous excitement flashed across their faces as the redeeming entourage materialized at the camp's open gate.

General Anders, limping and leaning on a cane, approached our stiff ranks with measured steps. Towering, skeletal and pale, he looked haggard after the severe and protracted hardship he had endured. His wrinkled, oversized uniform clung loosely to his desiccated body. With great effort he succeeded in holding himself militarily erect for his soldiers' parade. The sight of their tortured, peerless commander only strengthened his soldiers' admiration for him.

General Anders came to a halt opposite the paired ranks of silent, taut soldiers, waiting for their liberator's first words. Slowly, with pronounced concentration, he reviewed the ranks and paused for a few seconds beside each and every man. His eyes, glittering like tongues of flame, explored each soldier's face penetratingly and significantly. He would not allow the value of this historic moment to be lost on anyone.

To his right, also at erect attention, stood General Szyszko-

Bohusz. He had represented the London-based Polish government-in-exile in signing the agreement that permitted the Polish
army to re-establish itself on Soviet soil. General Szyszko-Bohusz,
a tall, strapping, broad-shouldered man, was conspicuous for
his handsome, crisp, and well-fitted uniform. His general's stars
and silver jacket buttons glittered in the sun's rays that broke
through the clouds of the sub-Arctic north. His natty, impressive
appearance and his smiling, robust face, stood in sharp contrast
to the wasted, creased features of his desiccated commander.

After reviewing the ranks, General Anders' entourage posi-
tioned itself in the centre of the parade. Anders delivered a
short speech, wasting no words, about the responsibilities of
the Polish fighter on alien soil. It was his duty to struggle to
liberate his occupied homeland, now under brutal Teutonic
repression. It was every Pole's immediate mission to disregard
past memories for the sake of ultimate victory.

The entourage's Russian host, General Zhukov, stood motionless beside the speaker, his fat, rigid face expressing restrained
satisfaction at what he had heard.

The soldiers, enthused, burst into a thunderous and rhythmic
chant: 'Hurrah! Long live Poland!' Thus they expressed their
respect for and admiration of their commander, whose advent
augured their freedom. Their cries reverberated into the distance.

The high-ranking visitors shook hands with several senior
officers whom they had long known, and left the camp. The
commander's remarks and the thunder of the soldiers' fervent
cheering reverberated in the void of the camp for some time.
The men were in no rush to disperse; they wished to savour
these moments of happiness as long as they could. Everyone
was fully satisfied and confident that the liberation process would
continue. They looked forward to the future and its promised
freedom.

We were all aware of the desperate, hopeless situation that
had been ours in the past. We perceived the unbelievable event
we had witnessed as a rare miracle bringing golden expectations
for the future in tow. The event left an indelible impression on
the POWs. The men conversed endlessly late into the night;
many stayed awake until morning.

The next day, the men were divided into two convoys, each heading for army organization centres in the southern USSR. I was assigned to a group including my friend Dr Merenlender. This pleased me, for I hoped that our continued trek in the hostile surroundings would thus be easier.

We spent the next few days tending to personal affairs: repairing clothing and shoes, and disposing of unnecessary items that had accumulated in our packs during our two years in boxcars and camps. Events proceeded at a dizzying pace, and every hour brought new information on how we were to leave the camp for good.

Amidst the hundreds of glowing, jubilant faces were several confused POWs who had not yet fully appreciated the import of developments. They paced about slowly and purposelessly as if daydreaming, eyes agape, looking about apathetically. Their faces radiated perplexity and disbelief in the vision-come-true.

Freedom

On 2 September 1941, the gates of Griazoviets were thrown open, and as if chased away by a magic wand, the armed guards vanished from their elevated posts around the barbed-wire fences. The NKVD interrogators and petty officials disappeared. Camp administration was handed to us.

Towards evening, we lined up in ranks of four, each column assigned to a different rail car, and the lengthy line of liberated men began to file down the dirt road leading to the camp gate. Mighty renditions of hackneyed marches from the 1920s – 'We're the Men of the First Brigade ...' – split the air. The marching men were delirious with joy at this unexpected gift of fate. Intoxicated at this moment of exaltation, no one noticed the raindrops that had begun falling from the overcast sky.

Some two dozen officers stayed behind in the camp. Several had refused to join Anders' Army because of their leftist opinions and past experience, preferring to offer their services to the Soviet authorities. These comrades, and a few good friends from our times of hardship, now stood at the side of the road and watched us march away. Their faces expressed pronounced astonishment as we insisted on pacing in the conservative, traditional Polish style.

The group encountered bitter disappointment from their Soviet patrons. The Red Corner men's efforts to join the Red Army did not pay off. After a lengthy and nerve-wracking wait, they were expelled from Griazoviets and had to fend for themselves, migrating, hungry and cold, across the vastness of Russia. Several of them joined Anders' army after friends intervened on their behalf; the rest eventually volunteered for the 'Red' Kościuszko Division set up under Colonel Berling.

As for the members of the Nazi 'barbershop club' and their leader, the scales of justice had the upper hand. These POWs had proclaimed their German nationality in hopes of quick liberation. Traitors who had sacrificed their dignity for short-term gain, they now snivelled in disgrace and shame under the bushes lining the path where the happy men marched. They had made the mistake of their lives, and they knew it. Handed over to the security authorities, their track now led to the far north. Their arrogant commander hanged himself on a tree in the camp, knowing what awaited him in the circumstances.

As the autumn sun set behind the barren expanses, the relentless drizzle gradually developed into a driving, cold, and unpleasant rainstorm. Down the muddy path the jubilant liberated men marched, their worn shoes sinking into the treacherous puddles. Alongside the rustic dirt road were humble shacks with closed shutters and rotting straw roofs. Poverty and neglect were evident. At the edge of the village stood an old woman wrapped in a black kerchief. Observing the column of soldiers, she raised trembling hands and murmured an inaudible blessing.

Exhausted, we reached the railway on its elevated bank. A collection of rickety shacks, piles of scrap metal, sundry filth, and mud marked the depot. Despite the authorities' promises, there was no sign of the rail cars that were to transport us.

Fierce rain, pelting hail, and driving wind forced us to scatter in the dark void. Some of us found shelter under a rickety thatched structure; others leaned against the boards of a tottering fence. Wandering some distance down the tracks, I and several comrades discovered a boxcar. On its wet floor surface we devised an improvised, temporary shelter from the deluge, and tried to take off our clothes, saturated with water and sweat.

Hour after hour the men waited. Spirits remained high despite the cold and spattering rain that penetrated from every direction, the ear-shattering thunder, and the lightning that flooded the overcast sky with blinding light. By midnight, most of the men had found refuge from the elements. Just then we heard people calling out unintelligibly in the distance. As they approached our position, it became apparent that they were looking for me.

Leaning out of an opening of the boxcar, I discerned Dr Tamara Alexandrovna in the gloom of night. With bated breath the Soviet physician asked me how I had known about our imminent liberation about a year before it actually occurred.

The question caught me off guard. A year before I had been sitting at a table and drinking tea with Alexandrovna, Professor Szarecki, and someone else. During our random conversation, Professor Szarecki asked Alexandrovna how long she thought our detention might last. Surprised, the physician paused for a moment of thought and whispered that it would probably last about 20 years. This struck the interlocutors like a clap of thunder. The 70-year-old professor was shell-shocked. After months of missing his loved ones and fearing for their fate, he took on a look of confusion and began to weep.

I was the youngest of the four at the table. Wishing to provide some relief, I remarked in jest that I thought we would leave the camp within about a year, singing, with a band playing in the background.

My spontaneous and meaningless answer met with no response at the time, as was proper in the circumstances. None of those present imagined that my naive reaction would become a prophecy that would come to pass one rainly, stormy night at the faraway Griazoviets rail station. But the Soviet doctor never forgot the conversation.

The people of the Soviet Union have an entrenched consciousness of spies everywhere. They are so intrinsically suspicious as to be ridiculous and illogical. To Dr Alexandrovna's mind, then, my pack must have been full of documents pertaining to a mysterious conspiracy involving the transmission of state secrets. In vain I tried to convince her that I had been speaking innocently and thoughtlessly. Even in the dark I could sense her suspicious glare. After a moment of sceptical rumination, she parted from me with a restrained, disappointed expression of farewell. My neighbours in the boxcar had been listening to all this, and to satisfy their curiosity I explained the background of the affair.

Our travel boxcars arrived at dawn. This mode of transport was something of a parting act of abuse by the camp authorities against the POWs who had miraculously slipped out of their clutches. Wet to the bone, haggard and spent after a lengthy sleepless night, we hurried through the driving wind to locate the boxcar to which we were assigned. It was important to secure a comfortable position for the trip that awaited us. This time, the cars were wide open and unguarded.

Heading south

On 3 September 1941, the train embarked on a six-day journey to the southern part of the USSR. Anders' Army, we were told, was being organized in the Volga River area.

The rain tapered off and the sun peered from behind the gloomy grey clouds. The men burst into gleeful renditions of folk-songs, and the feeling of freedom was perceptible.

One afternoon, the train stopped at a town called Yaroslavl. The station bustled with soldiers carrying weapons and heavy backpacks. Their clothes were tattered, and their shoes, held together with bits of rope, were caked with sticky mud accumulated in the course of a lengthy march. They were waiting for transportation to the front. Among the multitudes were wounded soldiers returning from the front with dirty, long-unchanged bandages. Others limped along on crutches.

The pushing, shoving crowd included old and young Poles

recently liberated from labour camps. They had come from
the far north – the Kola Peninsula and the Vorkuta area on the
Arctic coast – and were en route to reception centres for the
army in formation.

In a long column we advanced parallel to the station buildings
towards a workers' restaurant, quartered in a spacious wooden
structure. The place was tidy and clean. The walls were bedecked with Soviet leaders' portraits and slogans such as: 'Fight
the Fascist Invader'. The tables were set with wicker baskets of
sliced black bread. We were served thick, hot, delicious soup
with groats and chunks of potatoes and meat. It was our second
tasty meal in two years. A large samovar stood in a corner of
the hall, and men with canteens took the occasion to fill them.

Their tension alleviated, the satiated, happy men returned to
the train to resume the journey. Thereafter the stops were
frequent, attesting to heavy traffic of military trains headed for
the front.

After a long night of protracted stops and abrupt starts, we
reached Ivanovo. The noise and commotion on the platforms
brought an Oriental market to mind. Crowding was terrible:
multitudes of soldiers of various ages, refugee families with
children and wailing infants in mothers' arms. Thousands of
families had abandoned their homes, left everything behind,
and migrated south to save their lives from the advancing enemy.

Many Poles and Jews, liberated from the labour camps,
engaged us in conversation and appealed for help. Some had
been petty clerks and artisans before the war; falsely accused of
speculation and subversive activity, they had been sentenced to
years of exile and hard labour when the Soviets invaded eastern
Poland.

We helped starving men, women, and children, dressed in
rags and trembling with cold, with some leftover food and bits
of clothing in our packs. At this station we were not offered hot
meals; in their stead we received canned green peas and a chunk
of black bread. Dessert consisted of hot water and a sugar cube.

As we headed south, the landscape gradually changed. Around
us were vast fields of grain, with harvesting still in progress. The
villages became more affluent as we progressed. Stone houses

were surrounded by vegetable gardens and fruit trees, and domesticated fowl fluttered around the yards. We passed forests, green groves, and meadows populated by grazing sheep.

Reaching the Arzamas station, we came upon a sad scene of war devastation. Standing on sidings were dozens of cars and locomotives, burnt out, soot-covered, doors gaping open. They had been salvaged from the front. The steel frames, perforated with bullets and ripped apart by aerial bombardment, had become pieces of twisted junk. Multitudes of carelessly dressed soldiers clustered on the platforms. Angry men and women jostled, fearlessly and openly cursing the authorities for transporting 'cannon fodder' to the front. Throngs of labourers, despair evident on their tired faces, passed by on their way to the station restaurant. Mounted on the rooftops of the station structures were banners calling for the triumph of socialism, improvement of labour productivity, and eradication of the fascist murderers.

Our train bypassed the Moscow area, which was under enemy pressure, and continued south. We entered a fertile region with large, rich villages and forests stretching into the distance. Children played along the streams, and elderly fishermen bent patiently over the calm waters.

At Ruzayevka station, near Moscow, our transport was split in two. One part headed for Saratov, on the Volga. The other, including myself, branched to the east, toward Syzran.

We came to a large station and marshalling yard at the edge of town, with tracks winding in every direction. Here we beheld the grievous material damage caused by the Germans' aerial bombardments. Mammoth pieces of industrial machinery, pulled back from the front, had been dumped on banks of earth along the platforms. The massive steel frames and sophisticated gears stood there in the rain, exposed to the ravages of dust and sand.

At the platforms, trains passed without stopping, disregarding the impatient mobs waiting to board. Thousands of soldiers and civilians milled about purposelessly, enveloped in dense smoke and dust. Inside, sweaty people elbowed their way towards the ticket cashier. A queue of confused men and women, two and three abreast, trailed from the single ticket window open to the public.

On the stone floor in the unlit waiting room, hundreds of women and children, with their belongings, sprawled or sat in various postures for days and nights, waiting for a train heading south. The place was awash with filth, poverty, and despairing, hopeless people.

The disgruntled mob raged, fumed, and cursed. They fearlessly disregarded the security police, who kept themselves at a safe distance. Now and then somebody uttered sympathetic remarks about the Nazi occupier, intimating that he was preferable to the existing Soviet regime.

Refugees from the front delivered shocking accounts about the Red Army's crushing defeat. Their critical and heretical comments spurred many of the Poles to seek revenge. For the Jews, who viewed events differently from their neighbours, the same reports induced profound distress.

The general atmosphere was one of frustration and helplessness as everyone watched the massive existing order collapse. The situation was surreal, and those caught up in it could face the morrow only with terror and fear.

In the meantime, our train left the area and flashed past fields of standing grain that stretched to the horizon. Part of the bountiful harvest had been brought in; the rest had been left in the fields for lack working hands.

As we continued southward, traffic on the line lessened and our trip went faster. The landscape gradually changed, and beyond the tracks we beheld the endless flatlands and beautiful pastures of the Kazakhstan wilderness.

Vast stretches of land along the Don and Dnieper Rivers at the foot of the southern Urals had for generations been the exclusive domain of freedom-loving Caucasian tribes, the Cossacks, which paid no heed to the sovereignty of the central regime in Moscow. They lived by war and plunder, and earned a reputation for valour and cruelty. Because of their sublime skill in manipulating their horses and sharp swords, acquired in childhood, they had been the Russian army's select cavalrymen in both the Tsarist and Soviet periods.

After racing through the night, the train clattered over a long trestle spanning the Volga River. The river was more than three kilometres wide at that point, and its other side was invisible in the distance. Lushly vegetated islands could be seen vaguely near the horizon.

Once across the impressive river, we found ourselves on a desolate plain, with sparse vegetation and no sign of trees or cultivated fields. The southern sun gently stroked the men's faces, and the temperate weather imparted a sensation of freedom and calm.

Rapidly the train approached the large city of Kuybyshev, previously known as Samara. During the fateful days of the war, when Moscow came within range of Nazi artillery, this city had served as the government's temporary refuge. In the past it had been the capital of Kazakhstan, one of the largest republics in the Soviet Union.

In the distance we saw minarets, roofs of tall buildings, and factory chimneys. The Kuybyshev rail station was cavernous, and there was no crowding as at the previous stops. The atmosphere was relaxed, and the sensation of being far from the front was palpable.

Powerful loudspeakers blared the happy strains of folk-songs and military marches in all directions. Country women clutching braided baskets were selling watermelon, cucumbers, milk, and cheese. Our men were attracted to these delicacies, and began to barter with what remained of their used clothing.

The journey resumed. Relentlessly the train raced through the desolate, monotonous wastelands of Kazakhstan.

7

Totskoye

On 8 September we reached a small rail station named Totskoye. Exhausted, the men slowly climbed down from the boxcar and lined up with their belongings. We were to continue by foot.

Again we marched in a chilly drizzle. None of us ventured a guess as to what awaited us in our new-found freedom. At dusk, after a two-hour hike along a narrow, twisting road that wound up a steep hill, we reached a desolate field with a few wooden shacks visible in the fog. Fatigued from the hike and indifferent to our surroundings, we sprawled out on the dusty floor of one of the rooms. Everyone fell asleep at once, and noisy snoring could be heard in dead of night.

The next morning at dawn, the air reverberated with general commotion and the sound of friends calling out to one another. The area came to life. Outside was a barren expanse, bordered on the east by a picture-postcard hill that blocked the horizon. The locals called it 'Gold Hill', and older natives remembered the days when the fertile soil produced two harvests per year – the normal one and an abundant winter crop.

Our destination, Totskoye, was halfway between Kuybyshev and Chkalov (Orenburg). For generations the area's badlands had served as training grounds for regiments of Orenburg Cossacks. The region was known for its harsh inland climate. In the winter, unsheltered areas were afflicted with fierce cold and brutal blizzards known as *burans*, which smothered the light of day and produced mountains of snow that concealed every path and road. In the spring the wilderness burst into vigorous life, and vegetation sprouted prolifically in the endless meadows. In the sizzling summer, the blazing sun consumed every trace of flora, turning the expanse into a desert sparsely punctuated with patches of green along river-beds.

One of the shacks had been set aside as a primitive camp clinic. A long, unlit corridor led to the treatment and dentistry rooms and the doctors' living quarters. From the day the clinic opened, a relentless flow of patients began arriving from all the army units gathered in the vast camp. The outlines of men materialized in the distance. Approaching, they proved to be dressed in tattered, soiled clothes. Some were virtually barefoot, legs swollen with lesions caused by malnutrition, clad in rags held together with string. Many months of suffering, hunger, and hard labour in the Arctic cold had reduced them to skeletons covered with folds of dry skin.

Some came through in relatively good condition because they started out in uncommonly good shape. Even they suffered from a shortage of basic nutrients and proteins; many of them contracted pellagra as a result. With no fresh fruit and vegetables, a lot came down with scurvy, accompanied by gum infections, lesions, and loss of teeth. Many of those who turned to the clinic for care should have been rushed to hospital.

There actually was a hospital, situated at the edge of the camp in a cluster of old cabins next to a river-bed. Its director, Colonel Funk, was a veteran physician who brought human sensitivity and devotion to his responsible position. Many volunteered as auxiliaries or janitors, because these duties augmented the regular ration with a bowl of hot soup and a chunk of bread.

Hospital conditions were bad. At night, the cold and wind penetrated through cracks in the windows and doors. There was no heating, and beds and bedding were in outrageously short supply. Thus patients shivering with fever had to lie shoulder to shoulder on sheetless straw mattresses tossed on to the freezing stone floor. The authorities provided as small an inventory of medicines as they could, and the doctors allocated it only after making every possible economy based on priorities of patients' needs.

Some patients suffered from active tuberculosis and severe dysentery. Malaria and typhus epidemics claimed thousands of army and civilian victims. Malnutrition made all illnesses worse and claimed many casualties of its own.

Jews among the recruits

The army units in formation also had to content with harsh housing conditions. Living on top of each other in huts and tents exposed to the cold and wind, the men fell into arguments and disputes accompanied by fistcuffs. Theft of clothing and food was routine until supplies from Britain began to arrive. Jews were heavily represented among the victims of theft and insult. Hostile commanders disregarded the complaints, and enlistment committees used the reports as pretexts for rejecting Jews who sought to join the army.

Although Jewish candidates were stringently filtered for physical fitness and education, they accounted for almost half the men in several units. In the Fifth Division, some ultra-nationalist junior officers refused to command platoons with high proportions of Jews. Their superiors, apprehensive that the formations would lose their national character, imposed further restrictions on Jewish enlistment.

Camp headquarters began to place the Jewish recruits in separate units and accommodate them in rickety shacks with inferior supply conditions. Local villages and towns began to spread rumours about 'Totskoye Ghetto'. Thousands of Jews tried to enlist and were turned away; bitterly disappointed, they had to return to their places of residence and continue struggling for existence.

Despite the general hardship and hostility, there were only a few cases of escape to the nearby villages in search of work and food. One Jew's desertion provoked malicious accusations aimed at the entire Jewish people, fanning the flames of anti-semitism.

There were several senior officers of liberal convictions, who objected to the manifestations of hostility and took action to restrain them. One such commander was Colonel Galadyk, former head of the officers' supplementary training centre. Others were Colonel Leopold Okulicki of the general staff,[15] Captain Władysław Broniewski,[16] a leftist author, and other enlightened people. Their rational views often tipped the scales in favour of rescinding orders discriminating against Jews.

Soviet officers liaising with the Polish command adhered to their policy of supplying the new units slowly and under tight control. In this crucial period of the war, the front claimed highest priority. The Polish army was supplied with worn-out uniforms, some of them Czech, Estonian, and Lithuanian, with rusted metal buttons. Having been kept for years in musty warehouses, the clothes were rank with moss and mould. Despite these disadvantages, the tattered clothing was indispensable for the men coming out of the labour camps, dressed in rags and freezing in the harsh winter cold.

The first parade

Not all the recruits were issued with uniforms; many had to settle for improvised work clothes that they procured in various ways by their own initiative.

Those drafted into the first units, now gearing up for order drills, looked like products of a world of fantasy with their mixed, multi-coloured collection of fur hats, wollen hoods, and semi-standard army caps. An assortment of house slippers, torn sandals, and army boots held together with string protected their otherwise bare feet.

Eight units, each with about 200 men including several Jewish privates and officers, marched at the first ceremonial parade in honour of General Anders, who arrived in November to review the nascent army.

General Anders and his own staff officers, General Zhukov, and senior Soviet officers, mounted an improvised dais in front of the wooden command hut. The guests tensely watched the former POWs parade, as if beholding something wondrous and astonishing.

However miserable they may have looked, the soldiers

marched four-abreast with exemplary order and *esprit de corps*, clutching obsolete Russian rifles or wooden poles. The parade traversed the length of the frozen road, as the soldiers, proud of the pageant they were staging, sang hackneyed marching tunes. As they passed Anders' stand, some broke into spontaneous cheering in honour of the commander and the motherland.

Many soldiers could not take part because their physical condition or state of attire were not suited to the solemn event. They looked on in frustration, nursing their disappointment upon having missed out on a moment of happiness.

The parade finished, the two VIP entourages vanished into the command shack to toast the event with Russian vodka. The soldiers dispersed to their unheated shacks for a brief rest, which they needed after great effort and profound excitement. The routine of camp life resumed, and the Jews felt increasingly estranged in view of their growing ostracism in the holiday atmosphere that had become dominant.

Making friends on foreign soil

The flood of men who reached the camp every day included well-known public figures, doctors, academicians, and former Polish government ministers and officials.

I had a fascinating encounter with Meir (Marek) Kahan, a lawyer and journalist from Warsaw. Kahan was a versatile man of broad horizons and with total devotion to public activity on behalf of his people. He was an active member of the Zionist – Revisionist Party, and a member of the editorial board of Warsaw's large-circulation newspaper *Der Moment*. In one of our talks, he let me in on a secret: he had been working actively to establish a legion comprising Jewish volunteers whom the enlistment committees had arbitrarily turned down because they were Jews. The idea was to transport the men to Mandatory Palestine with their weapons, where they would endeavour to set up a state.

To everyone's great surprise, Kahan's relentless efforts met

1 The author as a Polish army officer before the war.

2 A unique photograph of the Kozielsk POW camp seen from the outside, with two Soviet physicians strolling outside.

3   Dr Merenlender, Major Berg and the author in their room at Totskoye, in October 1941.

4   The author reading a medical book sent from home, October 1941.

5 Drawing of the author by Jozef Czapski at the Griazoviets camp,
   5 August 1940.

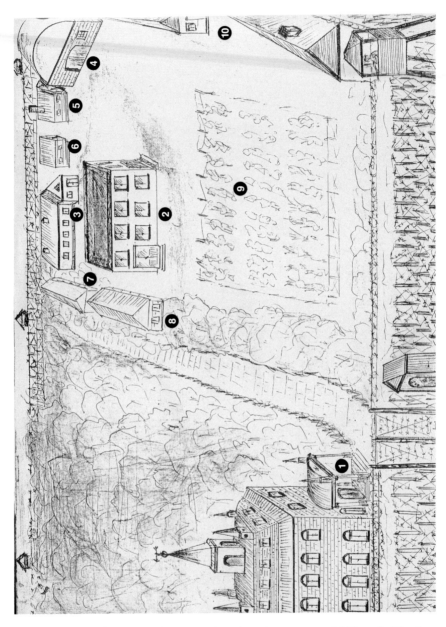

6 Author's drawing of the Pavlishchev-Bor camp, 1940. 1 Headquarters   2, 3 Prisoners' dwellings   4 Dining-hut   5 Kitchen
6 Stores   7 Bath   8 Ambulatory   9 Gardening corner   10 Stores.

7   Inaugural parade of the Polish formations in Totskoye, November 1941, with the Poles still in Soviet uniforms and without weapons. The Soviet General Zhukov and General Anders are standing on the porch in the background.

8   General Anders in Jangi-Jul in Uzbekistan, 1942.

9 Staff Headquarters of General Anders in Buzuluk, Kazakhstan.

10 In Iran in 1942, with Iranian officers related to the Shah. The Derbent Mountains are in the background.

11 Archbishop Gawlina, General Anders and General Szyszko-Bohusz in Jangi-Jul, 1942.

12 Professor Szarecki with the Lincoln sedan given to General Anders by Stalin.

with growing sympathy among the senior Polish officers. Pressing his plan constantly, he succeeded in persuading several generals and colonels that his idea had merit, even though they had previously regarded the Jews with anything but sympathy. The plan ultimately fell through because of stubborn objections by leftists and assimilationist Jewish circles. For me, Kahan's creative imagination brought on flickerings of hope at times of perplexity and pressure on foreign soil.

One day a surgeon, Dr Ernest Penski, reached the camp. He had been a standing army officer and head of a surgical department. Now he limped along with the last of his strength, leaning on a cane. He had arrived by a difficult route from the Arctic. Formerly rugged and masculine, he now looked like a living skeleton – his pale face deeply creased, his lips pressed together, and his wondering eyes squinting through slits behind red, swollen eyelids. His chest was shrouded in what remained of a filthy shirt, and his worn trousers, held up with a piece of rope, hung from his skinny hips.

It was sad, embarrassing, and shocking to behold this miserable man, whom I had known in his heyday. My sorrow overcame my selfish feelings; without hesitation I offered him the only shirt remaining in my pack. Perplexed, Penski could not cope with his own excitement. He stared at me in surprise and wiped his damp face. Cautiously picking up the precious gift, he paced to a corner of the room and swiftly ripped off the torn, flea-infested rag he was wearing, rolled it up carefully, and hurled it into the fire in the iron stove. Then he washed himself carefully with ice water at the spigot at the end of the corridor. This done, he returned to me with the crisp shirt, smiling jubilantly as if reborn.

Colonel Penski quickly found work in his profession. One day, years later, I encountered him as director of a military hospital in Kantara, east of the Suez Canal. He was once again a conspicuously handsome man, given the conditions of the Egyptian desert. He had not forgotten my offer of the shirt; it was one of the first human gestures he had met with after liberation. When I asked him for help, he returned the favour.

Another Soviet victim was a former commander of the large

Polish submarine *Orzel* in the Baltic Sea, who had gone through some fascinating adventures. During the war with Germany, he had sunk an enemy battleship and two supply vessels. The commander, a muscular, strong man and a superb athlete, then sensed a surprising gradual decline in his ability to concentrate and command his crew. Putting into Tallinn port, in Estonia he went to the hospital for tests. The diagnosis: protracted exposure to a lethal nerve poison. The discovery caused a sensation. It transpired that the commander's food had been systematically laced by the submarine's cook, acting in the service of German espionage. With much effort, the doctors succeeded in saving his life.

After the Soviets annexed Estonia, while he was still lying in hospital in Tallinn, the submarine commander was arrested and exiled to a POW camp. The ship and its crew slipped out of port in the dead of night, passed through the Skagerrak and Kattegat Sounds, joined the British navy, and continued fighting the Nazis.[17]

Another new acquaintance at Totskoye was Major Berg, former chief supply officer of the Polish police, who related embarrassing details from the first days of the war. Although Jewish, Berg had risen to a senior position in the command headquarters in Warsaw, and had witnessed the Polish government's escape to Romania when the war broke out. After Germany occupied the country, he escaped by fleeing to the east, where he was arrested by the Soviets and brought to a POW camp.

Berg was a pleasant, intellectual type and an expert in his field. His devotion to the Polish authorities knew no bounds. Notwithstanding his immense experience, he was not attached to Anders' Army, but accepted an appointment to the responsible position of director of a refugee absorption centre in the Central Asian town of Barnaul. Thousands of miles from army headquarters, Berg had thus committed himself to a kind of voluntary exile for the sake of the Motherland. After relations with the Polish government-in-exile soured, he miraculously succeeded in reaching eastern Africa with a group of civilians and children.

My room-mate, Dr Merenlender, introduced me to an old

friend of his, the owner of the prestige men's boutique Old England in Warsaw. His customers included ambassadors, aristocrats, the wealthy, foreign diplomats, and Foreign Ministry officials. A handsome man, he played down his Jewishness and had circulated in the glittering, gay circles of pre-war Warsaw high society. Even now his appearance was immaculate and his conduct flawless. Because he was also a brilliant conversationalist, we would have him over now and then for a cup of tea.

I ran into him by chance shortly after reaching Tel Aviv. Chatting briefly, he asked me for an urgent loan in pounds sterling for a few days. Knowing his past, I complied without hesitation, although that was all the money I had at the time. We parted amiably, expressing hopes of meeting again soon. Years of suffering had taught me to appreciate others' hardships.

The elegant man disappeared. About a year later I learned that he had flown off to his wealthy daughter in the United States after stopping temporarily in Egypt. When I reminded him of his debt, he replied, to my amazement, with an arrogant letter which demonstrated how blatantly false this 'nobleman' was. Safely overseas with my money, he never had the privilege of experiencing my reaction.

The 'Kołtubanka Ghetto'

The anti-semitic atmosphere that prevailed in the Totskoye camp was somewhat restrained by the proximity of the staff headquarters in Buzuluk. In Tatishchevo, where the Fifth Division was being organized, the situation was especially grim. There, in a place known as Kołtubanka near the city of Saratov, tents had been thrown up in a desolate field surrounded by snowy mountains. No one bothered to anchor them in the frozen soil, and there were no heaters against the bitter cold.

There the scantily clad, poorly fed Jewish soldiers were quartered. The tents constantly toppled under their heavy mantle of snow and the force of the night winds. Work tools were not provided freely; one needed approval of the central district authorities in order to obtain a rake or hammer.

To keep warm at night, the recruits had to light bonfires with wood gathered in a nearby grove. The situation deteriorated rapidly and disease proliferated, as did cases of frost-bite resulting in amputation of limbs. The patients lay on the ground; some died for lack of medical attention.

An air force training camp had been set up near the 'Kołtubanka Ghetto'. Its new tents, brought in from Britain, were dug into the ground, properly insulated, and equipped with heaters. The neighbouring camp was lined with access paths, bordered with stones painted in various colours. Field kitchens turned out plenty of hot food. The Jews in Koltubanka fumed with jealousy at the sight of the air force men's new winter clothes and warm boots. The Jews themselves had nothing, and were at the mercy of junior officers who pulled rank at every opportunity.

The inhabitants of the 'ghetto' were not allowed to set foot in the pilots' camp, and individuals who violated the directive met with insults and epithets from the cadets of the elite force. The Jewish chaplain, Rabbi Leon Szczekacz-Rosen, submitted repeated grievances to the army commanders and officials at the Polish embassy in Kuybyshev; these fell on deaf ears. The Jewish soldiers in Koltubanka were not given the privilege of greeting supreme commander General Sikorski when he visited the nascent formations in December 1941.

The Soviets were surprised and displeased with the massive turnout for induction. A persistant rumour circulated to the effect that the Soviet government was about to bestow Soviet citizenship on all the national minorities of eastern Polish origin. As Soviet citizens, they would not come under the general amnesty, and would not be allowed to enlist in Anders' Army. Such a decree might adversely affect the rights of Ukrainians, Russians, and Lithuanians. No one, however, would be more threatened by it than the multitudes of Jews, for whom loss of rights would result in danger of extermination. Thousands of soldiers could then expect to be expelled from the army.

A vigorous save-the-Jews campaign was launched on the initiative of public figures including Meir Kahan, Ludwik Seidenman, the journalist Bernard Singer, and others who had access to the embassy in Kuybyshew. Others interceded with the Polish government-in-exile in London.

Dr Retinger,[18] General Sikorski's adviser and friend, embarked on his own diplomatic activity with the authorities in Moscow, as did the ambassador, Professor Kot.[19] Together they succeeded in softening the worst of the decree.

A few months later, when Anders' Army was transferred to Central Asia, for further coalescence which they needed after harsh Soviet condition, the Kołtubanka camp was wound up. At this stage many Jews were discharged on shape organization and integration or get into battle order, to be shaped up various pretexts. A few of them succeeded in leaving the Soviet Union with the army by obtaining auxiliary positions or sneaking aboard transports of women and children to Persia, India, and eastern Africa.

Thousands of Jews, however, were left behind. They remained under harsh conditions in the cities, villages, and kolkhozes spanning the vast USSR, waiting for the first opportunity to flee. Eventually, young men in good physical condition joined the Kościuszko Polish Division, a force under Soviet patronage commanded by Colonel Berling, formerly a member of the Griazoviets camp 'Red Officers' group.

The latter army, too, was rife with anti-semitism. Contrary to official proclamations of equality of all citizens, Jews were filtered out and subjected to serious restrictions in their efforts to enlist. Despite the difficulties, Jewish officers and others with professional or university training succeeded in joining the Division. Many of them subsequently rose in rank on the battlefield, and returned to Poland wearing medals of honour. These did not help them during the wave of anti-semitic persecution that swept the cities of Poland after the war. After post-war 'democratic' Poland was established, the Jews were gradually squeezed out of the army and dismissed from their civilian positions, notwithstanding the merit they had earned in helping liberate their country from Nazi occupation.

8

The Jewish Legion Plan

Manifestations of anti-semitic hostility and discrimination surfaced as soon as the army began organizing, and from the moment Polish citizens throughout the Soviet Union began to receive assistance.

Some of the men liberated from the camps were public figures who knew about the inductees' deteriorating circumstances and realized that the situation placed multitudes of Jewish families in the USSR in mortal peril. One of the public activists who reached Totskoye was Meir (Marek) Kahan.

After being liberated from a hard labour camp in the far north, Kahan had followed a route fraught with hardships until he reached the induction centre. Contemplating the problem of the throngs of Jewish soldiers in the army formations, he put forward the idea of establishing a combat formation that would act to liberate Mandatory Palestine. Thus Anders' Army and the Polish leadership would be absolved of accusations of anti-semitism. The measure would also conform with the Soviets' policy of driving the British out of the Middle East.

In the course of his pre-war public activity, Kahan had made the acquaintance of General Karasiewicz-Tokarzewski, commander of the Sixth Division at Totskoye. With the latter's consent, Kahan invited several senior officers to a lecture on 'establishing a legion within the framework of the Polish army, for the struggle against Hitler'.

The officer corps was familiar with the idea of a Jewish legion following battles waged by Jewish soldiers under Colonel Berek

Joselevicz, during General Kościuszko's Polish insurrection at the end of the eighteenth century.[20] Furthermore, the poet laureate Adam Mickiewicz had made efforts in the nineteenth century to establish a Jewish legion for the purpose of liberating Palestine.

The lecture was unexpectedly successful. The spacious cabin was full of officers, with several generals and colonels seated in the first rows. Many unable to enter had to listen to the fascinating lecture through the open windows.

With consummate skill Kahan presented his idea to the audience; at the end of encounter, many expressed their willingness to command and train such a unit. Among the enthusiastic supporters of the idea were Colonel Jan Gaładyk, and Colonel Pstrokoński, one of Anders' senior staff officers. This support for the pioneering notion was tremendously valuable in the circumstances.

Elsewhere other activists who supported the idea were Miron Szeskin, former leader of B'rith-Hachayal (the Jewish Ex-Servicemen's Alliance), Rabbi Leon Szczekacz-Rosen, and the journalist Fried.

On 10 October 1941, the sponsors presented General Anders with a memorandum spelling out the details of their proposal to establish a Jewish legion under the army's structure and the command of Polish officers. The paper described the Jewish problem that troubled the command corps and its officers, and mentioned the economic difficulties the Soviets were encountering in meeting their obligations to the Polish army. Emphasis was placed on the difficult situation of the multitudes of citizens in need of urgent help; of the 600,000 homeless people in the vicinity of Tashkent in Uzbekistan, some 500,000 were Jews.

Kahan and Szeskin proposed that well-known figures be recruited for information and propaganda activities in the Jewish communities of Great Britain, the United States, Argentina, and South Africa. It was stressed that this action would result in greater willingness to assist the army. The need to safeguard the legionnaires' civil rights was also mentioned. The sponsors suggested that cooperation be fostered with the American Joint

Distribution Committee and the Hebrew Immigrant Aid Society (HIAS); this, it was believed, would further the cause of the Polish army worldwide.

Anders took a sympathetic view of the memorandum. Preparations were made to forward it to the commander-in-chief General Sikorski, who would soon visit from London to review the army being established on Soviet soil.

Word that a Jewish legion was about to take shape spread rapidly among the soldiers. Their hope of its realization became a ray of light in the atmosphere of depression and disappointment.

Members of the diplomatic corps in Kuybyshev embarked on an information and persuasion campaign for the Jewish Legion idea. Professor Kot, the Polish Ambassador to the Soviet Union and a confidant of General Sikorski, was sceptical. He feared that appeals to world Jewry would be misconstrued and would harm Poland's reputation, just as Poland had reached a fateful juncture in its struggle for resurrection.

The sponsors of the idea were dealt setbacks by some anti-semitic officers in Anders' staff headquarters in Buzuluk. This was expected. Less so was the feverish anti-legion activity waged by a clique of leftist Jews who had influence over Ambassador Kot. Among them were a socialist named Freid and two leftists, Henryk Ehrlich and Wiktor Alter, who were Bund leaders in Poland and members of the executive committee of the Second Socialist International.[21]

These dignitaries valued their allegiance to long-held political views more highly than the urgent needs of multitudes of Jews facing extirpation. In their stubborn struggle against the legion's proponents, the Bundists called on assimilationist groups who had made inroads with the embassy staff, including several members of the ambassador's inner entourage. Persistently these circles fostered their self-imposed estrangement from the Jewish people, their appearance as Poles belonging to the Mosaic faith, their disgust with any flickering of national awakening.

British government circles fully understood and appreciated their activities abroad. The legion's opponents overcame the efforts of the handful of resourceful visionaries in favour of it.

The initiative was nipped in the bud. It is unlikely that the Kahan memorandum ever reached General Sikorski for study and consideration during his visit to staff headquarters at Buzuluk.

While I was visiting Kuybyshev on a procurement mission for the staff headquarters clinic, Internal Security officials suddenly ordered Alter and Ehrlich out of the Grand Hotel restaurant to an urgent meeting. At that point their traces vanished. After repeated international appeals to the Kremlin, it was disclosed later that the two had been shot.

In a letter dated 23 February 1943, the Soviet Ambassador to Washington, Maxim Litvinov, informed the American labour leader William Green – in reply to Green's letter about Alter and Ehrlich – that the two had been sentenced to death in August 1941, for anti-Soviet activity. Following an appeal by the Polish government, they were released in September 1941. Then, as the Red Army engaged in pitched battles against the *Wehrmacht*, the two men were rearrested and sentenced to death in December 1942.

The Soviets viewed the Jewish legion idea with disfavour. It was liable to end in a manner that was dangerous for its initiators, because of the suspicion of espionage that dominated everything. At that time, Moscow was becoming more apprehensive about the Polish formations' willingness to fight alongside the Red Army. Polish leftist circles, headed by the writer Wanda Wasilewska,[22] began to prepare for the establishment of a 'Red Polish' division named after Kościuszko and commanded by a man we had known in the POW camps, Colonel, later General Berling.[23]

After the Jewish legion idea failed, its initiators found themselves in a dangerous situation. Rumours circulated about the Soviets' intent to take punitive measures against the 'nationalist reactionaries'. It was urgently necessary to spirit the activists away from the vicinity of staff headquarters, which swarmed with Soviet security people. Meir Kahan fled to Kitab-Shachrisiabs in Central Asia, where the Sixth Division was being organized. From there he succeeded in escaping the Soviet Union to the Middle East with the Polish army. Miron Szeskin found refuge with Colonel Bolesławicz's Ninth Division near the city of Margelan, also in Central Asia. The commander, an enlightened man from a long-established Protestant family in southern Poland, was true to the liberal views he had manifested in the POW camp, and energetically opposed the junior officers' anti-semitic displays. Risking his personal prestige, he extended his patronage to many Jews, including Menachem Begin,[24] and enabled them to reach the Middle East under his command.

Rabbi Szczekacz-Rosen met with a different fate. He was dismissed from his position and had to remain in the Soviet Union after the army was dispatched to the Middle East. He continued to help refugees under the auspices of the Polish mission in Samarkand in the southern USSR. After the Soviets severed diplomatic relations with the Polish government-in-exile, he joined the 'Red' Kościuszko Polish Division and reached the United States after the war.

9

Staff Headquarters in Buzuluk

My stay in Totskoye came to an end after two months. Officers at Anders' staff headquarters in Buzuluk who knew me from the POW camp, headed by Professor Szarecki and the architect Professor Sinicki, had taken vigorous action to open a clinic alongside the staff. On 20 November 1941, I boarded an army truck with my possessions for a three-hour dash along snow-covered roads to my new assignment.

A fierce blizzard greeted me upon my arrival in this typical Russian town. Chimneys protruding from its one-storey wooden houses with their sloping shingled roofs spewed thick black smoke. On the main road, peppered with bumps of frozen mud, a few poor, sad civilians rushed by.

At the edge of the headquarters compound I noticed the towering steeples of a demolished church, bearing remnants of crucifixes and shattered stained-glass windows. The church square had long been used as a junkyard, and glistening marble pillars could be seen through the open, unguarded main gate. Oil portraits of the Holy Trinity, mounted in worn gilded frames, still hung on the church's buckling walls.

Staff headquarters were located in the magnificent town hall building on a downtown street corner. The Soviet authorities had handed it over to the Polish army as a goodwill gesture. The two-storey edifice, built before the Revolution in Empire style, had prominent plaster ornaments over the lintels of the tall windows. In the rundown surroundings, the well-tended white building stood out like a legendary palace.

Stone stairs and gleaming white pillars at a corner of the building led to the main entrance, which was strictly guarded by armed sentries to prevent uninvited entry by ex-POWs, who streamed to army headquarters from all corners of the Soviet Union. Carved wooden portals led from the long, wide corridor to spacious rooms of the various staff departments. At the end of the corridor was a kitchen and dining room with tables and upholstered chairs. Upstairs was a large auditorium, with an artistic mosaic floor made of variously stained chips of wood that emitted a delicate rustling sound as one crossed.

My transfer to staff headquarters increased the range of my work; it also represented a promotion in status. With the large number of senior officers who arrived from London in their new, ironed uniforms, accompanied by aides and secretaries, the place exuded a festive atmosphere. One's spirits soared at the thought of fulfilling a national mission of the highest order.

Each day the army units reported to the medical department on health of their ex-POW recruits. Some of the reports aroused concern, especially when we began to hear of a rising number of typhus victims. Two varieties of typhus claimed thousands of lives, especially among the civilians. The situation reached epidemic dimensions in centres such as Guzar and Kermine, where every day dozens died and hundreds contracted malaria, tuberculosis, pneumonia, and dysentery. Professor Szarecki, concerned about the menace this presented to the multitudes of civilians rescued from the camps, worked energetically with the government offices for reasonable allocations of medicines, blood serum, and pesticides to fight the plague.

Fortunately for us, shipments of drugs, bandaging material, oils, vitamins, powdered milk, and soup began to arrive from Britain. The headquarters medical corps toiled around the clock, opening the carefully packed wooden crates, apportioning and sorting the medicines, and sending them on to the reception centres, hospitals, and army units in the field.

It was most satisfying to observe the happy face of famous comedian and singer 'Lopek' Krukowski when he dropped in to thank us for the vitamin pills that had strengthened his teeth, which were becoming loose as a result of scurvy. Once again he could enjoy life while performing for his admiring audiences.

I spent my first few days in Buzuluk looking for a place to live. The residents of the distant town had not forgotten the Soviets' constant pre-war propaganda about Poland and its bourgeois government, and were not inclined to rent rooms to Polish officers. After scouring the town, I found a room in a miserable country house near headquarters. The front door opened on to a dark kitchen with a dirt floor and a large brick oven that filled half the room. The air was fetid, damp, and mouldy. A wooden stool supported a rusted tub and a copper jug; next to these sat a metal pail with icy water from the well. Cooking utensils, sundry tools, and a giant axe, glittering and razor-sharp, were suspended on nails driven into the sooty walls.

The guest room was furnished with a bulky wooden desk, heavy chairs, and a rustic dresser. A long sheepskin and a winter hat with large earflaps dangled on a hook in the door. High felt boots with thick rubber soles stood in one corner. Next to the window was a small holy icon and a little oil lamp that the tenants sometimes lit on Sundays.

My landlord was an elderly, taciturn rail worker. His old wife was preoccupied with the household; she also walked into town several times on market day to buy some food. The predominant characteristic of the house was coldness and sorrow. No young voices were heard. No children were seen playing in the nearby yards. The landlord's daughter had married and moved far away, and his two sons had been drafted.

My tiny room, a narrow chamber next to the guest room, was equipped with a creaking fold-up metal cot and a straw mattress. Along the wall stood a little desk and an improvised cupboard that went back to the children's days. The square windowpanes were blanketed with a layer of ice, leaving the room in semi-darkness. During the long evenings, a little electric lamp attached to a point near the ceiling would illuminate the room dimly. Inside, it was warm. The fierce cold of the winter nights, which regularly plummeted to −40° Celsius, was imperceptible.

Professor Szarecki was accommodated in a spacious room in

an old downtown hotel. Both the conveniences and the heating system had long been out of order, and the water pipe was frozen. Thus the elderly physician came down with a cold and a high fever after only a few days there. In response, I offered to share my little room with him.

Because there was no room for a second bed – as if one were available – I spent a few nights sleeping on the floor. It was worth it; my modest living conditions quickly restored my guest's health. The old doctor profoundly appreciated my sincere devotion and contribution to his rapid recovery.

Our acquaintance, which dated from the initial period as POWs, and my having been at his side during our wandering from one camp to the next, strengthened his awareness that I was a person whose dedication could be relied upon at times of hardship. The venerable Catholic liberal disregarded the anti-semitism that prevailed at staff headquarters, and displayed his attitude towards the only Jew among the gloriously battle-tested senior officers. With my status in command circles, I was able to help many acquaintances and friends who approached me for favours when times were hard.

A few of the elite command officers, I found, harboured profoundly humanistic views. Colonel Wiśniowski, General Anders' deputy, was a sensitive and courteous man willing to help others in any circumstances, irrespective of religion and world view. Captain Ślizień, Anders' adjutant, helped me respond to some pressing requests for treatment of serious cases Colonel Okulicki, director of staff headquarters, was charismatic and liberal. His tough military mantle concealed a personality of rare goodness and helpfulness. He volunteered to parachute into Poland and command the underground forces there. After succeeding in this dangerous mission, he was summoned to Soviet command headquarters, whence his traces vanished.

A mission to Kuybyshev

Many of the staff officers had emerged from their prolonged confinement in the camps with seriously impaired health. Long deprived of basic nutrients and vitamins, they suffered from gum infections, loose teeth, and digestion problems.

Professor Szarecki instructed me to establish a dental clinic for staff headquarters. Armed with a written letter of introduction from the chief liaison officer, General Zhukov, I was sent to the main warehouse in the district capital of Kuybyshev for the requisite clinic equipment and instruments.

I set out on a cold and snowy day in December 1941. At the rail station I met by chance a Polish officer, also en route to Kuybyshev on business pertaining to the army legal bureau. The train was not crowded; the passengers rode in comfort. Access to Kuybyshev was strictly controlled at the time, because the Soviet government had relocated here when Moscow came under siege. According to rumours, Stalin himself had abandoned the capital. In general, refugees streamed toward the country's south, far from the theatre of battle.

I seated myself nest to an old Jew with a thick grey beard, dressed in a black coat. Profoundly miserable, he nevertheless commanded respect. His large eyes, full of sadness and worry, peered into the distance. He was a man whose world had gone dark.

I whispered something to him in Yiddish, and his face lit up. Eventually I succeeded in extracting a few sentences from him. Overcoming his suspicion of me as a uniformed Polish officer, he leaned toward me hesitantly, and, lips motionless, whispered a few fragmented sentences into my ear. He had fled Moscow during the German onslaught, after the capital had been abandoned and the government offices transferred to Kuybyshev. The city had been left to its own devices for a few days; in the absence of government and police, groups of rioters and soldiers broke into homes and shops of civilians and plundered the property of the thousands of Muscovites who had fled their homes. Hundreds of Jews had been killed or wounded in ways that recalled the pogroms of the Tsarist era.

This said, my neighbour's pallid face again took on its look of despair. Letting his head slump on to his chest, he retreated to his world of silence.

My other new acquaintance, the legal bureau officer, observed me from across the compartment, intrigued about my interest in the old Jew. A lawyer as a civilian, he had a Jewish name. After he took off his army jacket and loosened his uniform collar, I noticed a cross dangling from a thin gold chain, showing that he was a practising Catholic.

As we conversed, he proved to be an abundantly urbane, witty man with a never-ending supply of pithy sayings and a marvellous sense of humour. Yet he did not look impressive. His short build, pinched face, and sad, protruding eyes lent him the appearance of a provincial Jew, rather than a talented lawyer from the big city. His forceful manner of speaking and his overabundant self-confidence were his undoing among the Polish officers.

However well-educated and talented he was, he nevertheless entangled himself in the illusions widely harboured in nationalist circles. These had to do with the Polish people's historical calling as the leader of a federation of Eastern European peoples that would purportedly come into being after the war. Despite everything we had witnessed, his way of thinking had not changed.

Our lively conversation during long hours seated on the wooden bench of the third-class compartment made the trip pass more quickly. As the outskirts of Kuybyshev appeared on the snowy horizon, I still could not fathom the thinking of my neighbour, who had adopted the Catholic faith in order to advance his career and aspiration to assimilate into a society that wanted no part of him.

In the afternoon we reached the large city of Kuybyshev. Fierce cold and driving wind whipped our faces with spattering snow and stabbing, piercing ice. To secure a place to stay and obtain some advice on our enquiries with the Soviet offices, we headed for the Polish embassy.

Inside the massive, grey embassy building, dozens of high-ranking officers, recently liberated from faraway prisons and camps, scurried hither and yon. Along with them were famous people from all over the world, including professors, former government ministers, members of Parliament, foreign correspondents, and British liaison officers. The VIPs were quartered in rooms that ordinarily served as offices, and many other visitors were accommodated in the basement and underground carpark. In the embassy kitchen they made light meals consisting of jelly sandwiches.

The embassy staff taught me the techniques of intercession with the government officials and equipped me with the documents I would need for my task.

That evening we had dinner at the Grand Hotel restaurant, ordinarily reserved for foreign residents. An armed sentry at the entrance snapped 'closed' to anyone who approached. Though they could hear the strains of a dance band through the open ground-floor windows, even senior Soviet officers refrained from testing his assertion.

Inside the restaurant, the band produced background music as impeccably dressed waitresses brought servings of fine caviar and wine, as ordered from a printed menu. Flowers bedecked the tables, and antique crystal chandeliers gave off blinding light.

The restaurant had a snack bar at which one could buy top-brand cigarettes and chocolate, which were unavailable in town. Among the restaurant's regular customers was the American Ambassador, who would show up in casual clothes – no jacket, shabby trousers, and sandals – as if to display superiority and contempt towards those present.

Two of the hotel's guests at the time were activists of the World Jewish Bund, Henryk Ehrlich and Wiktor Alter. They were among the first men to be freed from confinement, and were now on their way to London. As the representatives of Polish Jewry in Sikorski's government, their tragic fate was sealed by their hosts, who helped them organize an 'anti-fascist committee' based on authors, artists, and intellectuals including Ilya Ehrenburg. One evening, Ehrlich and Alter were invited to an urgent meeting with the secret police. Setting out in their car, they vanished en route. More than a year later, it was learned that they had been executed.

The next morning, I strode down the snow-covered streets of the large city on the Volga to the offices of main medical equipment warehouse. The interior was packed to the ceiling with instruments, implements, and materials, sorted and arranged on shelves along the walls. A clerk greeted me with restrained courtesy and explained that my requisition would indeed be forwarded for handling, but only after the Health Services director gave his recommendation and the chief quartermaster his approval.

After rushing from one office to another, I returned to the warehouse, armed with a stack of little notes of approval. This time I turned to the clerk in Yiddish, describing my home town of Wilno, now under Nazi occupation, and the Jews who were subjected to mortal peril and persecution. At this, the clerk became deeply agitated. After giving the documents that I had procured with great effort a cursory glance, he passed my requisition on for urgent handling.

In a vastly improved mood after this triumph, I headed for the embassy to prepare my trip back to Buzuluk. Traffic was light that winter day. Most pedestrians were men in army uniform; the few civilians were dressed in bulky clothes with large fur hats and heavy boots. Everyone was serious, deep in thought, and taciturn. Although there were some youngsters around, none of them showed any inclination to youthful smiles or joy.

On a street parallel to the Volga I came upon a splendid sight of ships, freight barges, and various craft, passing slowly and with enchanting grandeur, emitting sharp and deafening whistles. Back at the embassy, I met my partner in travel. Together we set a time for our return to Buzuluk the next day.

Rising early the next morning, we strode down the chilly, deserted streets past City Hall Square and its massive statue of Stalin, to the rail station. There a saddening sight awaited us. The giant waiting room was packed with men, women, and children; hundreds of families sprawled on the stone floor with their possessions in desperate crowding. Access to the ticket office was blocked by the bodies of people in various prostrate postures. Skinny bare feet protruded in the air, and the swollen faces of crying children gaped all around. Mothers exposed their breasts to nurse, and changed their babies with masterful agility. Men scurried about in search of hot water from the station washrooms or from locomotives that stopped for a few seconds.

The rabble had been waiting there for many days and nights, expecting this or that train to come. The waiting room buzzed with unending noise and commotion. The people were like busy bees in a honeycomb, preoccupied with their labours in the cloud of smoke and haze that filled the chamber. The air was dense and humid, reeking of sundry vapours. Disappointed and despairing, we fled the scene and approached the station manager. As army men on duty, we were admitted to his private office and offered hot tea and dry rolls. With the manager's recommendation, we were equipped with rubber-stamped notes by virtue of which we could board whatever train we needed.

In fact, many trains slowed down with a screech of brakes, but none of them stopped. After exhausting hours of waiting, we saw there was no chance of embarking on our trip, and we left the area. Back at the embassy, they told us that travel was a difficult proposition and that we would have to try our luck at the station for several days until the train we wanted materialized.

The next day we rushed to the station before dawn, when morning mist was still suspended in mid-air. The terrible, surrealistic scene in the waiting hall had intimidated both of us. The dreadful overcrowding, and the absence of order and control, made it easy for German spies to plant parcels containing typhus-infested lice among the would-be passengers. This is just what they did. The epidemic gathered momentum and filled the hospitals, which were already packed with war casualties.

Experienced by now, we bypassed the station complex, skipped over platforms and tracks, and raced towards a grand passenger train that was pulling into the station. Luck went our way this time; the train stopped far away. Radio wires were draped over the green roofs of the carriages, whose doors were guarded by young officers.

Rushing to one of the cars, we asked permission to come aboard for a few stations. The junior officer quickly reported to his commander, whose positive reply spared us the need to continue exposing ourselves to the disease-infested waiting room. We happily boarded the train and stood in the corridor.

Peering into the compartments, we saw set tables and bottles of wine. Senior officers in dress uniform sat with lavishly dressed women, bedecked with jewels and elaborately coiffured. As we stood in the corridor, a woman in her fifties approached us. Her appearance commanded respect. As we talked we found that the train had been requisitioned by the engineering corps command to transfer the main institute for war materiel studies from Moscow to the southern part of the country. Her husband, an engineer, was the institute's director, and all the men aboard were engineering officers.

My interlocutress told about her origins in a Jewish family in Warsaw. She had married an engineer at the end of World War I, while studying art in Moscow's Lomonosov University. During the Revolution, she stayed in Russia with her husband and her two children. Contacts with her family in Warsaw were severed many years ago, but to that day her memories of her youth remained engraved in her memory, and she longed for her many friends.

As we listened to her story, intrigued, one of the officers passed by several times, openly attempting to break off this contact with 'foreigners'. The torrent of her words in pure Polish attested to her fierce desire to express herself freely on this rare opportunity in front of 'Westerners', as the Russians called us. Delicately she pulled out of her purse a silk kerchief with flower patterns and dried off her face. Several jewels embedded into gold rings flashed on her fingers. The talk was finally broken off with the screech of the train's brakes at the Buzuluk station. We parted with a handshake and stepped down to the platform.

We returned to the ramshackle town in the dark of the winter night. I was truly depressed, in view of the general misery everywhere. I lay down on my creaking bed and found myself unable to sleep. The hours dragged on, accompanied by pictures repeatedly flashing across the veil of darkness as if it were a movie screen.

The morning after my return from Kuybyshev, haggard, I

reported to Professor Szarecki and described my successful mission. Then I returned to my office duties, where I had been given the responsible task of organizing the staff headquarters clinic.

In many long nights in my narrow room, I had visions of the women and children packed together in the train station, followed in repeated sequence by the apparition of the elite's luxury passenger car. The stinging disparity between citizens in the USSR, which purports to be fulfilling the vision of social equality, has always made me heartsick.

Young officers just off the train from England clustered in the staff building. Their uniforms were new, and their faces gleaming and lively. The older officers, prematurely aged in the POW camps, went about heavily in worn uniforms, and their faces attested to the years of suffering they had endured. Many of them were in poor health; they were not accepted for active duty and were transferred to a reserve unit.

At the entrance to the staff building one November day, I ran into a desiccated, spent man whom I hardly recognized. It was Miron Szeskin, former honorary consul of Honduras in Warsaw. He had been active in Jewish public affairs and commanded B'rith Hachayal – the Jewish Ex-Servicemen's Alliance in Poland before the war. Now liberated from protracted detention, he had overcome the difficulties presented by the army guard contingents and reached headquarters.

He described the hardships he had endured, and asked me to find him a job in the army. Immediately I approached Professor Szarecki and asked him to grant Szeskin an interview. I depicted my acquaintance as active in the highest echelons of public life, and as a man of integrity who could help further the Polish cause in the free world.

After conversing with Szeskin, Professor Szarecki made enquiries with General Anders, who agreed to employ Szeskin as a civilian in uniform in staff headquarters' service.

For Szeskin, in his worn-out clothing, this was a quantum leap. During his tenure within the army's framework he was able to collaborate with Meir (Marek) Kahan in the latter's efforts towards setting up a Jewish formation in the Polish army. He also helped enlist the support of influential senior officers for the original proposal.

Looking for missing men

A special section of staff headquarters was set up to locate missing men, act for the release of prisoners, and provide aid for families uprooted throughout the country. The man appointed to head the Missing Persons Section was one Captain K., an ultranationalist.

The Soviets obstructed rescue efforts, refusing by various ruses to disclose the whereabouts of the detention camps. Nor would they hand over lists of prisoners. The new section at headquarters painstakingly collected names of missing men as reported by others who had been liberated and succeeded in reaching the army formations.

The office organized reception facilities and health centres in the large cities. Their employees, known as *delegats*, maintained contact with local Soviet authorities to promote the prisoners' liberation. They also kept stocks of food and clothing, for distribution to ex-prisoners upon their arrival.

The Soviets occasionally provided basic commodities, although in negligible quantities compared with the great needs. Supplies improved when Britain sent some basic relief items, along with uniforms and equipment for the formations in the field.

The reception centre for the northern USSR was established in the city of Kirov. It attracted a stream of men liberated from the camps across the Siberian tundra at Pechora Bay, Vorkuta, Kotlas on Arctic coast, and the Kola Peninsula on the White Sea. A few survivors arrived from the mining camps around Kolyma, near the Bering Strait in the Far East. Reception centres for the southern region were established in Tashkent, Samarkand, and Alma-Ata, in the Central Asian republics of Uzbekistan and Kazakhstan.

Special representatives were dispatched to the rail stations. It was their task to guide the ex-POWs and prisoners to the reception centres and induction committees.

In many sections, the desperate situation of multitudes of Jewish ex-POWs and detainees became evident in its full gravity. Families had traversed vast distances to reach the reception centres, in hope of relief and guidance from the *delegats* of their government. A bitter letdown awaited them in some of the centres. They were confronted with a double dose of abuse: anti-semitic discrimination by the Polish representatives, and studied in difference on the Soviets' part. The latter had washed their hands of the liberated men, arguing that it was now the Polish authorities' duty to care for them.

Most of the reception centre *delegats* and rail station representatives were public figures, officials, or retired officers, of whom only a few were Jewish. How much help ex-prisoners received depended on the emissaries' judgement and good will. A few ex-POWs, after great effort, succeeded in obtaining urgently needed relief or temporary shelter for their families. Animus toward the Jews also dominated the section's main office at headquarters in Buzuluk. Petty officials made no effort to empathize with the throngs of Jews, and refrained from intervening with the Soviet authorities to liberate their family members.

I shall never forget a Jewish teenager who, after a difficult journey, succeeded in confronting the section director in hopes of helping his parents. They had been exiled to the far north, and their requests for liberation had been met with refusal by the Soviets. Trembling in agitation, the boy faced Captain K. and pleaded for help. The response was so offhand as to surprise the people in the room. Contemptuously he shoved the flabbergasted youth out of the door and into the long corridor. There he stood motionless, head down, consumed with despair. He told witnesses that his affluent family had long been friendly with the director in pre-war Kraków and for years had offered him its support in times of trouble. Recovering from his shock, the boy picked up his pack and hurried away. This shameful treatment exposed the section director's twisted mind and left the eyewitnesses disgusted.

The section stepped up its hunt for missing men as Anders' Army was being transferred to the Middle East. It was instructed to draw up lists of civilians and children who would be considered for transfer to the Middle East, India, and Uganda. By making a great effort, one could get a limited number of Jews on to the list. Sometimes this was accomplished by listing them under false names as Roman Catholics. The Jewish Agency participated in an operation known in Hebrew as *Yaldei Teheran* ('Teheran Children'); its intent was to gather up Jewish children in Iran and take them to Palestine.

Once the army moved on to Iraq, however, the section's activity was decreased. It ground to a total halt when the Katyn Forest massacre was discovered and Soviet diplomatic relations with Sikorski's government-in-exile were severed. A few civilians succeeded in reaching Ashkhabad, a town in the Republic of Turkmenia, and crossed the mountains to the Iranian town of Mashhad. An alternate route was from Samarkand in Uzbekistan to Afghanistan, and thence to the Middle East.

Polish citizens were able to leave the Soviet Union after a repatriation agreement was signed between the USSR and 'democratic' Poland. Once back in Poland, some Jewish refugees left for destinations overseas; some reached Israel in the late 1940s as the 'Polish Aliya'.

At a meeting with Stalin, General Anders mentioned that his army had encountered a shortage of officers. Where were some 15,000 POWs who had been in three camps – Kozielsk, Starobielsk, and Ostashkov? In reply, Stalin asserted that all the POWs had been released in accordance with the agreement, and that the officers must have slipped out of the country by way of the Far East.

This only provoked further dread about the missing men's fate. Anders asked for Stalin's help in locating the officers who had been in the three camps, and Stalin promised to do his utmost to promote the search. It had been a 'friendly' meeting, and Stalin marked it by giving Anders a pair of thoroughbred riding horses and an American Lincoln luxury car.

General Anders returned from Moscow with promises and an agonizing toothache. He fell into a deep slumber in the patient's chair in my clinic. I was concerned at the sound of his snoring when I had to wake him up after the treatment. His nervous adjutants, waiting impatiently for their commander, helped me bring him back to alertness.

The Culture and Propaganda Department

The Culture and Propaganda Department at staff headquarters in Buzuluk became a bailiwick of creative talent liberated from the camps – well-known artists, authors, journalists, etc. The department had an entertainment section in which actors and singers who had been famous in pre-war Poland participated. Many of them were assimilated Jews, who maintained no more than symbolic affiliations with their origins. They represented themselves as Poles of the Mosaic faith. Most of them had fled Poland when the Germans invaded, and were arrested by the Soviets.

On the department's staff were the well-known comedian 'Lopek' Krukowski; the actors Zimand, Bielski, Tom, and Kersen; the famous singer Hanka Ordonówna; and the actresses Zofia Terne and Różyńska. Heading the department was Professor Aleksandrowicz, assisted by Captain Czapski. Active participants included Wittlin, Herz, Pruszyński, and Broniewski.

When performing at staff headquarters and for the army formations across the Soviet Union, the troupe had to keep its political colouration undercover because of strict Soviet control. The public, recently emerged from protracted confinement, treasured the performances as cultural events of great value.

The army symphony orchestra, under Ludo Philipp, achieved genuine artistic success. Participating in it were conductors and composers such as Gold and Petersburski, and performers such as Schütz and the Front brothers, who were renowned for their virtuoso performances at the prestige Adria Café in Warsaw before the war. The composers produced many tunes and songs during that time. One became famous: 'Our Tiny Country' by the talented composer and fiddler Gold.

The Culture Section published newspapers for the army and bulletins and information pamphlets for civilians. The department was active extensively – in Palestine, Egypt, and later in Italy. The entertainment troupe and orchestra performed successfully for civilians in the major cities of Palestine. The section also established several schools for the Polish émigrés' children. Regular high-school studies were offered, and some of university age were sent to the American University in Beirut for medical studies. Jewish youngsters did not gain much from army-sponsored study. Although a few attended university in Beirut or Britain with Polish army assistance, most of them enrolled in local schools in Palestine.

At the end of the war, arrangements were made to open a medical school and hospital in Scotland, at Edinburgh, which was named after Paderewski. The Polish immigrants' organizations in the United States donated all the necessary equipment. The initiators, Professors Szarecki and Aleksandrowicz, took vigorous measures to bring it to fruition, and drew up rosters of lecturers and department directors in the various medical disciplines. Among the candidates were Drs Merenlender, Tadeusz Cytrynik, Otto Finsterbusz, Mark Mozes, myself, and others.

These preparations went to waste when the British officially recognized the 'Democratic' Polish government in Warsaw and gradually dismantled Anders' army-in-exile. The hospital equipment was auctioned and off purchased by the Israeli Ministry of Health, thanks to the activity of the late Dr Aharon Bejlin. When the Israelis opened the crate, they found modern hospital equipment and instruments.

Indeed, the turns of fate …

The Department of Religions

The Headquarters Department of Religions was under the supervision of Bishop Gawlina, who had come from London after the Soviet authorities had agreed to this in a bid for American and Allied public sympathy.

After years of repressed religious sentiments in the detention camps, the soldiers' yearning for religious ritual was more profound than ever before. On religious feast days, the leading clergyman, bedecked in a purple velvet robe, a cope adorned with gold and silver, and a glittering mitre, clutched a shining cross that could be seen at great distances as he blessed his flock.

His appearance at solemn field parades, accompanied by the military band, turned these events into impressive displays charged with an atmosphere of sanctity and exaltation. His influence over his flock was tremendous. It even affected the Soviet liaison officers who attended the rites; their leader, General Zhukov, treated the Church's representative with marked deference. The department dispatched clergymen to the field units around the country and made sure they had all necessary devotional implements.

For the thousands of Jewish soldiers – especially the Orthodox ones – the dominant atmosphere was one of deprivation. The Jews were provided with no religious guidance and had neither prayer-books nor calendars marking their own holidays. Dr Meir Kahan assumed the formidable task of rectifying this. With Father Cieński's active assistance, his efforts succeeded. The priest was a charismatic personality, and an intellectual, broad-minded man whose liberal views were rare among the clergy. With his support and that of several staff officers, Rabbi Leon Szczekacz-Rosen was appointed Jewish chaplain and given officer's rank. A private named Neuman, husband of the film actress Nora Ney was appointed as his aide.

The short, withered rabbi made no outstanding external impression. The staff and officers of the Department of Religions, viewing him as a symbol of his downtrodden, persecuted people, did not appreciate him as his status should have warranted. His ability to restrain the manifestations of abuse and hostility towards the Jewish soldiers was minimal.

Because of the circumstances and the hostile environment in which the rabbi was supposed to discharge his duties, his efforts were limited to conduct of burial rites and observing Jewish holidays. These he performed with supreme devotion. He was very active among the uprooted families across the USSR.

Moving south

In early December, 1941, the Prime Minister of the Polish government-in-exile, General Sikorski, arrived from London to review the formations of his nascent army on Soviet soil. Accompanied by General Anders and Ambassador Kot, General Sikorski was received for an interview with Marshal Stalin in Moscow. The visitors complained to the Soviet leader about the intolerable conditions that confronted recruits in the new army. After years of suffering and hardship in the detention camps, the soldiers were quartered in rickety tents in the harsh winter, and suffered from serious deficiencies in food and clothing. As a result, both soldiers and civilians were increasingly susceptible to disease.

After hearing them out, Stalin agreed to transfer the army to temperate Uzbekistan in the southern USSR, and to improve food and equipment supplies. The first of these promises was honoured without delay; in early 1942 all regular and reserve formations continued organizing and drilling in various parts of Uzbekistan, southern Kazakhstan, and Kirghizia.

Staff headquarters were established in the town of Yangi-Yul ('New Way'), in a spacious two-storey building that had previously accommodated the central agricultural institute of the south. A broad entrance staircase led into a waiting hall, and well-lit offices branched off the corridors. The building was surrounded with lawns, and a grove of fruit trees followed the banks of the Kurkuldiuk River into the distance. The river meandered through a valley framed by hills and uninhabitable bluffs created by the area's frequent earthquakes. Irrigation canals ran from the river to the lengthy rows of aromatic trees and grapevines in the garden, and their gurgling sounds had a relaxing effect in the silence all around.

The fertile clay soil of the area produced unusually large fruit. The splendid peaches had velvety skin of interesting hues. Pears swayed on their branches like jars of honey. Bunches of grapes sagged heavily to the ground. A fierce heat wave broke out at harvest time. At twilight the ranks of laden trees sank into a mysterious haze, and one could almost hear the fruit ripening.

This was the so-called 'Uzbeki garden'. On a path running through it, General Anders and his adjutant would enjoy a morning romp on the thoroughbred horses that Anders had been given after his interview with Stalin.

The staff officers were housed in little wooden cabins in a residential quarter near the main building, amidst green lawns and well-tended flower-beds. There lived Generals Anders, Szyszko-Bohusz, and Zhukov.

The clinic was set up in an isolated hut. On its staff were Dr M. Panzer and myself, two nurses, and an orderly named Artek. The latter endeared himself to all his patients with his devotion.

With my personal contacts, I was able to alleviate the hardships of many patients in the process of leaving the Soviet Union. One of them was a distinguished army rabbi whom I had known before the war in his luxury apartment in Grodno. Another was a dermatologist from Wilno, a well-known Zionist activist, and a lady who belonged to the WIZO administration in Wilno.[25] People in need of help, starving and dressed in rags, came from vast distances with the last of their strength. Providing them with some bread and bath-water was tantamount to saving their lives. No less important was to assign them aliases and include them in the lists of persons leaving the Soviet Union.

The situation at the front was grave. Powerful Nazi forces were advancing into the southern USSR, at tremendous cost to the Red Army in personnel and property. Transportation came under increasing disruption, interfering with army supplies. Food rationing became more stingent than ever; for the first time it was applied to industrial workers.

As the front approached, multitudes of ex-POWs and refugees migrated under conditions of starvation. Economic hardship and typhus epidemics fuelled growing disgruntlement, which sometimes took the form of angry outbursts that threatened public order.

The hospitals were full, medicines were in short supply, and living conditions were crowded. Thus the epidemics rampaged unchecked. Every day the staff headquarters medical service received distressing reports about growing morbidity in the army units. Ultimately more than half of the men were affected.

Casualties from the Yangi-Yul area were sent to the crowded hospital in Ak-Altyn. On our frequent visits, we found the wards packed with unconscious people with high fever. The Soviet nurses worked with supreme devotion, and the doctors had to contend with stringent rationing of medicines and bandages.

Professor Szarecki, distressed by the situation, worked relentlessly despite his advanced years. He raced from one population centre and army unit to the next, exhausting himself to provide urgent guidance in efforts to combat the plague, whose victims mounted into the thousands.

Shipments of medicines and food had begun to arrive in greater quantities from Britain via Iran. They saved thousands from certain death in the vale of hardship and suffering.

10

Leaving Russia

In March 1942, General Anders requested another interview with Marshal Stalin. Obstacles in the army's training activities were impeding its efforts to attain the level of fitness it would need before leaving for the front.

While admitting that the Soviet Union had promised Anders' Army more food than it was getting, Stalin noted that the Soviet Union itself had wheat supply problems because the German fleet was sinking Allied ships; implementation of the agreement would have to wait. The host went on to assert that the Polish forces were refusing to fight alongside the Red Army. Thus he had no objections to its transfer to theatres outside the Soviet Union.

This answer took Anders by surprise. He had long suspected his host of intending to send the Polish units to the front before they were trained, whereupon they would be wiped out in a tide of blood. Stalin, however, reached this decision after efforts to persuade senior Polish commanders to collaborate with the Soviets had failed. In the meantime, endeavours to organize Polish units under the Red Army, commanded by Colonel (later General) Berling, were progressing well.

The Soviets took a dim view of the army being trained by the Polish nationalist Anders. This force had become a nuisance, exacerbating supply problems that had worsened in any case due to conditions on the front.

In compliance with Stalin's decision, Anders' formations, to-gether with groups of civilians, were transferred to the Middle

East at an increasing pace. The lists of civilian candidates for transport, drawn up by the Emigrants' Aid Section, included a small number of Jews.

Some of those transferring to the Middle East went by train to the Caspian port of Krasnovodsk and continued by ship to Pahlavi, Iran. Many additional transports advanced overland to Samarkand, Bukhara, and Ashkhabad in Turkmenia, whence they crossed the mountains to Mashhad and went on to Tehran. Stalin's word was law. Within a week, much of the army had been sent on its way to Iran and Iraq.

Anders' Army, with its supplies constantly reduced, could do no more in support of civilians, and such food shipments as arrived from overseas were not enough for the starving multitudes. In August 1942, the rest of Anders' Army was sent to the Middle East. This included the headquarters officers, the clinic team, and several hundred civilians.

A long train pulled out of the Yangi-Yul station and raced southward through the endless wastelands of Turkmenia. Finally it crossed the Amu Darya River and plunged into the barren wilderness at the approaches to the Caspian port of Krasnovodsk.

So dazzling was the sun in this area that one could hardly take in the monotonous scenery, which met with the clear blue sky on the horizon. En route we caught sight of Colonel Berling, stiffly erect in his grand uniform and a forced smile plastered across his face, in the company of two shapely, fair-haired young women. His function as the Soviet government's representative irked the senior Polish officers, who deliberately turned aside, making pointed remarks – in such a way that he could hear them – on cooperating with their eternal enemy.

Port warehouses along the desolate coast were filled with crates of supplies – canned food, milk powder, medicines – from overseas. Native inhabitants and their starving children scurried about the barren expanse at all hours of day and night, in search of edible leftovers from the barrels that had been tossed into the army's garbage enclosures.

From the train we walked down a slope to the shore, using

a makeshift gangway to board a ship that would take us south to the Iranian port of Pahlavi.

General Szyszko-Bohusz and a team of officers remained behind at headquarters in Yangi-Yul, hoping to continue the recruitment drive and provide aid to the multitudes of civilians who had not been attached to the two transports. Anders' liaisons in the reception centres across the USSR were providing less relief to ex-POWs than before. The indigent were left to their own devices in coping with the harsh conditions of the country's state of emergency.

The Soviet attitude toward Anders' representatives deteriorated, and their appeals were rejected. Stores of food and medicines that had arrived from Britain were confiscated, and public activists found themselves under arrest for 'subversion' and 'espionage'.

Soviet–Polish relations reached a deadlock after the German radio announced, in April 1943, that a mass grave of Polish officers had been discovered in the Katyn Forest. The Soviet Union severed diplomatic relations with the government-in-exile in London, and the two erstwhile allies embarked on mutual accusations just as the war reached its decisive stage.

The Polish army left the USSR in the shadow of disagreements and gossip-mongering between General Anders on the one hand and Sikorski with his ambassador, Professor Kot, on the other. Anders, with plenty of personal experience, assessed the Soviets' Western policy at close quarters, while Sikorski and Professor Kot were far from the scene of events and could not estimate the Soviets' considerations.

Sikorski and Kot adhered to their agreement with Stalin, calling for the integration of the Polish units in the war effort against Germany. By contrast, Anders believed the army would be wiped out in battle before reaching the motherland. The best thing to do at the time, he said, was to take the army out of the Soviet Union. General Anders acted on this assessment, contrary to his government's policy, and received Sikorski's consent *ex post* – as the troops were heading south. Subsequent events proved that he was right, and thousands of people owe their lives and freedom to his decision.

Iran

With a jarring screech, the anchor of our ship was hoisted and its stern pulled away from the pier. The jubilant passengers cheered thunderously, convinced that their ordeal on Russian soil had come to an end.

Tightly my fingers gripped the bulky steel deck railing as the ship slowly slipped away from the desolate coast. For the first time in years, I felt free. The calm waters and clear blue sky filled me with sensations of happiness and well-being. As if having sprouted bird's wings that were taking me high into the vastness, I thrust aside a heavy melancholy. Remaining deep inside was a suppressed grief, which gnawed away as I ruminated about my familys home and the tragic situation that must have been prevailing there at that moment. Sleeplessly I paced back and forth on deck, in the pale light of the crescent moon, until dawn's first glow appeared on the hazy horizon.

That sun-drenched afternoon, after 24 hours at sea, a strip of land came into sight – Iran, land of freedom. A short time later the ship docked at a pier, and the cheering passengers promptly stepped ashore.

The younger men dropped their belongings on to the sand, stripped hastily, and leaped stark naked into the refreshing water. The sun's rays caressed the bodies of the newly freed men. At that mighty, unique moment after years of isolation and suffering, the general release of tension was perceptible.

Pending our arrival, large tents had been set up in long rows on the flat, sandy shore. There were shower huts, and field kitchens were turning out meals that included plenty of white bread, for the first time in years. Medical service people diagnosed cases of contagious diseases. After these were examined and recorded, we were left there until the time came to resume our journey.

The doctors among us were invited to work with the permanent staff, inoculating and sorting the transports of army and civilians that continued to reach the transit camp. We also joined the camp physicians on an outing to the nearby town of

Resht. On the way, we stopped near a towering wall of basalt stones, which surrounded an abandoned harem owned by a rich Iranian. Protruding over the wall were chalky-white domes rising atop the flat roof of a structure as picturesque as anything in a children's fairy-tale. The owner had taken his entourage and concubines to his second residence in India, far from the war zone.

Through a narrow gate we entered a spacious court with a blue marble pool and a magnificent fountain. Exquisite white marble statues of women stood all around. Entrances to quarters reserved for women were concealed behind greenish marble pillars with Corinthian capitals. Glistening stone steps twisted upwards towards the roof, where the guards and servants lived.

It was a hot, sunny day, but a cool, refreshing breeze blew in from the sea. The heatwave and haze everywhere else could not be felt in this isolated corner of the desert. A vast garden with fruit trees, towering palms, and thick shrubs stretched in every direction. Flower-beds in a pageant of colours gave off the intoxicating scent of jasmine.

On the other side of the wall was an arid expanse crossed by crooked paths leading to a nearby village at the base of a tall, steep hill. Flocks of birds chirped endlessly on rock-strewn slopes visible in the distance. With its clear pastel colours, the splendid pastoral landscape conveyed a surreal aura of idyll.

Crossing the Elbrus Mountains

After a week of quarantine on the beach, we moved on, packed in large military Dodge trucks, via the city of Casvin toward the Elbrus Mountains. We were heading for the capital, Tehran. Mountain elevations in northern Iran, peaking at Mt Demavent, reach 5,000 metres. The mountain road, twisting in hairpin bends, was riddled with dangerous and, at times, nearly impassable potholes. Taking care not to tumble into the abysses that lurked at every turn, the drivers manoeuvered skilfully up the slope on the narrow track; the passengers beheld a dizzying sight of tortuous paths spilling down into the valley, flanked by precipitous stone wall on the verge of toppling into the void. Donkeys and camels, laden with heavy sacks of crops from the harvest, paced slowly through a box canyon toward the huts of the nearby village. Sheep and goats wandering about on the green hillsides added life to the otherwise sterile landscape.

The roadside, upholstered with green grass, red poppies, and wild flowers, abutted a pine forest. Rock outcrops and piles of stones at the higher elevations looked like monsters or primeval creatures. Occasionally we passed an orchard or ornamental garden that gave off intoxicating aromas. An exhausting and fascinating day's trip was nearing its end. The setting sun spread a crimson blanket over the horizon. The mountains quickly donned a mantle of fog and a veil of violet darkness, until their identity vanished altogether into a single mass of eerie blackness. The area settled into utter dark, a terrifying thing to behold considering the richness of nature all around. Just a few lights flickered in the distance. We spent the night sleeping deeply in the bowels of nature; at dawn the convoy moved forward in a thin line, making its lengthy, steep descent.

On the way, we passed a few villages, some pasture, and corn and sunflowers growing in clusters on the mantle of sand. On rare occasion we encountered little groves of willows and poplars with thick trunks and outstretched branches.

Tehran

As we approached the great city, the terrain became flat and monotonous. The paved road led through a desolate landscape of little mounds of sand until we reached the outskirts of the Iranian capital.

At midday we reached a large transit camp, packed with previous transports. Across a vast field stood several massive, tall buildings reminiscent of army barracks, surrounded by ranks of residential huts and warehouses. The camp gate was open, and the men organized outings and visits to the town about three kilometres away.

The next day, I was assigned with two other doctors to the

Red Cross hospital in Tehran. The city's main streets were clean and quiet. The population was a diverse mosaic of national, ethnic, tribal, and religious groups. With the variety of languages and dialects they used, neighbours occasionally found it hard to talk with each other. Most of the people were merchants and artisans. Some were fantastically wealthy, and had wayward children enjoying a life of luxury in the capitals of the world.

The aristocracy and the wealthy landlords lived in vast, grand estates on the slopes of the Derbent and Shemran hills that loomed over town. Their homes were miniature Western-style marble palaces, hidden behind lush, multi-coloured flowering shrubs and stylish, meticulously tened flower-beds.

Because residential space in the teeming city was in great demand, I had to engage in protracted foot-slogging to find a room in an apartment owned by an old Armenian woman. Her husband, employed in one of the Persian Gulf oil emirates, was a rare guest in his own home. His illiterate wife had to remind her husband to send her some money for her sustenance, and she needed help to do so. An elderly woman next door would translate what she said into halting French, and it was my job to phrase her requests in the kind of English that a simple labourer would understand. The postal money orders that arrived from the devoted husband proved that I had done my job well enough.

A cool, fresh northern breeze from the summits of the snow-clad Elbrus Mountains caressed the summer-scorched higher elevations of the hills. Desert landscape embraced the parched, sun-drenched city, swathed in dust that blew in from the desert. At sunset the horizon gradually darkened, exchanging its greyish colour for a deep blue, and the indistinct wailing of jackals and the hollow hooting of owls floated in from a great distance in the eerie void.

A ruler-straight main street bisected the city, and construction work progressed round the clock all along it. Most of the houses were three storeys tall and had been erected in recent years. The building boom reflected the pressure of multitudes of military and service personnel who arrived from various countries during the war.

From dawn to dusk, labourers with rag-clad, barefoot children could be seen unloading sacks of cement from their donkeys. Then, with amazing agility, they would carry them in woven baskets across scaffolds at the building sites. Methods were primitive, and no modern machinery could be seen.

Chilly water flowed around the clock in open gullies at the edge of the main street. It emanated from springs in the area and melting snow in the mountains. Pipes led the water into deep stone cisterns under the houses.

The gurgling of the water in the canals produced a barely audible and monotonous sound that gained volume at night and imparted to the environs a fascinating and relaxing feeling of rustic tranquillity. The labourers and their children leaned over the edge of the gully nearest the construction zone whenever they needed to drink, shave, bathe, wash their clothes, and water their donkeys.

Tehran's population, with its many children, dwelt in stark poverty, shoulder to shoulder in shacks and dug-out caverns on the outskirts of town. Their conditions stood in blatant contrast to the fantastic wealth of the aristocracy and the affluent class. The Soviets, ever on the alert, knew of their abject economic circumstances. Soviet embassy propagandists occasionally visited the square in front of Parliament in Tehran and, with pronounced generosity, handed out loaves of bread and cigarettes to the multitudes.

Luxury hotels and restaurants with dance bands sprouted like mushrooms in the capital, as did performances by various musicians, dancers, and artists. Entertainment spots hummed until morning with melodies of all the world's peoples and loud conversations of British, American, Russian, and other officers.

Wartime Iran was of paramount importance as a vital conduit for the transport of equipment to the Soviet Union. Material was shipped to the Soviet port of Krasnovodsk from the Persian Gulf and the Caspian Sea port of Pahlavi.

Shah Muhammad Reza Pahlavi was the country's unchallenged ruler during the inter-war period, and he did much to develop his country with generous German support. When the war broke out, the Red Army took over the northern part of his country and the Caspian coast, while the British dug into the southern part and the Persian Gulf. The pro-German Shah was forced to abdicate in favour of his son, and Tehran came under joint Soviet-British occupation.

The Soviet embassy in Tehran had the largest foreign presence in the city, it controlled a vast compound, encased in a high stone wall. Inside were entire streets with residential buildings, workshops, warehouses, garages, and army vehicles. Thousands of soldiers and secret service men scurried about town, and everywhere one could hear Russian being spoken.

As a rendezvous of Soviet, Allied, and German agents, Tehran became a world espionage centre. It was the site of unexpected incidents and exceedingly dangerous surprises for the innocent civilian.

One autumn day at twilight, I was heading home from the hospital along the main street, in the last feeble rays of the setting sun. At some distance I noticed a man in civilian dress, impudently harassing two hospital nurses who were trying unsuccessfully to evade the nuisance. Being in uniform, I went up to the man, who had a deeply creased face, and ordered him to desist.

To my surprise, he pulled a pistol, aimed it at me, announced that I had insulted a Soviet security officer, and ordered me to follow him. Seeing no way to defend myself on the deserted street, I submitted. On the way, I warned him about his unbecoming behaviour towards a hospital physician on duty.

We approached the wall of the Soviet Embassy fortress. At the sight of it, scenes of the intelligence services and kidnappings of Polish officers, whose traces vanished opposite the entrance to headquarters in Yangi-Yul, flashed in my memory. Soundlessly I considered how to slip out of my escort's grasp before we reached his own 'turf'.

Fortunately, I mentioned my name as we talked on the way. At the sound of it, the agent stared at me long and hard, replaced his hand-gun in its holster, and looked around. Then, as if disclosing a secret, he blurted his name in a hoarse whisper: Arkadi Fridman. Choosing his words carefully, he explained that he had lived in the city of Homel in Belorussia before the

war; his next-door neighbour was my uncle, whose family had
lived there many years.

I told him what I knew about my father's older brother, a
man of rare talents and a prodigy in the famous Mir Yeshiva.
At an early age, he left his parents' home in a village in the
vicinity of Brest, and after migrating across Tsarist Russia, settled down with his family in Homel. From fragmented reports
during the Revolution, we learned that his sons had attained
senior government positions. The conservative Polish regime
prohibited any contact with relatives in the Soviet Union. Now
I feared that my uncle's entire family remained in the Nazi
inferno.

My interlocutor grew excited as I spoke, and went on to
describe the atrocities committed by the murderous Nazis against
the Jews of Homel. We continued conversing in the dark, whispering, until after midnight. Finally, we bade each other an
emotional farewell in the heavy fog that blanketed the deserted
alleyway.

Just past us was an illuminated little gate in the rampart of
the Soviets' threatening citadel. So short was the distance between myself and a different ending to the chance encounter.

The hospital

The Red Cross Hospital in Tehran was quartered in a massive,
opulent government building whose construction was nearly
complete. The structure had been erected at the end of the
city's main boulevard, Shah Reza, named for the Shah's father.
Next to it stood a large marble monument with a life-size
statue of the old Shah, ringed with flower-beds. A dirt road led
from the site into the desert that stretched as far as the horizon.

The hospital was organized very quickly. Its staff of expert
physicians, selected personally by Professor Szarecki, included
Drs Tiepelt, Stanistaw Frank, Zygmunt Kurlandski, and Resnikov,
and the surgeons Srokowski and Malofieyev. The large wards
were packed with patients, most suffering from protracted
malnutrition, tuberculosis, malaria, and neglected malignancies.

The medical and nursing equipment that had arrived from Britain was modern and superb. The instruments and medicines were top-notch and made the doctors' work easier. In these auspicious circumstances, I succeeded in organizing a full-fledged department with a staff of doctors, technicians, and nurses, all devoted to their tasks. Hundreds of senior officers, including major Allied commanders, were astonished at the quality of organization and service provided to those in need. Among the clinic's patients were General Anders and his entourage, and several British and American generals.

The hospital physicians were faced with horrifying scenes. Some of the patients had arrived in transports from the Soviet Union in critical condition, after suffering from protracted starvation and cold in remote villages of Kazakhstan. Among them were desperate men and women, living skeletons clad in dry, parchment-like skin, and victims of pellagra, long deprived of proteins and other nutrients.

The surgical department received dozens of cases of malignancies totally ignored for years. I shall never forget the desiccated face of a prematurely aged young woman suffering from advanced breast cancer. The exposed, gaping, pus-infected lesion was infested with worms and flies that nested in the blood that oozed from the festering ulcers. Another case was a facial cancer. Through a large cavity in the cancer-eaten cheek tissues I could see into the mouth and the teeth that had turned yellow with caked blood. Night shifts in the wards were usually saddening, overwhelming affairs, replete with cases that no extent of medical care could treat.

Helplessness in confrontation with the angel of death robbed the doctors of their sleep for weeks. However, some of the frustration and depression were offset by the great satisfaction of having successfully brought some of the survivors back to renewed life by means of thorough, devoted care.

Yearning for relief from their intensive labour, the doctors began to explore the fascinating attractions of this land of fable. On one such occasion, we organized a group for trip about 300 kilometres south to Isfahan, the capital of ancient Persia. The city was famous for the grand edifices that rulers of the Orient

called home. Here was the palace of a thousand pillars, a splend-
idly beautiful and architecturally fascinating structure with its
integration of many-coloured forms of marble. The mosque of
Msidishah featured a wealth of complex, picturesque mosaics
created by master artists and superb architects.

One day while exploring the attractions of Tehran itself, I
met by chance two senior Iranian army officers who were related to the Shah. As we conversed over a glass of wine in the
company of their wives, my hosts produced a map of the country
and pointed at vast territories owned by themselves as family
inheritances. They had never visited most of these lands. The
villagers there were sharecroppers, and had been paying high
rents for generations. The owners spent most of their lives
frolicking in the casinos of the world's capitals.

The Shah's palaces in Tehran abounded in fabled treasures
that had accumulated for generations. His major residence, a
twelfth-century palace, was one of those sights that left visitors
speechless. Accompanied by our Iranian acquaintances, we went
up the broad marble stairs to the grand entrance area, at whose
facade stood two giant vase-shaped pedestals rising full-height
from the ground floor. They were chiselled out of extremely
rare green turquoise. The officers of the Shah's Cossack guard
would race up the stairs on their horses at full gallop for the
daily palace roll-call.

A mosaic floor was installed in the spacious guest hall. Over
it was a vast silk carpet, embroidered in decades of work by
expert craftsmen. Threads of pure gold embellished its fringes,
and the ruler's family tree, with life-size portraits of his forefathers
and their offspring in bright colours, was embroidered in its
centre.

The Shah's throne stood at the front of the hall. Enclosing
it on all sides was a screen with thousands of pearls and precious jewels as large as a man's eye. Hundreds of rubies, sap-
phires, emeralds, topaz, and amethysts winked at the visitors
with their myriad colours. Some had long since vanished.

Antique crystal chandeliers suspended from the vaulted ceiling
scattered blinding light in every direction. Heavy curtains descended to the floor from the edges of the windows and doors.

In the corners of the hall stood ancient armchairs of carved wood, upholstered with flowery velvet.

Between the tall windows stood glass cabinets, full of *objets d'art* and collections of gifts from governments and rulers of states. On the shelves were dozens of spears and swords with diamond-crusted handles and golden blades, daggers, crystal goblets, and gold table ware.

The real heart-stopper was the huge, glittering gold samovar with handles carved out of ivory, a gift of Tsar Alexander III of Russia to Shah Muhammad Reza Pahlavi, father of the young Shah.

Nor was the visit devoid of surprise. One of my courteous hosts plunged a hand into his pocket and whipped out a large emerald with rare bands of purple, a gem of inestimable value. He confessed, 'I saved one from the Russians.'

11

Iraq

The summer of 1942 was a fateful watershed in the course of the war. The Germans were advancing on the Soviet front towards the oil resources of the Caucasus, and in North Africa toward Palestine. Thus they threatened to trap the Allied forces in the Middle East in a massive pincer movement. Had this happened, all supply lines to the Red Army would have been cut. Axis agents engaged in subversion in the rear, trying to provoke a general Arab uprising against Great Britain and to drive the British away from the oilfields.

Polish formations transferred from the Soviet Union to Iraq were quartered in camps near the cities of Mosul and Kirkuk. Their mission was to defend the oilfields in the northern part of the country. Additional camps were set up in desert oases along the road to Baghdad. The camp near the village of Kana-Quin, near the Iranian border, was about 200 kilometres from the capital. The second largest camp was near the village of Ksil-ribat, about 100 kilometres from Baghadad; General Anders established his staff headquarters there.

Other camps and hospitals were scattered across the desert expanses; these belonged to the British and Indian armies. The Polish formations were reinforced with British officers, including many Jews and doctors who had signed up with General Kopański's Palestine unit, which they reached at the beginning of the war.[26] This unit took part in the fighting in North Africa, taking heavy casualties in the Libyan desert. Many Jews, including the son of the Warsaw journalist Bernard Singer, were killed or wounded in Tobruk.

The Red Cross hospital in Tehran functioned for only about half a year, after which the great effort invested in establishing and getting it running went to waste. The Allied supreme command suddenly decided to transfer the hospital to Mosul. The equipment was packed up within a few days, and the entire staff set out by train southward, to the Iraqi port of Basra. From there it continued to the northern part of Iraq.

The Iranian railway had been built recently by German engineers, who chose the most scenic route available. The train snaked through long tunnels blasted through rocky mountains that towered into the clouds, and crossed trestles soaring over canyons and rivers. Breathtaking scenery could be admired from the cars, much like the view from aircraft. Deep fissures in the earth attested to the lethal earthquakes that frequently shook the area. Splashes of green appeared in the canyons, and desert oases were bordered with gorgeous groves of palms.

The train crossed the region inhabited by the Bakhtiar: tribes, known for their carpets. Then it went through Isfahan and skirted Ahvaz. Finally it reached Abadan, the sprawling southern oil port at the the mouth of Shatt al Arab, the waterway where the Tigris and the Euphrates converge before spilling into the Persian Gulf.

At the approaches to the city protruded large oil tanks alongside refineries and pumping stations to the tanker ships anchored in the port. Supply vessels and oil tankers plied the Gulf incessantly, bearing the liquid that had become the lifeblood of our time. Crossing the river, we reached the Iraqi port of Basra, considered the hottest point on earth. A dense forest of palms stretched along the coast, their intertwining crowns creating an impermeable roof against the sizzling sun. Semi-darkness and primeval silence reigned in the forest, and no vegetation was able to sprout in the arid ground underneath.

Mosque minarets and the domes of wealthy sheiks' palatial homes punctuated the coast. The timeless tranquillity of this forgotten corner of the world, together with the deep blue sky and the blinding white hue of the endless stretches of sand, carried the visitor into a fantasy-land and a state of relaxation, divorced from reality.

After several days of idleness in this paradise of the south, we

were ordered to continue by Iraqi train to Mosul, an oil city in
the northern part of the country. It was a boring, monotonous
trip. We passed through the Baghdad station and reached Mosul,
at the foot of the Kurdistan mountains near the Syrian – Turk-
ish border.

The residents went to great lengths to maintain the city's
Arab character, shunning the influence of Western progress.
The streets began to bustle early in the morning, people crowding about on the pavements and under the shade of the houses'
arcades and pillars. The streets were narrow, twisting this way
and that with no particular order. Heavily laden camels and
donkeys progressed slowly, and worn-out wagons and modern
American luxury cars manoeuvered past them. The horses were
bedecked with harness and chains of glittering copper with
tinkling bells. Horsehair fans were inserted into the harnesses
between the animals' ears to chase away the bothersome flies.

Smoke spiralled skyward as the locals roasted walnuts and
sunflower seeds; this odour blended into the aromas of strong
coffee and narghiles. Corpulent Arabs sat on stools, lay on
woven rugs, and bent over low tables, engrossed in back-
gammon. Women dressed in black, their faces swathed in veils,
marched erectly, balancing large baskets, heavy sacks, or earthen
jugs on their heads with astonishing stability.

The semi-lit streets at the approaches to town offered scenes
of eye-stopping poverty. Barefoot children scampered between
the adobe huts, either naked or dressed in rags, playing in
puddles of thick oil in the gutters. In the desolate fields, men
tended terrifying grey oxen with large heads and twisting horns.
After sundown, immense tongues of flame and twisting pillars
of smoke rose over the mountaintops and climbed skyward.
Innumerable oil wells in distant fields produced natural gas,
which was being burned off.

The Indian hospital

Our hospital staff was provisionally quartered in tents about
three kilometres outside Mosul, near the railway to Turkey.

There was an Indian hospital nearby, situated not in tents

but in an abandoned marble quarry in the middle of the desert – literally in the bowels of the earth. It was used by air force units posted in the area to meet emergencies. The hospital's sloping entrance was camouflaged against enemy aircraft. Long underground corridors led to the wards, operating theatres, and clinics. Until the order to open our hospital arrived, the doctors were attached to the Indian hospital, where they helped with the routine work.

Cut off from their families, the men could release tension, alleviate boredom after work and drive their pressing personal problems out of mind by retreating to the club, where card games were organized.

The 'champion' at this pursuit was the hospital commander, a corpulent giant of a man whose fat brown face never stopped smiling. At home he was head of the health service in Punjab province, with a population of more than 60 million. His family and his many servants remained behind in the Punjab capital of Lahore.

In addition to his high army salary, paid by the British exchequer, he received a fat allowance from his ruler, a wealthy maharajah. Still, he was a hard-driven card player whose success left his partners and opponents agape. Whenever his cards did not perform as expected, his face began to twitch for reasons at first unknown to us.

The games were played in something of a ritual, holiday atmosphere. An Indian soldier, a member of one of the massive subcontinent's many tribes, was placed at each player's disposal. They wore a variety of headgear. Some sported turbans atop their long hair, and embroidered kerchiefs of silk or fine wool were wrapped around the turbans. Others had moustaches and red tarbooshes. Still others had long black hair that tumbled down their backs, bedecked with colourful ribbons. The servants were most useful when preparing the standard drink: a weak concoction of brandy or gin with soda and ice cubes. They did this with tremendous skill and diligence.

One of the regular cardplayers was the head of the internal medicine department, a professor with the rank of colonel. As a civilian, he had lectured at the University of Calcutta, capital of Bengal province in eastern India. After graduating from a

medical school in London, he stayed in England for several
years of advanced studies, by which time he had acquired Western
culture and adopted a European lifestyle. Our men took note
of his impressive appearance and courtesy. He began spending
time with the Polish physicians when he fell in love with one
of the beautiful nurses in our hospital. The nurse, the daughter
of a well-known doctor from an esteemed family, swept all the
men off their feet – and evaded the brown-skinned officer's
persistent approaches.

One day, I was surprised to receive an invitation from the
professor to join him in an outing. Aware of his passion for the
beautiful nurse, guessed what he had in mind: to solicit my
help in his pursuit. At the appointed time the professor showed
up, together with one of his colleagues, in a late-model touring
car with a black chauffeur.

After driving for about an hour, we stopped in a broad
meadow blanketed with grass and abundant wild flowers. We
sprawled out on a long slope that reached to the horizon. It
was a remnant of the walls of the city of Nineveh, capital of
ancient Assyria. Nearby stood the ruins of the ancient city gate,
with lions etched in stone. Apart from the chirping of birds in
a nearby grove drenched in spring sunlight, all was quiet.

After a long monologue on ancient Indian civilization, the
professor went on the medical matters. Then he abruptly turned
to me with a personal and very secret request. He had been
informed that the hospital director performed so impressively at
cards because he used a fixed deck. A public scandal might
embroil many parti-cipants in serious complications. Would I
please persuade my fellow officers to stop frequenting the
club for the purpose of playing cards? He added that several of
his Indian friends had run up/heavy debts because of their
losses.

My colleagues were surprised to hear of this criminal behaviour by a senior commander with a high-ranking position, but
they agreed to forgo their visits with their Indian counterparts.
Idle and bored as the days passed and our own hospital was not
put into use, the doctors and other staff members became increasingly irritable – and hostile towards the handful of Jews.

The protracted inactivity undermined discipline and released impulses among the nurses and care workers, who began to slip into legendary, enchanting Baghdad on brief entertainment forays. There, throngs of officers from all the world's armies filled half-lit nightclubs and bars in wild quest for adventure and ways to blow the money they had saved during their stay in the desert.

The boom town's cunning Levantine merchants prospered as never before. Soldiers streamed in from great distances, greedily snapping up overpriced clothing and women's jewellery. Prostitution spread like wildfire. Some Polish women who had arrived with the army from Russia, yearning for amusement and easy profit after liberation from their poverty while in Soviet exile, became new practitioners of the ancient profession.

Polish prostitutes, in competition with local services, were in high demand. Baghdad's street urchins quickly realized this. In the congested streets they would grab soldiers' shirt-tails, offering them their imported wares in halting English and Polish: 'Pretty girl, Polish girl with hat....'

In view of the foul atmosphere, I applied for a transfer from Mosul. My friendship with the head of the medical services, Professor (now General) Szarecki – originating in our years together as POWs – helped me extricate myself from the embarrassing situation of life in a society I despised.

Hospital No. 2

A few days later I received transfer orders to Hospital No. 2 in Kana-Quin, halfway between Mosul and Baghdad. Our hospital commander was outraged by this circumvention of his authority. As we parted, he asked me to explain why I had abandoned my post. I revealed nothing.

I left boring Mosul feeling as if a stone had been lifted off my heart. I looked forward to heading for 'wide open spaces' and congenial surroundings. Disappointment soon followed. I quickly found that I had gone from the frying pan into the fire.

Crossing the desert, I came upon a vast area covered with a lengthy row of tents. It was the hospital. The Kerman-Shah mountains across the Iranian border were visible in the distance. Army units from Britain, Burma, India, and South Africa were stationed in the area. A short distance away was a British hospital, whose pretty nurses were tremendously popular with the doctors.

The commander of Hospital No. 2 was a regular army officer whom I had known at Griazoviets, which he had reached with the group of 'Lithuanians'. In the crowded quarters of the camp, the Jews had helped him survive the hardships by donating boards for his bed, sheets, and blankets to protect him during the Arctic winter.

Reporting to him now, I found an ungrateful man and a harsh commander, irrecognizably different from the person I had known. His features radiated hostility throughout, his narrow eyes gleaming cruelly. His lips were pressed together and his face expressionless, evincing no indication of our shared past.

His measured words breathed arrogance and pride of power. The anti-semitic officers in his headquarters generated a thick, poisonous atmosphere for the handful of Jewish doctors, most of whom were renowned specialists. They included Drs Merenlender, Jakob Goldinberg, Axelrad, Cohan, Essigman, and Józef Koch.

The Jews had to adjust to the circumstances, preferring to dine at a separate table in the officers' mess and refraining from arguments with their colleagues.

Despite the strained interpersonal relations, I succeeded in organizing a large department with a team of doctors, nurses, and such instrumentation and equipment as was suited to the desert conditions. Officers from various Allied formations crossed the desert to avail themselves of the department's services, and expressed their appreciation by inviting us to visit their clubs and tour the area.

Desert adventures

On one such occasion, I chanced to make the acquaintance of an Anglo-Indian officer with deep tan skin. The impressive, smartly dressed major came from a well-known English family; his father had spent many years in British government service in Bombay, and had married into the local aristocracy.

Despite their English education and customs, the offspring of English–Indian intermarriages were treated as inferior by English society. At the same time, they looked down on citizens of their Indian homeland.

My new acquaintance was commander of the detail of primary-care ambulances that served the regiments stationed along the desert highway from Baghdad to northern Iraq. He was in charge of dozens of trained teams equipped with resuscitation gear. At his personal disposal was a touring car fitted out with a kitchen and refrigerator with enough food for a few days' travel. Indeed, shortly after meeting him I was invited, together with several doctors and nurses from the hospital, to a desert outing towards the Iranian border.

Amidst the untamed expanses of undulating dunes, mountain slopes, and threatening cliffs – from whose crevices packs of howling jackals and hyenas would venture at night – we suddenly spotted an oasis, a seemingly artificial splash of green in the parched surroundings. In its centre, amidst dense, fresh vegetation of leafy trees, green bushes, and towering palms, stood a miniature palace with marble columns and vaulted windows. A splendid mosaic floor was visible through the stained-glass windows of the hidden sanctuary.

The pastoral tranquillity was accompanied by the relentless, furious rush of water in a narrow, twisting watercourse embraced in profuse vegetation and enchanting flowers. The cold waters of the brook of Yarshiran came down from the Kerman-Shah mountains, disappeared between the cliffs, glittered occasionally in the desert sun, and spilled into the Tigris. The shady banks of the stream provided wild animals with shelter from the arid desert, and at dusk they approached the water to quench their thirst.

The Qesar-Shiran palace had been erected in honour of one of the Shah's wives or concubines. In this God-forsaken place, pounded by desert winds and clouds of dust, the grand building looked like part of a film set depicting a fable.

Our fascinating outing left profound impressions. Heading home, we got lost in the vacant desert as the sun set behind the mountains. A solitary light bulb flickering at a great distance led our convoy to the road that took us, safe and sound, back to our tents.

Some time later, the commander of the Australian artillery corps extended a tempting invitation to hunt wild boar in the middle of the desert. A group of sharpshooter officers, including a paediatrician and former lecturer in a medical school, reported to the rendezvous point before sunrise with rifles and other kinds of guns. The organizer of the outing, owner of an estate and an experienced hunter, warned us not to stray from the group; if a boar went wild under pursuit, our hand-guns would not suffice to stop him.

The hunters dispersed at dawn, and I found myself alone with a friend in a patch of rocky desert. A weak chirping sound came from a deep fissure in the rock, and my curious friend peered in and pulled out three tiny, two-day-old jackal puppies.

From afar came reports of gunshots, calls of the hunters from their blinds, and terrifying lowing as the wild beast fought for its life. The hunters returned to the rendezvous point dragging a fat boar, blood oozing from its wounds.

Back in our tent at the hospital, my friend Dr Skorczyński assembled a cage of iron mesh as a home for the puppies. Experienced in caring for the newborn, my paediatrician colleague patiently nursed the infants with a baby's bottle. Our neighbours were amazed at how fast the little creatures grew. A few weeks later, their eagerness for the bottle waned. My friend offered them bits of fresh meat, which they spurned at first. Then he placed the meat in the sizzling desert sand and left it there. Once it began to smell like carrion, the little ones leaped upon it with astonishing greed.

At night, the growing puppies began to wail and struggle to escape their confines. Packs of adult jackals approached our tent after dark, and their howls intermingled with those of the puppies, scampering about wildly in their cage. The commotion deprived our neighbours of their sleep and threatened to frustrate my friend's scientific experiments.

Then the problem solved itself. One night, to our surprise, the jackals' wailing was replaced with a suspicious silence. The next morning, we found that the puppies had vanished. There was no indication of anyone's having broken into the cage. After investigation, we found a tunnel leading from the desert sand into the cage in our tent. Through it the puppies had been whisked to freedom.

The desert population

In the war years as always, the vast Iraqi desert was a transit route for nomadic tribes with their herds of sheep and goats, and for traders with their packs of camels laden with merchandise for and from the West. The nomads called the bright, sandy landscape stretching from the highway east to the Iranian border the 'white desert'; this distinguished it from the desert heading west, towards the Syrian border. That desert, strewn with black basalt stone and grey granite boulders, was called the 'black desert'.

Desert animals, predatory birds, and insects had worked for generations in perfect harmony to purify the wilderness from animal corpses and residual wastes. Giant vultures followed the herds of animals at high elevation, plummeting to earth and greedily tearing away preferred limbs with their sharp beaks and powerful claws. On their heels came other predatory birds. At dusk, packs of wailing, screaming jackals streamed to the site of the kill, shredding what remained of the prey and struggling bloodthirstily for the pieces. Their rivals, the hyenas, crunched and gnawed at the leftovers, the joints. The ants walked away with any remaining shreds of flesh and tendons. Night-time breezes dispersed bone fragments, and the next day's sun reduced them to dust that disappeared into the rolling hills of sand.

Thus, without the touch of a human hand, the desert maintained its pristine state for millennia.

Heatstroke

The desert heat reached its peak in the afternoon hours of summer days, and the monotonous, desolate expanse – thousands of square miles – became one great oven. The paved road crossing the area was the only sign of human presence in the endless wasteland.

Anyone out in the sun was at risk of heatstroke, and army orders indeed forbade such exposure at midday. Treatment of victims of desert heatstroke was no routine affair; it was the result of protracted research and experience in the field. Patients were resuscitated in a special structure built atop a broad surface of poured concrete equipped with stone tables. On the roof, water dripped from metal containers down wooden scaffolds on the high walls, coated with branches of thistle and various thorny desert plants. Powerful electric fans suspended from the ceiling caused the dripping water to evaporate even faster than otherwise. Thus the room was something like a giant refrigerator, equipped with requisite first aid accessories and medical instruments.

As duty officer one sizzling July day, I patrolled the kitchen to examine its cleanliness and the quality of the food being served to the men. Just then a shipment of eggs arrived from Syria. To my surprise, two chicks leaped out of one of the crates and began dancing around on the stone kitchen floor. They had pecked their way out of their eggs! The long, hot trip had turned the wooden crates into hatcheries. No longer surprised, I found that only a few eggs delivered to the officers' mess for consumption were edible.

12

From Baghdad to Haifa

Considering the large number of victims of serious wounds and dangerous war injuries for many months, I had been pondering an idea for a surgical instrument that could be used in the repair of facial fractures. Now, during those summer months in the Iraqi desert, I found the time to sketch it.

Conventional surgery under protracted anaesthesia caused the seriously injured patient great suffering and, at times, worsened his general condition. My device would make care under emergency conditions easier and quicker.

Having completed the sketches, I sought an opportunity to build a prototype and try it out on patients. I turned to my friend Professor Szarecki, head of the health services at command headquarters in Rehovot, in Palestine. He responded at once. Within a few days, an order came attaching me to staff headquarters. My departure caused the hospital director no sorrow, but I parted with my friends with a heavy heart, sad about the atmosphere in which they would have to carry on with their duties.

The route to Rehovot led from Baghdad across the desert to Damascus and thence to Beirut and Palestine. Transportation was provided by a British company, Nairn, which used a special rail car towed by a powerful but slow shunt engine. Its dozens of upholstered seats became comfortable beds by night.

As the bulky vehicle crossed the vast, flat desert and approached Damascus, the landscape changed. The wasteland yielded to signs of civilization – fields of vegetables and village houses with well-tended gardens. Syria was under French mandate at the time.

Reaching Damascus, I boarded a train that happened to be there, and after two hours of slow travel I disembarked in the dead of night at the freight depot of the Lebanese capital, where I reported to the British army transit camp, and caught a brief nap on the damp soil floor of one of the tents. My slumber was cut short at sunrise by a shout: the duty sentry announced that an army truck was heading for Haifa. Without hesitation I leaped aboard with my possessions, rejoicing at my good fortune.

The sun rising behind the mountains of Lebanon illuminated the picturesque coastal highway in its full grandeur. The dancing waters of the Mediterranean displayed a full spectrum of colours. A thin mist enveloped the enchanting landscape. The pastoral scene worked excitement alongside feelings of peace. A little later I noticed, for the first time, a sign in Hebrew on the wall of a rickety house: hayat ('tailor'). I had crossed into the Holy Land.

The Scottish driver stopped next to the rail station and announced curtly: 'Haifa. Get out.' The passengers grabbed their packs and scattered in all directions.

It was a suffocating morning, typical of the rainless autumn of Palestine's coastal plain. Sweating in my woollen army coat and heavy shoes, I boarded a bus for the trip to Rehovot, where Anders' Polish Army had established its Middle East headquarters.

The venerable General Szarecki greeted me warmly at the door to his office. After I presented the sketches and explained how the new instrument worked, the veteran surgeon looked up with an expression of profound satisfaction. With his rich combat experience, Szarecki was devoting what remained of his long life to putting medical know-how to work for others' sake.

Good news came through a few days later: the Army's supreme commander, General Anders, recommended that the prototype of my instrument be produced at a Royal Air Force workshop in the nearby town of Yavneh. Visiting the workshop, I found a selection of sophisticated machinery and devices for the production and repair of precision instruments. The engineers and technicians obediently followed my instructions on how to manufacture parts of the experimental device.

After the instrument was ready, I addressed a conference at the headquarters auditorium, attended by military doctors and surgeons from all units in the area. My description of the device and demonstration of its abilities, using a soldier injured in a traffic accident, were highly successful. At the end of the conference, Professor Szarecki expressed his appreciation for my activity on the army's behalf, and informed me that he had decided to send me to the British Medical Centre in the 15th Scottish Hospital in Cairo. There I would conduct a presentation of my instrument and undergo a period of advanced training. The Scottish Hospital was the top medical institution in the Middle East during the war years. The greatest British specialists treated casualties from all over the area.

Palestine was not a friendly place for members of the Polish army. The Polish officers' arrogance cast a shadow over personal relations, even though tens of thousands of Poles lived in the country, so there were many 'locals' who spoke Polish fluently. Animus towards the Poles was aggravated by hundreds of Jewish officers and men who had deserted their units because of anti-semitic treatment. These embittered men, taken in by kibbutzim and other non-communal farm villages, nursed deep grudges against their former comrades-in-arms. Jewish officers in Polish uniform met with an ambivalence quite unlike the hearty welcome offered to the Australians, New Zealanders, and South Africans, whom the local residents loved.

I stayed in Haifa with my brother, with whom I had been out of touch for years. This, and my impression of the way I was received following my lectures at Medical Association conferences, aroused and then strengthened my desire to settle in Palestine. Instructive meetings with the poet Abraham Brojdes, a friend from my youth at Tarbut high school, and other friends from 'Jordania', the Zionist fraternity in Wilno, gave me the feeling that I was in my own homeland, after years of rootless peregrination.

My profound excitement at the sight of the Eternal City, the introduction to Dr Yaski of Hadassah, and my visit to Professor Emanuel Olswanger – a long-time acquaintance of my parents in Grajevo, tipped the scales. However, I had to postpone my personal plans. My urgent trip to Cairo and the desire to continue contributing to the war effort prevailed.

After completing personal arrangements, I boarded the train to Cairo at Rehovot. With irritating slowness, the train crept southward, stopping frequently, crossing desolate dunes and miserable Bedouin shacks.

Together with me in the first-class car were four British officers, including a colonel who sat next to me half-asleep and silent. The bored passengers joked about how the train would stop even to give right-of-way to a cow or a donkey. At the Kantara East station, the colonel got off with a suitcase, and the train went on. Moments later, a pandemonium of angry shouting enveloped the area. The train stopped in the desert at the approaches to the Suez Canal. Angry military police officers leaped aboard the train, burst frantically into the car, and pushed their way into my compartment. After scanning it hastily, they whipped my suitcase off the shelf and, over my protests, announced that it belonged to the colonel who had got off the train at Kantara. Indeed it did. Although it resembled mine, it bore a business card with the colonel's name.

A few minutes later I received my suitcase, which had caused the incident. The colonel had realized his error after opening my suitcase, in which, to his astonishment, he found a skull and several human bones. I had used them in designing the prototype of my surgical device, and was bringing them along to the hospital in Cairo.

Palestine was in a state of upheaval at the time, with various underground groups busily engaged in sabotage. The Mandatory army was on constant alert, and extreme suspicion was the rule. Jewish soldiers and officers in the Polish army were known to train members of the underground and smuggle military equipment into the country for their anti-British struggle. The incident surrounding my innocent suitcase might have frustrated my plans in Cairo, had it not come to a happy end after intelligence people investigated the episode once I had reached my destination.

The Scottish Hospital in Cairo

Reaching the Scottish Hospital, I was taken to the commander in the customary fashion, and attached to the surgical department staff. For quarters, I was assigned a room together with two dark-skinned Anglo-Indian officers.

The hospital itself occupied a magnificent building on the Nile. A large passenger ship anchored at a pier served as nurses' quarters. Spacious hospital wards, outpatient clinics for follow-up care, and well-equipped operating theatres admitted war casualties from hospitals throughout the Mediterranean basin, embracing the fronts of Europe and North Africa.

The medical team included senior experts from medical centres in Scotland and England. It was performing the world's first experiments on human patients using a new drug, developed in England, called penicillin. After a few days in the hospital, the director of my department, Colonel Pulvertaft, opened a cabinet with great circumspection and showed me a bottle containing a bit of brown dust. It was penicillin. At the time, the wards were full of soldiers with open, pus-infested wounds. Taking great pains to economize, Pulvertaft and his aides deposited a pinch of the powder into the infected areas. Removing the men's bandages the next day, we were stunned to find the wounds disinfected and clear of pus. The wonder drug had been amazingly effective on our patients.

The medical staff was astonishingly devoted to its duties, resulting in a commensurate quality of care. One evening when I was on duty, I went through the department and, to my surprise, noticed a famous surgeon, Mr Oldfield, examining and sorting the delicate instruments that would be used for surgery the next day. He trusted no one else with this detail, he explained.

The people of Cairo were quite hostile to the Allied armies. Their sympathy for the Germans had not diminished after the pinnacle it had reached when Rommel mounted his stunning drive on Alexandria. Evidence of pre-war Nazi propaganda surfaced in small talk, the newspapers, and the many leaflets posted in display windows and street-corner kiosks.

The British officers usually treated the Egyptians with the kind of humiliating condescension towards the 'natives' practised in their colonies everywhere. They would ply the streets with batons, offensively demonstrating their superiority.

One day, as I shared a taxi with a British officer, the driver chose a roundabout route to run up the meter. The enraged Briton drew a whip and whacked the driver over the head. I steeled myself for the victim's response. To my surprise, he restrained himself, and, oozing murderous rage, uttered a juicy Arabic curse that no one understood. It was the disciplined response of a man aware of his humiliation and powerlessness.

Masses of Egyptians, who had thronged from faraway villages to the cities during the war in search of easy profits, began to hearken to their leaders' propaganda and stand up for their dignity. They chose to do this by being hostile to the uniformed aliens.

In Cairo's entertainment spots, nightclubs, and grand hotels, suspicious characters and Nazi spies mingled freely with Allied intelligence agents who spent their free time enjoying the great city's bands and Oriental belly dancing. Men in uniform had to behave with extreme caution in their contacts with the residents, refraining from dangerous entanglements with unexpected parties.

When my advanced training in Cairo was complete, I took the train back to Palestine for an assignment with the medical team of Hospital No. 3 in Kfar Bilu, a settlement near Rehovot. I looked forward to a protracted stay in the country. Again my hopes were quickly dashed.

13

Italy

I was attached to a new team of doctors, in which I had neither a friend nor a veteran acquaintance. Lonely, frustrated, and disappointed, I was aware that my own initiative had torpedoed my hopes of staying on in Palestine.

The hospital was due to sail to Italy, and the team set out from Rehovot on a lengthy trek southward to Port Said. On New Year's Eve 1944, a passenger ship set sail with several other vessels. They carried supplies for Marine units of the Anzio bridgehead, and for a concentration of formations in southern Italy gearing up for the attack on Rome.

The Mediterranean weather did not let us down. Even in January, many passengers spent the day on deck, taking in the sun's refreshing rays. Young soldiers, appetites whetted by the crisp air, engaged in a roll-eating contest with incredible results. At mealtime, they went through the menu indiscriminately, ordering and re-ordering canned meat, which was served in the form of 'hamburger' as hard as the soles of shoes.

The young passengers were in a good mood, confidently looking forward to action after protracted idleness. The older men, by contrast, listened tensely to the buzz of enemy aircraft engines and the clattering of their machine-guns as they circled overhead. Although the Allied air forces enjoyed supremacy, the Germans launched daring offensives in an attempt to disrupt the supply routes. Occasionally we could see pilots bailing out of their damaged craft.

After four days on calm waters, the ship docked at Taranto,

in southern Italy. From the dock, far from town, we beheld the magnitude of the destruction inflicted by the enemy armies' heavy bombing. Gutted ruins of high-rise buildings tottered and threatened to collapse. Piles of wreckage and heaps of rubble blocked the deserted main street. German graffiti – 'We shall return' – remained on the building walls, attesting that the enemy had quit the area only a few days previously. Military balloons with anti-aircraft defence nets were suspended over the shattered town.

Boarding army trucks, we drove west as far as Palagiano, on the shore of the Italian 'boot'. North of the town were hills that climbed gradually to the summits of high mountains. The white houses of the town of Motola clung to their slopes, seemingly suspended in mid-air. To the south, the calm Mediterranean lapped the shore. In all directions, after days of commotion and misery for the town's inhabitants, an eerie silence reigned.

The street that bisected the town was lined with the stone houses of well-to-do families; along the narrow, sandy alleys, scattered in disorder, were rickety wooden cabins tenanted by indigent, landless peasants with large numbers of children.

Looking for a place to live, I stopped with a new acquaintance, Dr Gustav Kimerling, at the handsome entrance of a house on the main street. A young woman approached us from a residential apartment. She was surrounded by children: an infant under one arm, a boy of about two under the other, and two little girls alongside.

They were intimidated by the sight of uniformed officers. The children's faces were covered in lesions indicating malnutrition. The landlady, a woman in her twenties, had the lovely face of a classical portrait – innocent expression, fair hair bundled in silk ribbons.

My friend, older and more experienced than myself, clutched a large chocolate bar and confidently uttered a sentence in Italian that he had learned from an abridged tour guide: 'We need a room with two beds and running water and central heating!' The woman, perplexed at the sight of the chocolate – my partner was pointing it at her oldest daughter – responded in the affirmative without hesitation, although she had heard of central heating only in stories.

Courteously she escorted us into a tidy guest room equipped with a sofa and armchairs in the local style, upholstered in flowery velvet. The room had long been out of use. Blooming potted geraniums lined the windowsills, and the window offered a view of the town church. A few old men were walking slowly to prayer.

We accepted these quarters. In addition to the sofa, we installed a fold-up military cot. Our presence brought the children no end of delight, as we occasionally treated them to sweets and military biscuits. We never met the landlord, and were told that he worked at the bombed-out railway station from sun-up to well past sundown. What he really did was probably something quite different; it may have had to do with the previous regime.

The people living on the main street, most of them elderly, could be seen each day walking to and from the church for prayer. The few young men were demobilized soldiers, nearly all of fascist persuasion. In our talks with them, they expressed yearning for times past.

Catholicism, the dominant faith in the villages of southern Italy, had adopted certain pantheistic affectations. Occasionally masquerade parades were held in the streets. The locals would turn out with their children in festive attire, carrying velvet flags, paintings, and colourful banners taken out of the church stores.

Hospital No. 3

Hospital No. 3 was set up on a broad plain that began just outside the village of Palagiano and stretched as far as the hills that gradually rose to the north and ascended into the Apennines. Dozens of large, neatly arrayed tents served as hospital wards for the thousands of wounded and sick. Other tents were residential quarters for the nurses, service personnel, and guards. Laundries, kitchens, and various warehouses were located at the edge of the plot.

The surgical department and operating rooms were located in the schoolhouse, a two-storey structure. The specialist physician staff adroitly sorted and accommodated the hundreds of casualties urgently airlifted to this hospital during the decisive battle of Monte Cassino and the harsh campaigns waged to take northern Italy.

Of the 200 doctors and service staff officers, about 20 were Jewish, including several heads of department and aides. (The heads of department were: Drs Mietek Ashkenazy-Niemczyk, Otto Finsterbusz, Martin Knobel, Marcel Panzer, Adam Graber, Tadeusz Cytrinik, Łabedź (radiologist), and Salomon Slowes. Department aides included: Drs Leo Kurcer, Huler, Johanan Weisglass, and Henryk Berger.) Although Jews were well represented in numbers and status, their colleagues blatantly shunned them. Many were openly anti-semitic. After regular work hours, relations between the two groups of doctors were weak at best.

The doctors were allowed to rent quarters in private homes in town, thus enjoying privacy and rest when off duty. A group of senior Jewish physicians rented an empty apartment, establishing a Jewish community centre that they called 'the Knesset'. On Friday evenings, many doctors would gather there to listen to the Voice of Jerusalem.

As the High Holidays approached, a group organized a trip to the synagogue in the nearby port city of Bari. There we met Jewish soldiers from the United States, Great Britain, and South Africa, along with men of the Jewish Brigade from Palestine.

Back at the hospital, a recuperation centre was set up on a nearby beach for discharged patients. The new establishment was headed by Dr Jacob Litmanovich.

After only a few weeks at work, I was ordered by staff headquarters to move temporarily to British Hospital No. 64 in Barletta, where I would serve as a liaison officer with the Polish units stationed in the area. The order alarmed my friends, since fierce battles were being waged in nearby Foggia.

Subdued, I headed north to my new destination in a jeep driven by a taciturn British major. As we approached the front, the booming of cannon, reports of detonations, and whistling of shells grew louder. Squadrons of attack aircraft circled overhead, shrieking deafeningly. Towering stockpiles of bombs and shells had been readied at the edge of the woods along the road. On the horizon, tongues of flame climbed skyward from giant fires all around, and signal flares sent blinding trails of light into the dying sun's haze.

"Reaching our destination at nightfall, we were quartered in the rail station hotel, which had been requisitioned by the hospital staff. The danger of working near the front line did not stop the doctors from organizing dances in the officers' and nurses' messes. Heads of the hospital were senior physicians and surgeons who had volunteered for overseas service. After work they would meet at the snack bar and drive their concerns out of mind by downing shot after shot of whisky or brandy, mixed with soda and chilled with ice.

The Polish army units, not yet seriously tested under fire, were concentrated in the rear. As drunkenness among the soldiers spread, venereal disease and crude outbursts by hospitalized soldiers began to proliferate disturbingly. The hospital's commanding officer, an elderly colonel, presided over a daily report at which he punished drunken soldiers who had brawled and smashed windows in the nearby village. It was my duty to translate everything he said. I found it no easy task to convey the need for restraint to these wild young men. I was pleased when the Scot who ran the officers' mess gave me a little bag of delicious sweets as a going-away present.

While in Barletta, I operated on an Italian teenager who had been seriously wounded in the face. After he recovered and was discharged, his father invited me to his home and, as a sign of appreciation, presented me with a superb, ivory-inlaid accordion. The boy's father, one of the richest men in town, owned a factory that manufactured musical instruments. The sound of this music, accompanying the wistful songs of the officers in the mess, helped them set aside their worries. Many of them were sorry to see me go.

Returning to the hospital, I found to my surprise that my colleagues, confident that I would not return from the front, had divvied up my personal belongings. I had to reassemble my property from these devoted friends.

That winter in southern Italy was spent organizing the Polish formations within the British Eighth Army. Notwithstanding fierce battles and heavy losses, the Allied armies failed to break through the Germans' fortified defence lines. The Polish army had been given many months of 'days of mercy', the term used by the author Melchior Wańkowicz in a lecture he gave to the hospital staff. These days now came to an end, and the advent of spring augured imminent combat action.

The Battle of Monte Cassino

The year 1944 began with Allied offensives meant to break through the German defence lines and capture Rome. This was a complicated task that claimed many casualties, since the area's mountainous topography permitted the Germans to mount an efficient and protracted defence of their fortified positions.

The Apennines overlooked two major roads leading to northern Italy. In the centre of the range was Monte Cassino, with an ancient Benedictine monastery on its summit. The mountain's slopes were fortified with steel-reinforced pillboxes carved into the rock and surrounded by minefields. The select German garrison force was equipped with banks of mortars and cannon, thousands of machine-guns, and flame-throwers.

The Germans' defensive front – the Gustav Line – ran down the valley of the Liri River. North of the valley, they had set up a series of camouflaged fortifications along the Sangro River as far as Mt Piedimonte. They called this the Hitler Line.

As the new year began, the Americans, together with French and British units, carried out a surprise attack on the enemy's fortifications. The offensive was repelled with many casualties, and Monte Cassino remained in German hands. The Americans tried again two months later, this time with select New Zealand and Indian units. Again they failed, taking heavy losses.

The futile attempts to capture the mountain gave rise to the belief that the mission was impossible. Deliberate engagements were kept at lower intensity, as the commanders reorganized the combat units and drew up plans for new offensives meant to open the transportation routes.

This difficult task was entrusted to the Polish forces under General Anders. Attached to them were British and American units. Anders' Army numbered 50,000 well-trained men. Some of them were young recruits who had enlisted two years previously after surviving the harsh Soviet detention camps.

The day before the fateful operation, the regiments staged a highly impressive military parade in the deep valley. Bishop Gawlina gave a prayer of thanksgiving to the accompaniment of a military band. In his stirring speech, General Anders stressed that behind the mountain ranges was Warsaw, awaiting liberation. Our families, he asserted, were praying for the success of this operation to save the homeland.

The first offensive against the enemy's battlements was lunched on the night of 11 May. It failed, despite impressive achievements in which the men had crossed the Liri River and temporarily captured several fortified hills.

After a week's regrouping, a second offensive was mounted. Following heavy artillery fire meant to soften up the enemy, infantry staged a general onslaught all along the front. Murderous enemy fire failed to halt the frontal offensive this time, as the men fought desperately and with supreme self-sacrifice. The Germans' fortified defence lines were breached, and the monastery of Monte Cassino was taken in hand-to-hand combat. The highway to Rome had been freed. The cost: more than 4,000 killed and wounded, including many Jewish officers and enlisted men. Among them were several senior physicians who tended to the casualties on the very line of fire, only few metres from the enemy. One of those killed was the famous surgeon Dr Adam Graber; Drs Mark Mozes and Panzer were among the wounded.

Polish troops were first to approach the ruins of the monastery; following them, appearing from the other side of the mountain, was a squad of Americans. A battle of daggers and fists broke out between the two groups of 'comrades-in-arms'. They had to decide who was entitled to hoist the national flag over the remains of the massive monastery. As if the war had not caused enough bloodshed, the soldiers' prestige caused a little more.

The US Air Force had a base along the coast near the hospital, with an airfield where squadrons of heavy bombers were stationed. As the air force's activity increased, large numbers of severely burned pilots needed long-term hospitalization and special treatment.

By order of the hospital commander, I was dispatched with two colleagues to coordinate procedures for transferring the casualties. As we toured the area, three Flying Fortresses landed after sorties against targets in Germany. The grey monsters were perforated by dozens of enemy strikes. The front of the fusilages bore the squadron's emblem, a rampant tiger with a tongue of fire flashing from its mouth. Further back on the fusilages were drawings of about a dozen bombs, symbolizing the number of sorties flown by the crew.

The field bustled with life. Ground crews and contingents of security officers ran about. The aircraft crews climbed down from their machines and walked slowly towards us. One pilot, a Dutchman about 20 years old, appeared to be on his last legs. Despite his youth, his face was withered and creased, his blue eyes alternately expressing anger and kindness. One could guess that his senses had lost their acuity after the tremendous tension he had endured a few hours before. We exchanged a few polite sentences and courteous smiles. Weakly the young man described the devastation of the Nazis' industrial installations and factories, despite the strong air defence they were still able to mount.

Another crew member was a Jew from Brooklyn, the son of a Polish-born Orthodox rabbi who had emigrated before the war. In our brief conversation, he disclosed that he had volunteered for the air force to avenge the blood of his family in Europe.

Heavy-hearted, we took leave from these heroes, who had pledged their lives to the Free World's war effort. The squad of exhausted pilots hurried off for soft drinks in their mess, and for a brief rest before resuming their duties. We returned to the hospital with our impressions of the visit. Overwhelmed and conscience-striken, we pondered just how much this handful of valorous young men was contributing.

Our hospital admitted transports of hundreds of casualties during the campaign. Its 2,000 beds were fully occupied for several months after the bitter battles had ended. With acute sorrow the doctors tended young fighters who had returned from the front in shock, missing limbs, and with contorted faces. Some belonged to General Anders' personal guard.

After the Monte Cassino campaign, we visited the battlefield. Awaiting us there was an apocalyptic scene of devastation and death. As an eerie silence hovered over the expanse, sooty fragments of walls and ruins of chimneys protruded over the mountaintop. They belonged to the massive monastery structure, now gazing coldly into the bloodstained valley below. The bridges over the Liri and Sangro Rivers had been destroyed, and we had to advance to the monastery by detours.

Clergymen and gravediggers were still at work in the field. Corpses, some still clutching their weapons, lay in various positions in the deep furrows of the fields and along the narrow roads twisting toward the higher elevations. Helmeted heads of dead men, face down, appeared in the bushes. On the hillsides lay soldiers who had fallen on mines in the last spate of hand-to-hand combat. Ravens split the air with their unnerving shrieks. Supply trucks, burned-out tanks, and pieces of artillery that tumbled down the mountain lay where they had fallen in the valleys.

The Allied armies entered Rome on 4 June 1944, and held a splendid victory parade. Senior Allied commanders began to gush with praise for the valour of the Polish fighter. Polish commanders were decorated with orders of distinction. President Roosevelt, in the presence of King George VI and Pope Pius XII, awarded General Anders the esteemed Congressional Medal of Honor. The hospital physicians were given 'Monte Cassino crosses'.

Today a military cemetery rests at the foot of the famous mountain. Some of the tombstones are embellished with Stars of David. After the heat of the bloody battle and its aftermath, not all the Jewish fighters had the benefit of being buried with citation of their faith. They had given their lives for a Poland that indeed survived the war, but almost without Jews.

The Germans, not deterred by their failure, dug into a rear defence position – the 'Gothic Line'. Having overcome the forces of the 'invincible' Reich, the Polish units emerged from the battle with *esprit de guerre* they had not known before. Ignoring their losses, they continued to engage the enemy. After fierce battles, they captured the Adriatic port of Ancona, the key to continued supplies for the units advancing north.

The 'Gothic Line' was captured in September 1944, and the *Luftwaffe* found itself unable to operate on the Italian front. The Americans' Flying Fortresses relentlessly bombed German industrial centres. The Polish air force participated in some of the sorties; its crews included several Jewish pilots recruited from Palestine and Britain.

As for the millions of Jewish civilians in Europe, the Warsaw Ghetto uprising, put down in 1943, sealed their tragic fate. The Nazi annihilation machine worked at full speed, and the infernos of death raced against the clock to complete the 'Final Solution'. Under pressure of public opinion and recurrent appeals by American and British Jewish community leaders, several forays were launched against two extermination camps, Maidanek and Auschwitz (Oświęcim). These were limited in scale. Because the camps were far from the airbases – Roosevelt said – the risk to the air crews was too great for anything more extensive.

It was then that the Poles in Warsaw rebelled against the Nazi occupier. The desperate fighters appealed for help, and the Allied armies responded with some parachute drops of equipment and medicine. The Red Army waited for the uprising to collapse and did nothing. After two months of hopeless street battles, the last of the rebels surrendered to the Nazi forces, and their commander, General Bór-Komorowski, was taken prisoner of war by the Germans.

The Polish fighters on the Italian front, advancing toward Bologna, were told nothing of this depressing news.

The *Wehrmacht* forces on the Italian front formally surrendered in the town of Caserta, north of Naples. Among the thousands of German POWs were some of Polish origin, who were attached to Anders' formations. This exacerbated anti-semitism among our forces. One of the new 'recruits' was a physician subsequently put on trial for conducting medical experiments in an extermination camp.

As a harsh winter set in on the eastern front, the Germans suffered heavy losses. The Red Army recovered from its earlier setbacks and dealt the Nazis crushing defeats. They drove them out of eastern and central Poland and advanced westward.

Participating in Poland's liberation were units of the Kościuszko People's Army, under General Berling. These formations had a large number of Jewish officers and enlisted men, previously rejected by Anders' Army in Russia. Warsaw was finally liberated in January 1945 and the army continued towards Berlin.

14

Peace?

The great illusion

The outcome of the war in Europe was the undoing of the Polish People.

After the victory at Stalingrad in 1943, Stalin met Churchill and Roosevelt at Tehran and presented tough demands. One of them was the annexation of eastern Poland by the Soviet Union.

Earlier that year, the mass graves of Polish officers were discovered in the Katyn Forest. Following this discovery, diplomatic relations between Moscow and the Polish Government-in-Exile were severed. British and American positions began to change. At the end of December 1943 the Polish 'People's' 'Government' was set up in Warsaw under Soviet patronage.

The Red Army's occupation of Eastern Europe and its decisive role in Nazi Germany's defeat strengthened the Soviet Union's political stance. During the meetings of the Big Three in Yalta and Potsdam, Stalin utilized the Red Army's triumphs to extract far-reaching concessions from his Western colleagues.

Poland's fate was sealed. Great Britain and the United States officially recognized the People's Government in Warsaw, and Anders' Army was left with no backing.

As battle ebbed, so enthusiasm for and appreciation of the Polish fighters' valour diminished. The Government-in-Exile was not invited to the San Francisco peace conference in April 1945. Anders' Army did not participate in the grand victory parade in London in 1946, except for a few combat pilots who had been attached to the Royal Air Force.

Thus the army whose fighters had done so much for the historic victory were unrepresented at the pageant, and the nation that had been the first to stand up to Nazi aggression emerged from the campaign defeated.

Under pressure of political constraints, the leaders of the Free World reneged on their pre-war commitments and proclamations about a sovereign Poland within its existing borders. The nations of the world gave Anders' Army no recognition for the sacrifice it had made, and forgot its role in the victory.

The Polish army, its future uncertain, was transferred to northern England and Scotland. In his parting speech to one of the formations in transfer, General Anders openly expressed his political views on the Polish question. The British government reacted by hinting at the possibility of dismissing him in the future.

Anders' Army had long hoped to liberate Poland and establish a sovereign government along pre-war lines. After the guns fell silent and the peace treaty was signed, these hopes were dashed. Poland had been liberated by the Red Army and the Polish People's Army units. Illusions harboured by Anders' fighters and multitudes of families around the world were shattered.

The Warsaw government formally revoked Anders' citizenship. The revered commander lost control of affairs, and reality passed him by. His way of changing the course of events had failed.

Tens of thousands of Polish soldiers and citizens in exile were left with the choice of returning to the motherland or remaining in displaced persons' camps in hopes of emigration. Some of those who owned property in Poland, or who were elderly, refused to return to Poland, fearing the communist regime's attitude.

Soldiers with families in Poland responded to the Warsaw government's invitation to return, and assimilated into local society. One of the first senior officers to return was General Szarecki, who believed that the place of every Pole was in his native country. The esteemed professor was appointed as chief of the army's medical service, and earned respect and appreciation for his great contribution to his homeland.

Many of the Jews in Anders' Army emigrated to various destinations overseas. Professionals, including doctors, were granted British citizenship and continued working in their fields. The British government, not forsaking the thousands of Polish soldiers who remained in the camps, set up a special rehabilitation and housing office. Thousands embarked on new lives as farmers in Canada or industrial workers in Great Britain. Many Poles who remained in England were connected with the White Eagle Club in London and took part in its social, cultural, and propaganda activities. Jewish members participated in its meetings and events under a mantle of liberalism and freedom.

A number of Polish intellectuals in exile took up residence in France and in Paris established propaganda centre, *Kultura*, and a publishing house that issued a monthly journal.[27]

I was one of those who opted to settle in Mandatory Palestine and struggle for a Jewish state. To extricate myself from a feeling of exile, I availed myself of my friendship with Professor Szarecki, who had me transferred to the hospital in Kantara, along the Suez Canal. The head of the hospital was Colonel Penski, who had not forgotten the shirt I had given him when he reached the army camp clinic at Totskoye from the Arctic north. Upon his recommendation, I was released from the service.

I reached Palestine in the midst of the Jewish underground struggle against the British, and found myself sucked into the tide of events. On the 'Black Sabbath' of June 1946, when the British tried to round up and arrest the underground leaders. I was searched and detained by a red-bereted unit of soldiers belonging to the Mandatory garrison force. On a sizzling summer day, I was transported to a compound on the Tel Aviv beach, where thousands of men and women were kneeling under a burning sun, heads down and hands up, awaiting their fate. Having been a Soviet POWs, I was familiar with this scene. The British soldiers were openly brutal, kicking women as they climbed down from the trucks and clubbing men over the head. This first encounter with freedom in my own country engraved itself deeply into my memory. Upon my release from detention, I resolved to do everything possible to prevent the recurrence of such scenes in the future.

15

The Mystery of Katyn

In early May 1940, the last of the POWs from Kozielsk, Starobielsk, and Ostashkov reached the Yukhnovo camp in Pávlishchev-Bor. They expressed grave concern about the fate of comrades who had been removed from the three camps before them.

Our entrenched suspicion about the Soviet authorities' malicious intentions was based on the Soviet guards' brutal, humiliating treatment of the POWs from the moment they left the three camps for transfer in small groups, under close guard, and in rail cars meant for criminal prisoners.

We first surmised that these thousands of comrades had been sent on to small camps such as the one in Yukhnovo. This was disproved after the men were allowed to resume postal contact with their families. A torrent of letters expressing worry began to arrive from the areas under Soviet and German occupation. They were written by families of POWs who had been with us, and from whom nothing had been heard since April 1940.

After the Germans attacked the Soviet Union in June 1941, Sikorski and Stalin signed the pact under which all the POWs were to be liberated and a Polish army established. A serious shortage of officers in the units being formed became increasingly evident.

Masses of liberated Polish citizens presented themselves at induction centres throughout the country. None of them had been in the three POW camps; nor did they attest to having encountered the missing officers.

Polish army commanders made enquiries with the security authorities about the release of the POW officers. They came away empty-handed. Receiving Sikorski for an interview in the Kremlin in late 1941, Stalin promised the authorities' full assistance in tracing the missing officers. On the basis of this promise, the Missing Persons Section in staff headquarters in Buzuluk gave top priority to vigorous efforts to locate the missing men.

The difficult task of plumbing government offices in various Soviet cities in search in the missing men was entrusted to Captain Czapski. His broad erudition as an author and painter, and his total command of Russian, made him the most likely candidate for success. In compliance with Stalin's advice, Captain Czapski, armed with letters of recommendation, set out for Moscow in January 1942. His destination was the NKVD, whose full assistance he had been promised.

His efforts to approach the head of internal security, Beria, or his deputy Merkulov, were in vain. Enquiries with the security services in Kuybyshev, too, quickly proved disappointing. After a fatiguing run-around from one office to the next, Czapski was referred to the supervisor of the Soviet detention camps (the Gulag) in Chkalov, formerly Orenburg. There, after great efforts, he succeeded in reaching General Nasiedkin.

At this point Czapski returned to Buzuluk from his travails in crowded trains and bitter cold. He came back with instructive details about the man who, according to Western estimation, kept in his hands the fate of some 25,000,000 prisoners in detention and forced labour camps across the Soviet Union.

After recovering from the hardships of his journey, he reported to the NKVD building in Chkalov. The lengthy corridors of secret police headquarters were muted with carpets, and soundproof doors kept anything said in the offices from leaking out. Czapski was asked to step towards a wall cupboard. It popped open; behind it was General Nasiedkin, the commander himself, relaxed and at ease in his upholstered armchair.

The tough general was conspicuously courteous and spoke in a quiet tone of voice. What he said, however, was disappointing. He had no knowledge of the whereabouts of the Polish POWs. Thus Captain Czapski returned to Buzuluk without having succeeded in his mission. The fate of the missing men remained a mystery.

General Anders brought up the issue again in a visit to the Kremlin in March 1942. Stalin adhered to his version of events: all the prisoners and POWs had been liberated from the camps, as agreed with General Sikorski.

General Anders' Army left the Soviet Union for the Middle East with a feeling of sorrow and frustration. Thousands of comrades from the camps were missing, and their whereabouts remained unknown. There were occasional rumours. Some thought the men had been exiled to the Arctic island of Nowaya Zemlya. Others intimated that they had been treacherously drowned at sea. Still another story was based on interpretation of a seemingly surprising utterance by a senior NKVD official, either Beria or Merkulov: 'We made a big mistake.' The reference, according to this version, was to the problem of the Polish officers' disappearance. This account intensified everyone's apprehension about our comrades' fate.

Then world public opinion was stunned by a terrifying discovery. In April 1943, Radio Berlin announced that a mass grave of Polish officers had been unearthed in the Katyń, Forest, about ten miles west of Smolensk in Belorussia. The grave was found as the German forces retreated under pressure of the westward-advancing Red Army.

The surprising news provided the Germans with an invaluable opportunity to embark on a high-powered propaganda campaign blaming the Soviets and the Jews for the despicable act. The purpose was to damage Soviet–Allied relations and gain occupied Poland's sympathy for the perpetrators of the 'Final Solution' against the Jews. After the horrifying report of the massacre was announced, the German and Soviet governments launched rising waves of reciprocal accusations about who had committed the slaughter, of whose kind nothing had been known in the history of war since the time of Genghis Khan.

To prove their case against the Soviets, the Germans invited representatives of the Polish Red Cross in Warsaw to the Katyn Forest. They organized guided visits to the scene of the massacre for delegations of journalists, British and American POWs, and works committees throughout Poland.

General Anders' men learned of the atrocity while in the Middle East.

The Germans set up an international committee of forensic medicine experts from Italy, The Netherlands, Switzerland, and other Western European countries. The committee, chaired by Professor François Neville of Geneva, was to examine the bodies and gather testimony to establish the perpetrators of the murder.

In May 1943, the committee explored the forest areas in the Smolensk district near the Dnieper River. The place in question was known by local inhabitants as Kozie Góry ('Goat Hills'), and had once been owned by the Koźliński and Lednicki families. The committee members beheld seven mass graves containing about 4,500 corpses of Polish officers. The victims had been shot in the back of the head at short range with rounds of German-made hand-gun ammunition. Many of the corpses were trussed up with ropes, and their military coats were pulled over their heads.

German newspapers published photos of the officers' exhumed corpses, among them General Smorawiński and others who were with us in Kozielsk.

After considering the corpses' state of decomposition, the committee concluded that the murder had been carried out about three years previously. That was 1940, the year when the three POW camps had been liquidated and contact with the officers lost. Thus the massacre had taken place about a year before the Germans attacked the Soviet Union.

World opinion was taken by surprise. Stunned by disclosures of the Nazis' brutality in oppressing the peoples of Europe, it had till then attributed guilt for the detestable crime at Katyń to them.

Now finding itself under attack, the Soviet government began to defend itself, exploiting the Red Army's progress toward the site. After the *Wehrmacht* retreated from the Smolensk area, the Soviets published various testimonies and pieces of evidence 'proving' that the Nazis had slaughtered the POWs.

In September 1943, the Soviets established an investigative committee of famous Russian scientists, headed by members of the Academy of Science, Professor Nikolai Burdenko and Alexei Tolstoy. The committee was attended by the chief pathologist of the Red Army, Professor Voropayev, and by renowned forensic medicine experts. After examining the bodies, deciphering documents found at the site, and taking testimony from local inhabitants, the committee published a booklet: *The Truth about Katyn: Report of the Special Committee Charged with Investigating the Circumstances of the Murder of the Polish Officers, POWs of the Fascist German Invaders, in the Katyn Forest.*

On the basis of their studies in the field, the authors rejected the conclusions of the Western countries' committees, and cited testimonials and documents to prove that the Germans had committed the massacre in late 1941. At that time, the pamphlet asserted, the POWs had been building roads along the German–Soviet frontier. After the Germans invaded the area, the POWs found themselves stranded for lack of transportation. The Nazis detained the officers and slaughtered them in 1941.

The warring countries' intelligence services laboured feverishly to discover details that would confirm the other side's guilt. Hostile witnesses were eliminated, and secret documents vanished from offices in countries around the world.

As the fighting in Italy ebbed, a Russian peasant named Krivozertsov turned up at Anders' headquarters. He was from the vicinity of Katyn and, he asserted, had been the first to inform German command of the presence of the Polish officers' mass grave.

As the advancing Red Army approached the Smolensk area, Krivozertsov fled to the West, adopted the name Loboda, and made his way to England under Polish army auspices. At the end of the war, this important witness was found hanged in mysterious circumstances.

In the war's last days the crates of documents and personal effects collected from the Katyn victims' clothes disappeared. Various countries' intelligence agents mounted a dramatic operation in search of them.

In June 1950, an American Russian-language newspaper named *Sotsialistichesky vestnik* published a letter to the editor under the headline 'Katyn', by one Professor Olshanski of Voronezh University. The writer, a friend of Professor Burdenko, had defected to the West at the end of the war after assuming an official function in the Soviet sector of Germany. His letter contained a revelation: Burdenko declared to him that the massacre had been committed in 1940, more than a year before the Germans attacked the Soviet Union.

Yet another public committee on Katyn was established in New York, chaired by the former US ambassador to Warsaw Arthur Bliss-Lane. Under his pressure, a special Congressional Committee was established in Washington, DC in October 1951. The Soviet Union, Democratic Poland, and East Germany refused to cooperate with it.

After collecting hundreds of testimonies, checking documents, and scrutinizing pieces of evidence in the cities of Europe, the committee unanimously pinned the blame for the murder of the officers at Katyn on the Soviet secret police.

After having signed a repatriation agreement with the Soviet Union in 1957, the Polish Communist government in Warsaw found itself in an embarrassing situation. Multitudes of Polish citizens returned to their place of birth. Not one of them, however, had been a POW in any of the three officers' camps.

Fifty years after the crime, its perpetrators have not yet been officially identified, as the traces of the massacre were painstakingly obfuscated. Until 1990 the mystery was shrouded in a fog of circumspection and perpetuated the anguish of thousands of the victims' families.

Epilogue

My purpose in bringing these matters to public knowledge is to shed some light on their Jewish aspect, which, however important, has been neither exposed nor even mentioned in analyses of the events of the time.

This tragic story reflects a fateful combination of Jewish and Polish aspects, so intertwined as to be inseparable, Above all, however, the following major questions remain unresolved:

1 When were the thousands of POWs murdered?
2 Who murdered the POWs, about 1,000 of whom were Jewish?
3 Why were thousands murdered and about 400 spared?

Question 1 The treatment by the Soviet guards, from the moment we stepped through the little hidden gate in the Kozielsk camp wall, was not only brutal but surprising. It was astonishingly unlike the attitude we expected, after weeks of false rumours originating in camp headquarters augured liberation. These rumours were meant to induce calm and favourable expectations among the thousands of POWs in the camp.

The guards' atrocious, vile behaviour towards senior officers and old men was of the kind invoked against defenceless, patronless people who had no avenue of redress – but who were earmarked for elimination. The guards were obeying orders, and knew nothing about the few transports that would be delivered to the rescue camp in Pavlishchev-Bor, near the town of Yukhnovo. The inscriptions on the walls of the prisoner cars were hastily scribbled by comrades in previous transports. Reading them, we were all apprehensive of the terrible fate in store for us. However, only the few who reached Pavlishchev-Bor were able to report on our ordeal during those fateful, endless hours of the trip to the rescue camp.

After the three POW camps were wound up in 1940 and postal communications with our families resumed, the men in Pavlishchev-Bor were inundated with letters, full of concern for the fate of thousands of our comrades, whose contact with families had been so abruptly severed. This was more than a year before the Germans attacked the Soviet Union. The Soviet publication *The Truth about Katyn*, asserts that the Germans had murdered the officers after occupying the area in 1941. This does not stand to reason. Are we to believe that thousands of officers went on existing without showing a sign of life for some 18 months after the camps were wound up, even though the Soviet Union and Germany were on friendly terms until war broke out in June, 1941?

Question 2 Several hundred of the 15,000 POWs in the three camps were Germans and *Volksdeutsch* who had been inducted into the Polish army from areas of western Poland bordering Germany. One of them was an officer whose duty would have been to command a camp of German POWs.

A large number of POW officers had well-formed political convictions before the war, and espoused German collaboration against the Soviet threat. These Polish citizens gambled everything on continued amity between the Third Reich and the Soviet Union. By stressing their German affiliations, they expected to earn quick liberation and repatriation. In fact, a few of them were liberated before the hostilities broke out, through intervention by the German embassy in Moscow.

The surprise German attack dashed the hopes of the remaining Germans and ethnic Germans. Their corpses were found in the mass grave in the Katyn Forest. It does not stand to reason that the Nazis murdered these hundreds of Germans and pro-Germans.

These facts were not brought to light in the investigating committees' deliberations. Among the survivors of the three POW camps who testified about their confinement and circumstances under which the thousands of officers vanished, none was Jewish.

Question 3 By partitioning Poland with Nazi Germany, the Soviet Union thought it was putting Polish political independence to an end once and for all. The Soviet leadership gambled everything on its unbreakable friendship with Germany. This conviction was expressed whenever Soviet officers conversed with the POWs.

When addressing the POWs, and in the notes they took during the investigations, the Soviet interrogators referred to them as 'former Polish army officers'.

The Polish leadership and intelligentsia – those with influence in the territories of occupied Poland – were systematically eradicated by being exiled deep inside the Soviet Union. The thousands of Polish officers in the three camps might have presented a serious obstacle in the process of establishing control over the Polish people; the decision to eliminate them had been taken at the highest echelons of the Soviet regime when they were first detained in the camps.

Several months before the German offensive, the camp commander at Griazoviets had recommended that we keep our uniforms in order because they might be of future utility. That was a most significant utterance.

Guided by the principles of dialectical materialism, the Soviets operated in two directions at the same time. On the one hand, they eliminated the thousands of POWs; on the other, they kept a handful alive for show, in case the political circumstances changed – as indeed they did.

Appendix I

Free translation from the Polish original:

General Władysław Anders
Commander-in-Chief, Polish Army in the Soviet Union
Via: Colonel Okulicki, Chief of Staff

Memorandum

We, the undersigned:

1 Engineer Miron Szeskin, Leader of the Jewish Ex-Service-men's Alliance 'B'rith Hachayal' in Poland, [and]
2 Advocate M. Kahan (editorial board of *Der Moment*, member of the Supreme Council of the Association of Publishers in Poland),

appeal to you on the matter described herewith:

The agreement between Poland and the Soviet Union liberated about two million Polish civilians.

After the harsh conditions they had endured until this agreement was concluded, they are at present in need of rest, long-term care, and therapy, before they can be enlisted into the Polish army.

As active participants in Jewish public life, we are duty-bound to call your attention to the fact that the Jews of Poland represent a significant proportion of all Polish citizens liberated in the aftermath of the aforementioned agreement.

We estimate their number at some 600,000, including 500,000 in the Tashkent area alone. The multitudes reaching the area thrust a serious burden on the reception centres, which are meant for the army's organization. Food, shelter, and housing, clothing and medical care set aside for army needs are being used for the urgent requirements of the civilian population.

Therefore, long-term care activity must be developed more broadly. Polish citizens should receive proper assistance and care; the military command must be released from such obligations. The Polish government will need financial help from various charitable organizations, since without this it cannot succeed in this endeavour.

The Jews of Great Britain and the United States, noteworthy for their generosity, have established the Joint Distribution Committee – a capable, powerful charitable organization. Undoubtedly they can accomplish this task. The propaganda invoked in appealing for the public's help will generate a response in the Polish émigré centres in the United States, Brazil, and Argentina. This will help the government of Poland marshal such funds as will be necessary to extend relief to Poles in the Soviet Union. The undersigned believe that their contacts with Jewish communities worldwide can serve as a point of departure for this action.

Our proposal does not accept any separatist intent. The Jews' suffering has greatly amplified their sensitivity to the sufferings of others.

Gentiles, too, will benefit from the long-term care to be obtained for the Jews of Poland, because we are all duty-bound to help one another in this time of emergency.

It would be a mistake, however, to concentrate on care only. As representatives of a political trend that espoused a humanitarian solution of the Jewish problem in Poland, one compatible with both the Jewish and Polish interests, we cannot disregard the fact that this problem, with all of its implications and results, still exists. We have no intention of forgetting the official proclamations and declarations of official circles in this matter. We simply establish a fact without venturing into the reasons underlying it. Because this is the reality, its existence must be taken into account. Events of recent times have reconfirmed that the only solution compatible with both Jewish and Polish interests as to the Jewish question in Poland is the Zionist idea. The importance of political and economic relations between independent Poland and Zionist Palestine, in which a large number of the population will comprise Jews of Polish origin, are well-known matters that have been explored and honed long ago. We shall only mention the Polish government's intervention in Middle East affairs in the context of the Palestine Mandate, and import – export activities by various bodies before the war. We should also note that a Polish military division reached Palestine during the war. For these reasons we must act today, so that the Palestine problem is resolved once the war ends.

For this reason we propose the idea of a unit to be sent into combat on the Middle Eastern front. Without entering into circumstances and reasons in the present memorandum, it is a fact that Jews' participation in the Polish military force is not viewed with favour. On the other hand, the Jews are entitled to serve in the army. We emphasize strongly that the Jews want to take part in the war against Hitler, our people's great enemy. Therefore a Jewish Legion operating within the framework of the Polish army meets the needs of the time, provided that the requisite political conditions are maintained.

Establishing the Legion should be guided by a favourable approach towards the Jews, and sympathy from the Polish government and the main command of its army for the Jewish national idea.

The Legion will not serve as a precedent for differential attitudes towards Jews and Poles. It will not impinge on the rights of the Jews as Polish citizens. Participation in the Legion to be established will be exclusively voluntary, and the Legionnaire will retain all his rights as a Polish citizen. We believe our proposal to be consistent with British interests in the Middle East.

We therefore propose the establishment of a body representing the Jews to advance the ideas spelled out in this memorandum.

Signed,

M. Szeskin   Buzuluk,
M. Kahan   10 October 1941

Appendix II

Free translation from the Polish original:

Original on file at the Hoover Institution on War and Revolution, Stanford University, Stanford, California.

Report on a talk by General Anders with representatives of Polish Jewry in the Soviet Union

At 11.30 a.m. on 24 October 1941, on the initiative of the Polish Ambassador in Kuybyshev, a talk was held between the Commander-in-Chief of the Polish Army in the Soviet Union, General Władysław Anders, and representatives of Polish Jewry, at present in Soviet territory.

Present: Professor Stanistaw Kot, Ambassador of Poland to the Soviet Union
General Władysław Anders
Representatives of the Bund: Henryk Ehrlich and Wiktor Alter
Representative of the PPS [Polish Socialist Party]: Advocate Otto Pehr
Representative of the General Zionists: Seidenman

The report was written by the press attaché of the Polish Embassy in Moscow, K. Pruszyński.

General Anders began the talk by expressing satisfaction at having the opportunity to discuss problems with representatives of the Polish Jews. He wishes to explain the conditions under which the Polish army is being established in the Soviet Union, with a substantial proportion of soldiers of Jewish origin. These conditions are harsh in the extreme. The Soviets intended to establish only one Polish division, while General Anders demanded that two divisions and a reserve centre be established. Consequently, the Soviets' food allocations for the Polish army are small, and are restricted to 44,000 portions. Of these, many are reserved for families of army men and for civilians who arrived in the army's wake. Hence conditions for the army are harsh, above and beyond housing difficulties and other problems.

In view of the aforesaid, friction has developed with the Jews, who filled the army ranks because Soviet policy favoured the liberation of Jews from the camps. As a result, the proportion of Jews in the army is greater than their proportion in Poland. Because the Soviets limited the number of soldiers, liberated Poles could not gain admission to the army, despite their qualifications and previous army service.

There is no doubt that some of the Jews are not very conscientous; for them, service under existing conditions is a refuge, at least until they go out to the front.

In the General's opinion, the Jewish population comprises two types: those from western and central Poland, and those from the eastern districts. The behaviour of the later during the harsh days of Poland's defeat was very bad at times. They stripped soldiers of their weapons and tore the eagle emblem from their caps. Anders relates that contrary to the surrender agreement, the Soviets gathered the Polish fighters in Lwów for the purpose of exiling them, and the Jewish residents there treated the prisoners of war insultingly. In the detention camps, there were many complaints about the Jews' attitude towards their Polish neighbours. These instances will not be forgotten, especially under the existing conditions of pressure. They must be taken into account.

The General will not tolerate anti-semitism, although he

cannot deny that it has manifested itself under the conditions that have come about. Jewish groups have attempted to foment political activity.

Two groups presented memordanda to the General on the situation of the Jews in the Polish army.

"A memorandum was presented by Revisionist circles represented by Engineer Miron Szeskin and Advocate Marek Kahan. In their memorandum they propose that anti-semitism in the army be prevented by establishing Jewish units in a legion under Polish army administration. The Revisionists intend to receive American assistance and transfer the legion to Syria. They estimate the number of Poles in the Soviet Union at about 2 million, including approximately 900,000 Jews, from which it is possible to establish a formation of 100,000 soldiers.

In the General's opinion, the proposal and the numbers specified are inaccurate. It is hard to determine the numerical ratio of Jews and Poles, but the percentage of Jews is in any case smaller than that cited by the Revisionists. Furthermore, the army is 7 per cent of the country's population, not 12 per cent.

Anders estimates the strength of the Polish army in the Soviet Union at approximately 100,000–140,000, and the Revisionists' estimate cannot be taken seriously.

The Poles' aim is different from that of the Revisionists. The Poles aspire to establish the Polish state, while the Revisionists aim to establish a Jewish state in Palestine. Accordingly the General presented them with the following reply:

I want no national formations in the Polish army, because this would lead to similar initiatives by the Ukrainians and Belorussians. The army should be unified and should fight for Poland.

A second memorandum was presented by Bund member Lucjan Blitt. He contends that the Jews and all other citizens must be treated equally, and that there are no grounds for establishing a separate Jewish army. However, Blitt would like to organize lectures and assemblies for the Jews. Anders did not agree with this view, because all events in the army must be uniform.

There is another unpleasant problem. Reports by the Poles and the NKVD indicate that many Jews are leaving Buzuluk for Tashkent, and are propagandizing against the Polish army. This is undesirable. The General does not object to their leaving the army for Tashkent, because some cannot withstand the harsh conditions under which the Polish army operates. Because food is in short supply, soldiers go into the fields barefoot to collect potatoes. In existing circumstances and because of the large number of recruits, those with military training leave the induction centres with the authorities' agreement. This requires official approval, which the Jews disregard, as in the case of the last group of about 200 men. This worsens relations.

The General will not countenance anti-semitism, but for this he needs the Jews' help.

Mr Ehrlich mentions the painful manifestations that surfaced in 1939. He himself encountered and witnessed the sympathy of the Jews of eastern Poland for the Red Army. These phenomena distressed him as a Jewish Bundist, just as they distressed the Poles.

Alter adds that these manifestations were isolated. The General counters that they were not.

Mr Ehrlich is of the view that such phenomena as occurred should be understood against the background of relations in Poland, which worsened during the period preceding the military defeat. Moreover, the Poles' attitude towards the Jews in the Soviet camps is anti-semitic too. Relations are bad on both sides. Ehrlich's party expects the Jews to be treated like all other citizens, and strives to prevent friction.

General Anders' position toward the 'Jewish Army' is consistent with the principles of the Bund, Ehrlich maintains: 'We Jews are fighting not for Palestine but for Poland, and wish to fight for Poland. We do not wish to be divorced from this war for any reason whatsoever.'

As for the Revisionists' activities, Ehrlich believes that, according to the recurrent results of municipal elections in Poland, this group is of no moment. Ehrlich knows the authors of the Revisionist memorandum, and refers to Kahan with disfavour as having been reprimanded in a resolution by Jewish authors and journalists after deviously taking over *Der Moment*. Summing up, he asserts that the Bundists' only desire is to act in conformity with General Anders' doctrine: a single Polish army with one goal – struggle for a new Poland.

Seidenman adds that as a Zionist whose position within his own camp is different from that of Ehrlich and Alter in theirs, he concurs with them, eschews segregation of Jews in the army, and opposes discrimination among Polish citizens. The Polish army should be uniform.

Mr Ehrlich believes that a Jewish advisory institution for all affairs should be established alongside General Anders. Anders rejects this categorically. The army's structure does not recognize an advisory institution; the army is apolitical. Politics belongs to the Embassy, and an advisory body can be set up with it. The General objects to politics and national discrimination in the army. Anyone who is not a soldier should be expelled from the army.

Mr Alter understands this position, and believes that propaganda and culture among the Jewish soldiers may be of great value.

The ambassador adds that the propaganda and culture section in London has a Jewish officer who represents the Jews' affairs.

The General will consider the proposal in the future, as part of the army's cultural section. The talk was preliminary in nature because of the General's lack of time. There would appear to be general agreement that the Jews in the Polish army should not be segregated, and that all Polish citizens in the army should be treated equally.

Press Attaché   Kuybyshev
The Polish Embassy in the Soviet Union   24 October 1941

Appendix III

About the author

Dr Salomon Slowes was born in Grajewo, near the border of Eastern Prussia; the family relocated to Wilno upon the outbreak of World War I. The author, a graduate of Tarbut Jewish high school in Wilno, completed medical studies and specialized in surgery. After advanced training in Vienna, he was appointed assistant in the Department of Face and Jaw Surgery of the University Hospital in Wilno. Inducted into the Polish army at the beginning of World War II, he was taken by the Soviets to the Kozielsk POW camp, and was one of the few who remained alive after the murder of officers in the Katyn Forest.

The author left Russia with General Władysław Anders' Army. As a military doctor, he directed surgical departments for victims of face and jaw injuries in Allied army hospitals in Iran, Iraq, and Palestine. He was awarded citations of honour for similar action on the Italian front.

After the war, Dr Slowes settled in Israel. During Israel's War of Independence he was a consulting surgeon with the Israel Defence Forces. After the war, on Israel Defence Forces recommendation, he went to Europe and the United States for advanced training. He has published professional articles and was admitted to the Association of Plastic Surgeons in Great Britain.

Returning to Israel, Dr Slowes directed the maxillo-facial surgery of the Tel Aviv–Jaffa Medical Centre. As a member of the Israel Association of Plastic Surgeons, he has been invited to lecture at scientific conferences and at Tel Aviv University Medical School. He has conducted advanced courses for Central Health Fund physicians and for counsellors with Israel's equivalent of the Red Cross.

After the 1967 Six-Day War, he published a book on the treatment of maxillo-facial injuries; after the 1973 Yom Kippur War, he directed a hospital department that cared for wounded Egyptian POWs.

In public activities, he spent many years as a member of the Israel Medical Association central committee. He also headed the Association's organizational department, and served as consultant and medical adviser to the Ministry of Defence and the National Insurance (Social Security) Institute.

Over the years, Dr Slowes has gathered and compiled information on the Katyn Forest massacre. The very idea that time would consign important details to oblivion, and the urge to fight the amnesia that would bury a tragedy of war, disturbed his rest and conscience. It was with this motivation that Dr Slowes wrote this book.

Editor's Notes

1 General Władysław Sikorski (1881–1943), pre-war politician and military figure. From October 1940, Prime
Minister of the Polish Government-in-Exile and from November 1940 Commander-in-Chief of the Polish Army.
Killed in a plane crash in Gibraltar in July 1943.

2 Professor Ignacy Moscicki (1867–1946), President of
Poland, 1926–39.

3 Marshall Edward Rydz-Smigly (1886–1941), Commander-in-Chief of the Polish Army in 1939.

4 Major-General Władysław Anders (1892–1970), Commander of the Polish Forces in the Soviet Union after his
release from the Soviet Union in August 1941, and later,
of the Second Polish Corps in Italy. Hated by successive
Polish Communist governments, died in exile in London.

5 A reference to the battle at Grunwald in which Polish and
Lithuanian forces decisively defeated the Teutonic Knights
in 1410. The battle marked the beginning of the decline
of the Order.

6 The Polish Government left Warsaw in early September
and moved eastwards. After the Soviet attack on Poland
on 17 September 1939, the government evacuated itself
to Romania where it was interned by the authorities.

7 Colonel Adam Koc (1891–1969), pre-war Polish politician and soldier. Left Poland after the defeat in September
1939. Participated in the Polish Government in Exile
between 1939 and 1942.

8   Semyon Timoshenko (1895–1970), Marshall of the Soviet Army and Defence Commissar. After participating in the attack on Poland he commanded the Soviet troops invading Finland.

9   Marshall Jozef Piłsudski (1867–1935), politician, head of state, Commander-in-Chief of the Polish Army. In 1919–20 fought a successful war against Soviet Russia. It was the only war the Soviet Union lost until the defeat in Afghanistan.

10 Pyotr Stolypin (1862–1911), Tsarist Minister of the Interior and Prime Minister. The special coaches were widely used for the transfer of political prisoners under the Tsars and the Soviets.

11 Lavrenti Beria (1899–1953), Soviet Minister of the Interior and Head of the Secret Police. Stalin's right hand, executed by his successors.

12 Jozef Czapski (1896–), well known painter, writer and journalist. Fought against the Red Army in 1920 and 1939. After the war settled in Paris where he was a co-founder of the *émigré* political monthly *Kultura*.

13 Garments worn by Jews during prayers.

14 See Janusz Zawodny, *Death in the Forest* (enlarged Polish edition: *Katyn*, Paris, 1989, p. 122).

15 General Leopold Okulicki (1898–1946), professional officer in the Polish Army, Chief-of-Staff of General Anders. Last Commander-in-Chief of the underground Home Army. Arrested by the Soviets in 1945, died in 1946 in a Moscow prison, probably murdered by the NKVD.

16 Władysław Broniewski (1897–1962), a great Polish Communist poet with colourful personality. Fought against the Red Army in 1919–1920, later supported the Russian Revolution. Imprisoned by the Soviet in 1940, released in 1941, left with the Anders' Army. After 1945 settled in Poland where he became the 'national poet'.

17 After the daring escape and the arrival in Britain, 'ORZEL' under the new captain, Jan Grudzinski (1907–40) patrolled the North Sea, sinking a Nazi transport ship 'Rio de Janeiro' with the troops on their way to Norway, and was herself sunk in June 1940.

18 Jozef Retinger (1888–1960), colourful political figure, active in Europe and Mexico. After the war an *éminence grise* of European politics and one of the architects of the Council of Europe. In 1941 a *charge d'affaires* of the Polish Government in Exile in Moscow.

19 Professor Stanislaw Kot (1885–19   ), Polish Ambassador to Moscow 1941–2.

20 Berek Joselevicz (1764–1809), Jewish merchant, Colonel in the Polish Army. Fought with Napoleon in Italy, Austerlitz and elsewhere. During the Kosciuszko Insurrection against Russia in 1794, organized and commanded a Jewish light cavalry regiment. Killed by the Australians during the battle of Kock.

21 Henryk Erhlich (1882–1942), Wiktor Alter (18   –1942), Polish leaders of *Bund*, a Jewish Socialist Workers Party. Executed by Stalin.

22 Wanda Wasilewska (1905–64), left-wing activist and writer. From 1940 a member of the Supreme Council of the Soviet Union. Red Army Colonel and Political Commissar. In 1943 chaired the Union of Polish Patriots set up by Stalin which became the alternative Polish government.

23 Zygmunt Berling (1896–   ), professional officer with left-wing leanings. After being released from Soviet prison in 1941 he served briefly under General Anders before defecting to the Communists where he commanded the First Polish Army in the USSR.

24 Menachem Begin, Israeli Prime Minister between 1977 and 1983. Imprisoned by the Soviets, left with General Anders, and reached Palestine together with about 3,000 Jewish soldiers. Out of this number, two thousand (including Slowes) went to fight the Italian Campaign and the remaining soldiers deserted in Palestine to fight for the Jewish state. Begin, who was a prominent Jewish politician, wished to stay in Palestine but refused to desert. He approached General Szyszko-Bohusz and obtained indefinite leave.

25 Women's International Zionist Organisation.

26 General Stanislaw Kopanski (1894–1978), formed an élite Polish Carpathian Brigade in Syria in 1940. The Brigade

fought under the British Command in Tobruk and Gazala, reorganized in 1942 in Palestine into a division, and took part in the Italian campaign. He became Chief-of-Staff of the Polish Army in 1943.

27 *Kultura* – the most influential Polish *émigré* journal, published in Paris since the war.

Index